The
Plain Language
DICTIONARY
OF
REAL
ESTATE

Barbara Cox
Jerry Cox
David Silver-Westrick

Bella Vista Publishing Company, Inc.

BELLA VISTA PUBLISHING COMPANY, INC.
San Clemente, CA 92672

ISBN 0-9718225-0-6

10 9 8 7 6 5 4 3 2 1

Contents

Keystrokes for the Real Estate master IIx®

Keystrokes for the TI-BA Real Estate™

Keystrokes for the HP10b®

Keystrokes for the HP12c®

Mortgage Payment Table

Cost per $1,000 Borrowed

Selected Real Estate Related Web Sites

About the Authors

A

AAA tenant — (also called "triple-A tenant") an especially credit-worthy or well-known commercial tenant whose presence will enhance the ability of the landlord to attract similar tenants. See also *anchor tenant*.

"A" paper — real estate loans for borrowers whose credit history fits within generally accepted mortgage industry standards of credit worthiness and whose income meets underwriting guidelines.

abandonment — the voluntary surrender of real property without naming a successor; disclaimer of ownership.

abatement — a decrease in level or intensity. An example is tax abatement, in which a taxing agency reduces, eliminates, or defers property taxes to encourage investment or promote home ownership.

absentee owner — a property owner who does not reside in or on the property.

absorption rate — an estimate or projection of the sales or rentals of a particular type of real property in a given area compared to the total supply of such properties during a specified period. The general formula is [*total inventory ÷ expected sales for the period*].

abstract — a summary of a longer document or documents, such as an abstract of title or an abstract of judgment.

abstract of judgment — a summary of a decision in a court case.

abstract of title — a chronological summary of all recorded grants, legal actions, wills, instruments, and proceedings affecting title to a particular piece of real property.

abstractor — a person who compiles summaries of documents relating to real estate title.

abut — to adjoin physically along at least one dimension. See also *adjacent*.

acceleration clause — a provision usually seen in a credit document, such as a note or mortgage, giving the lender the right to demand that the entire amount of the loan be repaid immediately upon the occurrence of a specific event, such as a breach of the terms of the loan contract or the sale of the underlying security.

acceptance — a legal term describing a clear expression of a selling party's intent to be bound by the terms of an offer.

access right — the right of a property owner to reach his or her property from an adjoining public road. See also *egress* and *ingress*.

accession — the acquisition of title

2

accommodation party   acquisition loan

by a property owner to additional land deposited by rivers or streams. Also, the acquisition of title to fixtures, such as fences and interior improvements, added to the property by a third party.

accommodation party — a person or entity who, without consideration, signs a credit document to enhance the ability of a third party to obtain the credit. A parent who co-signs a bank loan for a child is one example.

accommodator — the party who takes temporary title to a property in connection with a Section 1031 exchange. See also *delayed exchange*.

accord and satisfaction — the settlement of a disputed debt or obligation for less than the full amount claimed.

accounts payable — money owed to another by a business. See also *accounts receivable*.

accounts receivable — money owed to a business for goods or services performed in the ordinary course of business. See also *accounts payable*.

accretion — the gradual increase in area of a parcel of land from natural processes such as the movement of soil by rivers and streams. See also *alluvium/alluvion*.

accrual method — an accounting term describing the "recognition" of revenue and expenses in the account-

ing period in which they are earned or incurred regardless of when the cash is actually received or paid out.

accrued depreciation — (also called *accumulated depreciation*) an accounting term describing the dollar amount of depreciation claimed for tax purposes on an asset since it was acquired or placed in service.

accrued interest — interest earned but not yet paid.

accumulated depreciation — See *accrued depreciation*.

acknowledgment — a declaration made by a signatory to a document to an authorized official, often a notary public, that the signature was made voluntarily and without duress. Sometimes refers to the signature itself.

acoustical ceiling — ceiling made of, coated with, or covered by a sound-absorbing material.

acoustical tile — tiled material designed to absorb sound.

acquisition — (1) the act of securing ownership of an asset; (2) the asset itself.

acquisition cost — total cost of securing title to a property, including, but not limited to, the price of the property, legal and professional fees, appraisal costs, commissions, loan costs, and taxes.

acquisition loan — money borrowed for the purpose of acquiring title to a property. Contrast with money borrowed for purposes of making changes in the property, such as a construction loan.

acre – traditional measurement of land area equal to 4,840 square yards or 43,560 square feet. Allows size comparisons of irregular parcels.

acre foot – a unit of volume, typically applied to measuring large volumes of water for irrigation purposes, equivalent to one acre, one foot deep.

acreage – parcel of land consisting of multiple contiguous acres. See also *acre*.

act of God – random, unpreventable natural event, such as a flood, hurricane, drought, or civil insurrection. Acts of God are often excluded from property insurance coverage, requiring property owners to purchase specialty flood or storm coverage.

action – legal proceeding brought in a court of law.

action *in personam* – legal proceeding against a person as opposed to a property. Seeks a remedy involving some action by a named person, such as the payment of a debt or the performance of a service. See also *action in rem*.

action *in rem* – legal proceeding against a property or thing. Typical examples include a foreclosure or the imposition of a lien. See also *action in personam*.

action to quiet title – See *quiet title action*.

active participation – a specified level of personal involvement in the acquisition, management, and disposal of rental property. Tax laws provide more favorable treatment if active, as opposed to passive, participation can be demonstrated. See also *passive investor*.

actual age – an appraisal term meaning the chronological age of a structure or improvement. See also *effective age*.

actual notice – the receipt of a fact by a party to a transaction leading to direct knowledge by that party. Contrast with constructive notice, in which a party is deemed by law to have received the information. See also *constructive notice*.

actuary – a person trained in the analysis of the appropriate pricing and valuation of insurance premiums, annuities, and dividends.

ad litem – typically, a guardian appointed by a court "for the suit" to protect the interests of a party to the suit. Protected parties are commonly minors or persons judged legally incompetent.

ad valorem tax – tax based on the value of the thing to be taxed. Property taxes are a common example.

ADA — See *Americans with Disabilities Act.*

ADC loan — an acquisition, development and construction loan.

addendum — something added to and intended to be incorporated in a contract.

addition — an increase in the physical size of an improvement after its initial construction. Construction of a second story on an existing single-story house would be an addition. A cosmetic remodel of the existing kitchen would not be an addition.

additional deposit — an increase in the amount of the deposit tendered by a buyer to a seller of real property, usually intended to enhance the attractiveness of the offer or to compensate for an unusually long escrow.

additional space option — a lease term giving a tenant the right to lease additional space within a property during the lease term.

add-on interest — interest calculated for the life of the loan, then added to the principal. The sum of the principal plus the add-on interest is then divided by the number of payments to determine the amount of the periodic payment. For example, a $10,000 loan at 8% interest with a term of five years would have a total payment of $14,000 ($10,000 × 8% × 5 + the original $10,000). Monthly payments would be $233.33 ($14,000 ÷ 60).

adhesion contract — a contract deemed by a court to be so one-sided in favor of the party who prepared the contract that the court will not enforce it.

adjacent — physically near but not necessarily touching. See also *abut.*

adjudicate — to render a formal decision in a legal action in a court of law.

adjustable rate mortgage (ARM) — (also called a *variable rate mortgage*) a mortgage in which the interest rate changes over the period of the loan. The key components of an ARM are the start rate, the index, the margin, the adjustment period, and the note rate. The initial interest rate for the loan is called the start rate. The underlying interest rate to which the loan is tied is called the index. Common indexes include the rate on 26-week T-bills, the COFI (the 11th District cost of funds index), and LIBOR (the London Interbank Offered Rate). The index may change daily, weekly, monthly, quarterly, or upon the occurrence of some event, such as a Federal Reserve change in the cost of funds to member banks. The margin is a percentage added to the index rate to derive the actual note rate. The adjustment period is the time between note rate adjustments. The note rate is the actual effective interest rate on the ARM at a given point in time.

For example, assume that the

start rate for a particular adjustable loan is 5%. Assume that the index is the average interest paid on one-year Treasury bills for each year of the loan. Assume that the margin is 3% and the adjustment period is six months. The note rate for this particular loan would be 8% (5% + 3%). If the Treasury bill index increased over a six-month period to 6%, the note rate would rise to 9%.

The monthly payment may or may not change when the note rate changes. If the payment allowed by the lender in the loan documents is less than the current note rate, the loan is called a negative amortization loan. In a negative amortization loan, the deferred interest (the difference between the interest paid and the interest charged) is added to the principal balance. See also *annual interest cap, annual payment cap, Cost of Funds Index, deferred interest, LIBOR, lifetime cap, negative amortization, variable interest,* and *variable rate mortgage.*

adjusted sales price – the net selling price for a parcel of real property after all costs of sale, such as commissions, escrow fees, and title insurance, are subtracted.

adjusted tax basis – the tax basis equal to the original acquisition costs of a property plus the costs of any capital improvements, minus any accumulated depreciation. See also *accumulated depreciation, basis, capital improvement,* and *tax basis.*

adjuster – a person generally em-ployed by or contracted to an insurance company who is authorized to assess and settle insurance claims.

adjustment – an appraisal method that facilitates comparisons of similar but not identical properties. An appraiser will make additions or subtractions to dollar- value estimates because of differences between aspects of the subject property and the most closely comparable properties. For example, an appraiser might add $10,000 to the estimated price of a subject property because of an extra bedroom, or subtract $20,000 because of an inferior location. See also *appraisal, appraisal approach,* and *subject property.*

administrative regulations – rules issued by an agency of government that are deemed to have the force and effect of law. State departments of real estate and the Internal Revenue Service are examples of agencies that adopt and publish administrative regulations.

administrator/administratrix – a man/woman appointed by a court to settle the estate of an intestate decedent. See also *decedent* and *intestate.*

adobe – a mix of a type of mud found in the southwestern United States added to straw and used as a building material. Adobe may be applied as a coating or baked into blocks.

adult community – a housing development intended to be occupied by "older" persons. While age discrimination in housing is generally illegal, local, state, and federal agencies have made exceptions for qualified senior or adult housing. Minimum age requirements vary widely.

advance fee — money paid to a real estate broker before any service is rendered. Designed to cover the broker's cost of initial advertising and promotion of a listing.

adverse land use — open and notorious occupation of property contrary to the interests of another title claimant. See also *adverse possession.*

adverse possession — a method of acquiring title to property owned by another. Adverse possession requires open and notorious occupation of property contrary to the interests of another title claimant for a prolonged and continuous period of time. This statutory period of time varies by jurisdiction. The adverse possessor must exhibit the clear intent to exercise a claim of rightful title, and must exclude possession by the actual owner. In some jurisdictions, the adverse possessor must also have paid required property taxes for the period.

affidavit — a written statement made under oath before an official such as a notary public.

affirm — to confirm or ratify.

affirmation — a declaration indicating that a statement is true.

affirmative action — a general term describing various government programs designed to eradicate discrimination in housing, employment, and education.

affordable housing — a general term describing housing projects built for individuals or families who could not otherwise afford to purchase or lease similar housing. Often developed in conjunction with government or private subsidies, and subject to a variety of qualification rules and resale restrictions.

A-frame — a house design characterized by an A-shaped roof that also forms the walls of the house.

after-acquired property — property acquired by a judgment debtor after the judgment that is subject to a lien by the terms of the judgment. See also *judgment* and *lien.*

agency — a relationship in which one person or entity acts on behalf of another. An agency relationship between a principal and an agent imposes certain "duties of care" on the agent. Agency may be express or implied. Express agency is intentionally entered into by both the principal and the agent and is often evidenced by a written agreement. Implied agency is inferred from the conduct of the parties. An implied agent appears to be acting as the agent for another whose actions and statements are consistent with this agency relationship. See also *express agency,* *implied agency*, and *duties of care*.

agency agreement — a written or oral agreement in which one person or entity agrees to act on behalf of another. An agency agreement is an essential element of the relationship a real estate broker has with a principal. See also *agency*, *duties of care*, *express agency*, and *implied agency*.

agency by estoppel — the agency created by operation of law when an agent has overstepped the bounds of his or her agency through negligence of the principal. In an agency by estoppel, the principal is held responsible for promises the agent made on the principal's behalf, even though unauthorized.

agency disclosure — a written document given to the principal(s) in an agency agreement by the agent. The document summarizes the agent's duties and informs the principal(s) of the various duties of care attaching to the agent, depending on the nature of the agency relationship. For example, a single agent might owe the utmost fiduciary duty to his or her client, while a subagent might owe only what is called a duty of "good faith and fair dealing." See also *subagent* and *duties of care*.

agent — a person or entity authorized to act for another. See also *principal*.

agrarian — relating to fields or farms.

agreement of sale — one of the many terms for a contract for the sale of real property. See also *acceptance*, *deposit receipt*, and *offer*.

AIR — See *American Industrial Real Estate Association*.

air rights — the bundle of ownership rights to the use and enjoyment of the space above a property and any of its improvements.

AITD — See *all-inclusive deed of trust*.

alcove — small recessed portion of a room.

alienation — the transfer of an ownership interest in real property.

alienation clause — a contract provision, usually found in a loan secured by real estate, stipulating that the entire amount of the note must be paid, at the discretion of the noteholder, if the property is sold, contracted for sale, or leased for more than a specified period. See also *acceleration clause* and *due-on-sale clause*.

alkali — chemically a base as opposed to an acid. Alkalis can leach from soil and damage concrete foundations, plants, and crops.

all-inclusive deed of trust (AITD) — a junior mortgage with a face amount totaling the actual amount owed under the junior mortgage plus the amount of any senior mortgages. The mortgagee collects the total combined payment from the mortgagor, pays any senior mortgage obligations, and keeps the remainder. AITDs are most commonly used where the senior mortgage interest rate on a property is low. A purchaser of the property may wish to keep the existing mortgage in place, rather than obtain a new loan at a higher rate. Alternatively, the seller of such a property may wish to charge a premium over the actual cost of the underlying debt. See also *due-on-sale clause* and *wraparound mortgage*.

alluvium/alluvion — the material that builds up through accretion along a shore or riverbank, adding to the total land area. See also *accretion* and *diluvion*.

ALTA — See *American Land Title Association*.

alternative minimum tax (AMT) — a federal flat rate tax that applies to taxpayers with certain types of investment income and deductions when the AMT exceeds what would have been paid under their regular income tax schedule.

amendment — a modification of an agreement that does not substantially alter the essence of the agreement. See also *novation*.

amenities — features associated with real property that increase its perceived value. Examples include community pools, recreation rooms, views, and proximity to good schools.

American Industrial Real Estate Association (AIR) — an organiza-tion of real estate professionals who specialize in representing industrial property. See also *Industrial Multiple*.

American Land Title Association (ALTA) — (1) an association of title insurance companies that provides standardized title insurance forms for members use; (2) a form of title insurance.

Americans with Disabilities Act (ADA) — 1992 federal law mandating "equal access" to "public accommodations" for persons with a mental or physical impairment. Some effects of the law can be seen in the presence of ramps for wheelchairs into and in public buildings, wheelchair-accessible rest rooms, and parking spaces for the disabled.

amortization schedule — a list or table displaying the payment schedule for a loan, along with the amount credited to principal and to interest at each payment.

amortization term — the time required to pay off a loan with specific periodic payments. For example, many home mortgage loans have an amortization term of 30 years.

amortize — to pay off a debt over time in installments.

amortized loan — a loan in which at least some principal reduction is achieved through installment payments. A fully amortized loan is paid in full with the last installment payment.

AMT — See *alternative minimum tax.*

anaconda mortgage — a mortgage that secures all debts of the mortgagor that shall be due and owing to the mortgagee at any time.

anchor tenant — the principal, largest, or most prestigious tenant in a commercial project such as a shopping center. Large centers may have more than one anchor tenant. They are thought to attract traffic to the center, enhancing the ability of the landlord to lease the other spaces.

annexation — (1) a political process by which a city or county acquires additional territory; (2) the conversion of personal property to real property; for example, a bookcase that has been permanently affixed to a wall with screws has been annexed to the real property.

annual interest cap — the maximum allowable increase or decrease in the interest rate of an adjustable rate mortgage (ARM) during a 12-month period. For example, if an ARM with a 3% annual interest cap started the year at a 7% rate, it could go no higher than 10%, nor lower than 4%, during the subsequent 12-month period. See also *annual payment cap.*

annual payment cap — the maximum increase or decrease in the periodic payment of an adjustable rate mortgage (ARM). The annual payment cap, which is independent of the annual interest rate cap, is usually expressed as a percentage of the payment. For example, if the payment on an ARM in year 1 was $1,000/month and the annual payment cap was 5%, then the monthly payment in year 2 could be no higher than $1,050 and no lower than $950. See also *annual interest cap.*

annual percentage rate (APR) — the ratio of the total finance charge (including but not limited to the interest charge, points, and certain other fees) to the total amount financed or to be financed. APR is expressed as a percentage and is designed to allow consumers to compare different loan programs. Lenders are required to disclose the APR under Regulation Z. See also *Truth in Lending Law* and *Regulation Z.*

annuity — a series of equal payments over a period of years.

annul — to cancel or invalidate.

antideficiency laws — state laws preventing enforcement of deficiency judgments on purchase money loans. See also *deficiency judgment.*

antitrust laws — federal and state laws designed to promote competition and discourage monopolies. Applications in the real estate industry include prohibition against collusive fixing of commission charges.

apartment building — multifamily structure providing multiple residential rental units.

apparent authority — the reasonable conclusion on the part of a third party that an agent had authority to act for a principal. The principal may be bound by the actions of an agent acting with apparent authority. See also *agency by estoppel.*

apportionment – the assignment of prorated expenses such as property taxes, insurance, and association dues to the buyer and the seller of real property.

appraisal – an educated and informed opinion or estimate of value of real property by a third-party expert. Used for purposes of establishing value for tax and estate purposes, for lending, and for setting a realistic market price. See also *fair market value.*

appraisal approach – one or all of the three methods most commonly used to determine the value of real property: (a) the cost approach (an estimate of the actual current cost of replacing the property); (b) the comparable sales approach (compares recent sales of similar properties and adjusts for differences); (c) the income approach (compares income streams of various properties).

appraisal report – a written estimate of value by an appraiser including the factual basis and the method or reasoning employed to form the estimate. See also *appraisal* and *appraisal approach.*

appraised value – the opinion of

an appraiser concerning the likely market value of a property at a particular point in time.

appraiser – an expert on the valuation of real property.

appreciation – the increase over time in the value of real property.

appropriation – (also called *dedication*) the reserving of private land for a designated public use.

appurtenance – a thing that is not the land itself, but that increases the value or utility of the land and is deemed by law or agreement to belong to the land. Typical examples are easements, water rights, and condominium parking spaces.

APR – See *annual percentage rate.*

aqueduct – a large pipe or channel designed to transport water from one area to another. See also *irrigation.*

arbitration – an alternative to judicial resolution of disputes. Parties to a contract may agree in the contract to submit any disputes to a neutral third-party arbitrator, who will hear the dispute and render a decision. The decision may be binding (no recourse to judicial appeal) or non-binding (the losing party may litigate despite the arbitrator's decision). Typically, arbitrators are not bound by existing law or precedent in making their decisions. See also *binding arbitration* and *mediation* .

arbitration clause – a contract

provision calling for arbitration of any disputes between the parties to the contract. See also *arbitration*.

architecture – (1) the practice of designing structures; (2) the visual and structural style of a building.

area – (1) the number of square feet in a building or portion of a building; (2) a geographic zone, such as the "Southern California area"; (3) a portion of a structure, such as "sleeping area," "eating area," etc.

ARM – See *adjustable rate mortgage*.

arm's-length transaction – transaction in which all parties are able to bargain independently and without undue duress, restriction, or influence by other parties or external circumstance. An example of an arm's-length transaction is the sale of a home on the open market between an unrelated seller and buyer. A non-arm's-length transaction might be a private sale of a commercial building by a corporation to its wholly owned subsidiary.

arranger of credit – a person who facilitates the extension of credit by another person. Real estate brokers may be arrangers of credit if they broker a transaction with seller financing.

arrears – (1) a delinquency involving a debt; (2) installment payments made at the end, as opposed to the beginning, of a payment period.

arterial highway – any major highway or freeway.

artesian well – hole in the ground through which water flows because of naturally occurring water pressure.

asbestos – a natural fiber derived from rock and used as an insulator in residential and commercial construction through approximately 1978, when it was found to be a potential health hazard. Many states now ban its use and require sellers to disclose its presence to a buyer. Some jurisdictions require that existing asbestos be professionally removed upon the sale of a structure.

as-is – without warranty as to condition by the seller. In an as-is sale, the buyer is responsible for investigating the item (either personal or real property) and agrees to accept it in its present state. As-is language in a contract does not generally shield a seller from liability for misrepresentation.

asking price – the price at which a parcel of real estate is offered for sale. The term implies a willingness to negotiate on the part of the seller. A buyer may respond with a bid. Asking price is sometimes distinguished from a firm price, which suggests that no negotiation is possible. See also *bid* and *firm price*.

assessed value – the dollar value placed on real property by a government agency for property tax purposes. Assessed value may be more or less than actual market value.

assessment — (1) same as assessed value; (2) the actual amount of the property tax; (3) a special charge to a property owner by either a taxing agency or a homeowners' association. For example, a homeowners' association might require a special assessment from all members of the association for an emergency roof replacement.

assessment district — a geographic area delineated for the specific purpose of levying a tax. An individual property may be located in more than one assessment district.

assessment period — the period during which the assessment is completed.

assessment roll — the public record of the assessed values of the properties in an assessment district.

assessor — the public official charged with determining the value of property for tax purposes.

assessor's map — a map showing the assessor-assigned parcel number for each parcel of land in a county.

asset — anything that can be deemed to have value. A building is an asset, as is the goodwill of a business occupying a building.

assignee — person or entity who receives a tangible or intangible property right from another. An example is an assignment of rights under a lease from an existing tenant to a sublessee. See also *assignor.*

assignment — act of transferring some property right or interest from one entity or person to another.

assignment of mortgage — formal transfer of an existing mortgage from a seller of real property to its buyer.

assignment of rents — a security device by which a lienholder is given the right to collect rents directly from the property owner's tenants.

assignor — a person or entity who transfers a tangible or intangible property right to another. See also *assignee.*

associate broker — (also called a "broker associate" or "affiliate broker") a licensed real estate broker who works under the supervision of another broker. See also *broker.*

associate licensee — a licensed real estate salesperson working under the supervision of a broker.

association of Realtors® — See *board of Realtors®.*

assumable loan — a loan secured by real property that contains a provision allowing a seller of the property to transfer the loan officially into the buyer's name. The lender may require the buyer to qualify for the loan and may charge an assumption fee. The seller is relieved of all responsibility for the loan. A loan with an acceleration clause would not be assumable. See also *acceleration clause* and *due on sale clause.*

assumption fee — charge made by a lender to transfer an existing loan to a new party.

at-risk rules — income tax regulations limiting deductible investment losses to the amount the taxpayer has actually invested plus any borrowed funds for which the taxpayer is personally liable. Designed to discourage illegal tax shelters.

attachment — (1) a court order allowing seizure of property to secure payment of a potential judgment. See also lien. (2) a document that is attached to, and made a part of, a contract. See also *addendum*.

attestation — verification by a witness to a person's signature on a document that the signature is genuine.

attic — a space between the roof rafters and the ceiling joists that is accessible after construction is complete. (An inaccessible area is not considered an attic.) See also *garret*.

attorney-at-law — a person who is licensed to practice law.

attorney-in-fact — a person who is authorized to act for another by a power of attorney. See also *power of attorney*.

attornment — formal agreement by a tenant of an existing landlord to become the tenant of a successor landlord. The agreement creates a new tenancy.

attractive nuisance — a dangerous condition of real property that, by its nature, invites trespassers who may be injured or killed. Common examples include open pits or wells, unfenced swimming pools, and unguarded construction sites. Property owners are charged by law with taking special precautions to prevent harm caused by conditions deemed to be an attractive nuisance.

auction — a method of selling real or personal property in which multiple buyer bids are solicited. The property is sold to the highest bidder unless the seller has established a reserve (a price below which the seller will not sell the property) in advance. See also *reserve*.

avenue — a name for a road or street.

avigation easement — the right to use the airspace directly above a parcel of real property for taking off or landing aircraft. Restrictions may be imposed on the height and nature of structures on the property.

avulsion — sudden removal of land by the action of water. See also *accretion*.

awning — shade made of canvas, metal, or other material which projects horizontally from the outside wall of a structure over a window or door and provides protection from sun, wind, or rain.

B

back-end ratio – a lending term referring to the portion of a loan applicant's gross income that would be required to make payments on the proposed loan as well as any other long-term debt the borrower may have. Car loans, installment payments of longer than 1 year, and revolving debt, such as credit card debt, are included. For example, a borrower with a monthly gross income of $10,000 applying for a loan with payments of $2,500/ month who also has a car payment of $500/month, furniture installment debt of $500/month, and credit card debt of $500/month would have a back-end ratio of 40% (in other words, the ratio of the total monthly payments of $4,000 to the gross income of $10,000). Lenders use this ratio as a rule of thumb for underwriting loans. Lenders give back-end ratios careful consideration as a measure of a borrower's tendency to take on debt.

Different loan programs may have different back-end-ratio underwriting guidelines. Currently, typical back-end ratios acceptable to major home lenders range from 38 to 50% or more. See also *front-end ratio.*

back title letter – in states in which attorneys prepare title opinions, a document provided to the at-torney by the title insurer verifying the condition of title as of a particular date. The attorney is asked to research the state of title from that date forward. See also *title insurance.*

backfill – the replacement of earth around a foundation or into an excavated hole in the ground.

backup offer – an offer on real property made after another offer has been accepted by the seller. The backup offer may be accepted by the seller subject to the failure of the first offer.

bad faith – an intent to deal unfairly or to deceive. See, by contrast, *good faith.*

balance sheet – a financial table listing and comparing (balancing) the assets and liabilities of a business operation.

balloon framing – a type of wooden structural framing in which the vertical studs extend from the foundation to the second story roof. Second-floor joists are nailed directly to these studs at the second-floor level. It is not common today because of the additional cost of the longer lumber. It is now more common for each story to be framed separately.

balloon payment – a final payment on an installment loan that is substantially larger than the preceding payments. Balloon payments may be required for any loan that is not fully amortized. See also *amortize.*

baluster – a vertical post supporting a handrail.

balustrade – a unit consisting of a row of balusters, a handrail, and a newel post. See also *baluster*.

bank – (1) a commercial lending institution. Banks traditionally specialized in commercial loans, as opposed to home loans. The financial deregulation of the 1980s brought banks into the home loan business in significant numbers. See also *savings and loan association*. (2) the shore of a river or stream.

bankruptcy – a federal legal proceeding that allows insolvent debtors to escape further liability on the debts incurred up through the time of the filing of the bankruptcy petition. Secured creditors, such as mortgage holders, receive preference in the distribution of proceeds from the sale of the petitioner's assets. See also *insolvency*.

base and meridian – a grid of imaginary lines used by surveyors to locate and describe parcels of real estate. Similar to latitude and longitude, base lines run east and west, while meridian lines run north and south. See also *government survey method*.

base line – the east-west element of the government survey method. See *base and meridian*.

base period – a time period used as a benchmark against which events occurring in other periods are measured. For example, the first year of a commercial lease might be designated the base year and assigned a value of 100%. Increases in the cost components of the lease, such as rent, utilities, taxes, etc., would be compared to the base year and assigned values such as 104%, 112%, 110%, etc. Rent in the base year is $1,000. If rent increases to $1100 in year 2, its value is 110% of the base year.

base rent – a minimum rental amount in a commercial lease that has additional rental amount components, such as a sales percentage. For example, Abel leases retail space to Baker with a $5,000/month *base rent* plus 3% of gross sales as additional rent.

baseboard – a trim or molding covering the gap between a wall and a floor.

baseboard heating – an electrical or hot-water room heating system that radiates heat from the baseboard area.

baseline – See *benchmark*.

basement – the full-height or nearly full-height story of a building that is wholly or largely below ground level. See, by contrast, *crawl space*.

basis – dollar amount associated with an asset for purposes of determining depreciation, taxable gain, or loss. Basis usually refers to the cost to acquire less accumulated depreciation plus additions. See also *book value*, *capital gain*, and *tax basis*.

basis point – 1/100 of 1%. Used to describe and measure interest rates and interest rate changes. 50 basis points equal ½%.

bathroom – a room containing a toilet, a sink, and a bathtub. Conventionally, this is regarded as a full bath. A three-quarter bath contains a toilet, a sink, and a shower. A half-bath contains a toilet and a sink. A quarter-bath typically consists of an alcove or small room with a sink. See also *powder room*.

bay window – a window with three sides that project from the exterior of a structure The sides typically meet at either 90° or 45° angles. See also *bow window*.

beam – a large linear structural member made of steel, iron, wood, or other strong materials.

bearing wall – a wall that structurally supports another building component, such as a roof or an upper floor.

bedrock – relatively solid rock under looser soils.

bedroom – a room in a structure designed or designated as a sleeping space. Typically, bedrooms are distinguished from dens or bonus rooms in a house by the presence of a closet.

bedroom community – a residential neighborhood or community on the outskirts of an urban area in which the residents commute to the urban area to work and return home at night.

before-and-after method – a method of appraisal used to determine the value of a property that has been "partially taken" by some government action. This method compares the presumed value of a property before and after some action or change in the property that has reduced its utility. Used primarily to establish compensation for property owners who suffer damages as a result of government action that unfairly reduces the value of their property. See also *condemnation* and *eminent domain*.

benchmark – (1) a permanent physical marker used by surveyors to designate the elevation above sea level of a particular site; (2) a standard or criterion to which some change is compared.

beneficiary – a person designated to receive benefits through the actions of another person. For example, persons receiving income or property from a trust, loan, insurance policy, or will are beneficiaries under the terms of those documents.

beneficiary's demand – the written instructions from a beneficiary to a debtor under a deed of trust or a mortgage setting forth the amount that must be paid to receive a reconveyance from the beneficiary. For example, in a typical sale of a home with an existing mortgage, the escrow officer will contact the lender of record and ask that a written payoff demand be sent to escrow. It will take the form of a letter stating the amount required to satisfy the debt. When escrow closes, the specified sum will be conveyed to the lender who will then issue a document indicating that the debt has been paid in full. See also *beneficiary* and *trust deed*.

bequeath — to designate in a will the intended recipient of personal property. See also *devise*.

betterment — any capital improvement that substantially increases property value.

biannual — an event that occurs twice in a given year. See also *biennial*.

bid — the price offered by a buyer. See also *asking price*.

biennial — an event that occurs once every two years. See also *biannual*.

bilateral contract — a contract in which two or more of the parties exchange promises to perform or refrain from performing some act. A real estate purchase contract is a typical example. The buyer promises to pay for the property, while the seller promises to deliver title and possession. See also *contract* and *unilateral contract*.

bill of sale — a written agreement used to transfer an interest in personal property. Often employed in conjunction with a real estate contract to specify the personal property (such as washer, dryer, furniture) being transferred as part of the transaction.

binder — generally, an exchange of consideration leading to a commitment that falls short of a formal contract. Examples include (a) insurance binders, in which an insurer offers immediate temporary fire insurance pending a final review and approval by the underwriter; (b) the exchange of a deposit to evidence a verbal agreement to purchase real estate; and (c) a report issued by a title company evidencing a willingness to insure title to a parcel of property if certain conditions are met.

binding arbitration — a method of dispute resolution in which the parties to a contract agree to submit any disputes to a neutral third-party arbitrator, who will hear the dispute and render a decision. The decision is enforceable in a court of law and may not be appealed. See also *arbitration* and *mediation*.

biweekly mortgage loan — a loan in which the amortization provision calls for payments every two weeks, usually at half the monthly amount. The principal balance is reduced more quickly, resulting in lower total interest costs and a shorter term for the loan.

Blackacre — (also called Whiteacre) a fictitious name for a parcel of land, formerly used on legal documents to distinguish one property from another and to avoid confusion.

blacktop — a paving surface composed of gravel with a black oil-based binder.

blanket mortgage — a single mortgage covering multiple parcels of real estate, typically used by a residential developer who purchases a number of residential lots using one mortgage. The developer then builds and sells individual houses. The blanket mortgage will usually include a partial release provision, providing for partial principal reductions as the individual houses are sold. Another common use for a blanket mortgage is to offer extra security to a lender by pledging additional properties.

blended rate — a composite interest rate on two or more loans; often seen in a *wraparound mortgage*, in which an existing low interest rate mortgage is combined with secondary seller financing at a different, usually higher, rate. See also *all-inclusive trust deed* and *wraparound mortgage*.

blind — a shutter or shade covering a window.

blind nailing — a method of nailing

in which the nail heads are countersunk, puttied, and concealed from view.

BLM — See *Bureau of Land Management*.

block — (1) a parcel surrounded by streets; (2) one component of a legal description used in some states, such as Lot 29, Block 643, Tract 11825. See also *lot, block and tract (subdivision)*.

blockbusting — the illegal and discriminatory practice of generating residential real estate sales for personal profit through any representation that members of a protected group (such as those identified by race, gender, religion, physical or mental disability, familial status, or ancestry) may be moving into the area. Blockbusters generally imply that property values will fall if this occurs. Severe federal and state criminal and civil penalties apply for blockbusting.

blueprint — a large-format set of architectural, structural, and systems drawings intended to guide tradespeople as they build a structure. These drawings are called blueprints because historically the photochemical process used to copy the drawings results in dark blue lines on a light blue background. Such drawings now appear on off-white paper with black or dark blue lines.

blue-sky law — any of a broad package of federal and state legislation and administrative regulations designed to protect purchasers of securities against offerings as worthless as "so many feet of blue sky."

board – (1) piece of lumber 2 inches or less thick and 8 inches or more wide, of any length; (2) name for a variety of public or private management associations such as a board of supervisors, a planning board, a board of directors, or a board of Realtors®.

board foot – a unit of volume applied to lumber used in construction; equivalent to a plank of lumber 1 foot wide, 1 foot long, and 1 inch thick.

board of equalization – a local or state government agency charged with the task of ensuring that tax assessments are applied uniformly and fairly in the area of its jurisdiction. It has the power to adjust (equalize) assessments that are considered too low or too high in a given area.

board of Realtors® – (also called an "association of Realtors®") a local group of real estate licensees who also maintain membership in the National Association of Realtors® (NAR) and a state association of Realtors®. Local boards of Realtors® may own or operate the local multiple listing service (MLS), although the recent national trend has been to separate board and MLS organizations. Members are bound by a code of ethics in their dealings with one

another and with the public at large.

boilerplate – standard language in a contract that covers the most common provisions. Often pre-printed in the real estate contracts commonly used by agents and customized for local differences and needs.

bona fide – actual; in good faith.

***bona fide* purchaser** – an arm's-length purchaser of real property who exercises reasonable diligence in the purchase. *Bona fide* purchasers are usually accorded special protection against prior unrecorded claimants to the property.

bond – (1) an insurance arrangement in which an individual or business may be compensated for loss or damage by the failure of another party to complete some act or project promptly or properly. For example, in a construction contract, a completion bond may be used to ensure that the builder will complete the project on time. If the builder fails to do so, the proceeds from the insurance may be used to retain another builder to complete the project. See also *completion bond* and *performance bond*. (2) a form of debt instrument often used for financing public improvements such as schools, airports, and roads. An authorized agency may borrow money through the sale of bonds for an approved purpose, pledging specific or general revenues as repayment.

Bonds may be short term (up to 5 years) or long term (up to 40 or 50 years).

book value – for accounting and tax purposes, the value of an asset to an owner at a particular moment in time, generally equal to the *basis* (cost) minus *accrued depreciation*. See also *basis* and *depreciation*.

boot – a tax term identifying any additional value exchanged in an Internal Revenue Code Section 1031 exchange of like-kind properties to make the transaction balance. For example, if Abel exchanges his commercial building for Baker's apartment building plus $100,000, the $100,000 may be considered boot and would be immediately taxable. See also *Section 1031 exchange*.

boring test – the drilling of holes deep into the ground and removal of soil for analysis to determine its suitability as a building site.

boulevard – traditionally, a wide street lined with a pedestrian walkway; currently, any street or road.

boundaries – the legal physical limits of a parcel of land.

bounds – See *metes and bounds*.

bow window – a window that has a convex curved shape and projects from the exterior of a structure. It is distinguished from a bay window by its single curving side. See also *bay window*.

breach of contract – a failure, without legally sufficient excuse, of one party to fulfill the requirements of a contract. A breach by one party may lead to an award of money damages by a court or arbitrator. Alternatively, a breaching party may be ordered to perform the act they have failed to do, such as transfer title to property. This form of remedy is called *specific performance*. See also *contract*, *damages*, and *specific performance*.

break-even point – (1) the dollar rent or occupancy rate of an investment property at which the income equals the debt service and operating expenses; (2) the point at which accrued cash equals cash advanced for acquisition..

bridge loan – (1) a short-term commercial real estate loan intended to cover an interim period between two more permanent loans. A typical example is a loan to pay off a construction loan on a commercial project before more favorable permanent financing can be arranged. (2) a short-term residential real estate loan obtained by a buyer to allow the purchase of a new house before the buyer's existing house is sold, often collateralized by both properties. See also *swing loan*.

British thermal unit (BTU) – a measure of thermal energy, commonly used to compare the heat outputs of furnaces and heaters. One BTU is the quantity of heat required to raise the temperature of 1 pound (pint) of water 1 degree from the specified starting temperature of 39° Fahrenheit.

broker – a real estate licensee authorized under state laws to engage in the practice of real estate under his, her, or its own license and to supervise other licensees. A broker may be an individual, a corporation, or a partnership. See also *agent*.

brokerage – the practice of bringing buyers and sellers together and facilitating the sale of an asset such as real property. See also *broker*.

BTU – See *British thermal unit*.

buffer zone – a zoning term meaning an area of land separating one distinct type of land use from another and providing a transition. Examples include (a) apartment buildings located between a residential area and a retail area, and (b) a park area between a residential area and an airport. See also *zoning*.

builder warranty – a limited warranty, offered by a residential builder to a purchaser of a house. Builder warranties are required by law in many states and typically run one or two years. Structural warranties often run for a longer term.

building and loan association – See *savings and loan association*.

building codes – local and state building regulations having the force of law and established to ensure

minimum acceptable structural and safety standards for new construction. Building codes cover most common construction details, and also minimum and maximum structure size and height, parking, and lot size. See also *Uniform Building Code*.

building envelope – an emerging planning term describing both the total volume and shape of a structure. For example, a local planning commission might approve a 50,000 square foot multistory building with the requirement that the top floors be stepped back from the bottom floors to allow for a smaller visual profile or to protect existing views.

building inspection – periodic oversight of the construction process by an authorized public employee designed to ensure safety, health, and building code compliance. Typically, building inspectors visit a site after each major stage in the construction cycle, such as rough grading, foundation forms placement, rough framing, plumbing and electrical installation, etc.

building life – for tax purposes, the estimated useful life of a structure for depreciation purposes. Under current (2000) federal tax laws, nonresidential real estate may be depreciated over 31.5 years, while residential real estate is allowed a depreciation period of 27.5 years. See also *depreciation*.

building line – an administratively

determined line on a parcel of land beyond which no structure may be built. This line is typically established by the setback requirements in local building codes. See also *building setback*.

building permit — legal permission granted by an appropriate local government agency to build a specific structure on a specific site within a specified time period.

building residual technique — an appraisal term describing an approach to the valuation of improvements. The annual income that the vacant land would command is subtracted from the annual net operating income of the land plus improvements to yield the annual income attributable to the improvements. The income is then capitalized to determine the value of the improvements. See also *capitalization* and *net operating income.*

building setback — a municipally determined distance from a property line or street in which the building of a structure is not allowed. Setbacks are typically designed to decrease density, provide access, and/or preserve the character of an area, and vary widely depending on local custom.

build-to-suit — an arrangement by which an owner of land offers to build a suitable improvement for a prospective tenant in exchange for the tenant's agreement to lease the

property. Most common with commercial and industrial properties for which a tenant has very specific requirements.

built-ins — items of personal property that are deemed by law or local custom to be real property because they have been attached or affixed to the property or for which some special opening has been made. Examples include attached bookcases, light fixtures, and wood stoves for which an opening has been made in the roof for a chimney flue.

bulk sale — any sale of a major portion of the material, stock, supplies, or inventory of a business. Bulk sales are commonly encountered in connection with the sale of a business opportunity. They are closely regulated by the Uniform Commercial Code to prevent the defrauding of creditors in the course of a transfer. See also *Uniform Commercial Code.*

bullet loan — a loan with no amortization and a relatively short term of 5 to 10 years. The loan may or may not call for periodic interest payments. A balloon payment of the entire principal and any accrued interest is due at the end of the term. Prepayment penalties are common. See also *amortization* and *balloon payment.*

bundle of rights theory — the essential elements that define private ownership of real property. The "bundle" of rights attached to real property includes the right to access, occupy, and use the property, the right of "quiet enjoyment," the right to sell and devise, and the right to build structures, extract minerals, and grow crops. These rights may be divided with respect to a given parcel. For example, a parent may make a gift of real property to a child, yet retain a life estate with the right to occupy and use the property until the parent dies.

Bureau of Land Management (BLM) — federal agency charged with the task of managing those federal land holdings which are not part of the national forest and national park systems.

business day — a normal working day; not a federal holiday or weekend. Some real estate contracts specify performance in terms of business days.

business opportunity — any business offered for sale. If sale of the business involves a middleman and the transfer of real estate, a real estate license is generally required of the middleman. Business opportunities may also be subject to bulk-sale laws. See also *bulk sale.*

buy-back agreement — a contract provision obligating the seller to repurchase the property from the buyer at a stated price or following a price formula in the event that some condition occurs within a specified time. Typically employed for the pro-

tection of a buyer who is concerned that a job transfer may occur.

buy-down — a payment to a lender in exchange for a lower interest rate for all or part of a loan period; essentially, prepaid interest. For example, if a builder wishes to make his or her houses more attractive to buyers, the builder may offer to pay a fee to a lender in exchange for a reduction in the interest rate on the buyer's loan for the first year or two. A common example is a 2-1 buy-down, in which the interest rate is reduced two percentage points in the first year and one percentage point in the second year of the loan. From the third year onward, the interest rate would be the same as if the buy-down had not occurred.

buyer's broker — a real estate broker who is contracted by, and is usually paid by, a buyer. Many states now allow buyer–broker agreements in which the buyer agrees to pay a fee to the broker if the buyer purchases a property, whether that purchase is through an MLS listing, a for-sale-by-owner (FSBO), a lender foreclosure, or a probate sale. A buyer's broker owes a fiduciary duty to the buyer.

buyer's market — a casual term indicating a market in which the supply of property exceeds the supply of willing and able buyers. See, by contrast, *seller's market.*

buy-sell agreement — a contractual agreement in a partnership in which the partners agree to purchase the interest of a partner who leaves the partnership because of some specified event, such as death or disability. Departing partners agree to sell their interests to the remaining partners in such an event.

bylaws — organizational rules that form the framework for the organization's actions. Bylaws typically specify how decisions are to be made and by whom. Homeowners' associations are usually governed by bylaws.

C

cadastral map — a map used for title and tax inventory purposes, giving the location, description, boundaries, and owners of real property in a given tax jurisdiction.

caissons — vertical, poured-in-place concrete building foundation supports, extending from the surface to bedrock, often used on sloped lots or where surface soil is unstable. See also *pile*.

call provision — a clause in a loan document giving the lender the right to demand immediate repayment of the debt upon the occurrence of a specified event or contingency. See also *acceleration clause*.

cancel — to nullify or void. In a real estate contract, refers to the buyer or seller expressing the intent to withdraw from a transaction.

cancellation clause — a contract provision giving one party the right to withdraw from a transaction upon the occurrence or nonoccurrence of some specified contingency. An example is a provision giving a seller the right to cancel a real estate purchase contract if the buyer has not received loan approval by a specified date.

cantilever — the unsupported or projecting portion of a beam, truss, or other structural element.

cap — (1) abbreviation for *capitalization*; (2) a contractual limit place on a loan feature. Yearly (or periodic) and lifetime interest rate caps and yearly (or periodic) payment caps are common examples. See also a*djustable rate mortgage*.

capacity to contract — the legal ability of a person or entity to enter into a valid contract that may be enforced in a court of law. Minors have a limited capacity to contract: Contracts for essentials, such as food, shelter and medical care, may be enforceable; other contracts, such as the purchase of a car, may be disaffirmed by the minor, and will not be enforced by a court. Parties declared insane or incompetent by a court may not enter into enforceable contracts. See also *competent party*.

capital — money or property used in the production of goods or income.

capital asset — a tax term meaning

property not held for sale in a trade or business. Examples include business machinery, land held for investment, stocks and bonds, and a taxpayer's principal residence.

capital expenditure – (1) an accounting and tax term meaning money spent for an improvement that increases the value or utility of an existing fixed asset, example, new heating systems, swimming pools, and room additions; (2) money spent on the purchase of a new fixed asset, such as additional land for a farm. Repairs and routine maintenance, such as painting, are not capital expenditures.

capital gain – (1) positive difference between book value or cost and the proceeds from sale; (2) a tax term meaning the portion of the proceeds from the sale of a capital asset that is subject to taxation at capital gain tax rates. Capital gain is generally equal to the net sales price less the adjusted basis. Different tax rules apply depending on whether the gain is considered long term (assets held more than one year) or short term (assets held less than one year). At the present time (2000), the most favorable rules apply to the sale of a personal residence: Married couples can exclude from taxation as much as $500,000 from the sale of their primary residence. To qualify, the couple must have lived in the house at least two of the past five years. Partial exclusions may also apply. See, by

contrast, *capital loss.*

capital improvement – the improvement acquired or produced through a capital expenditure. See also *capital expenditure.*

capital loss – a tax term meaning the portion of a loss realized from the sale of a capital asset that is deductible against either capital gain or ordinary income. Different tax rules apply depending on whether the gain is considered long term (assets held for more than one year) or short term (assets held for less than one year). Losses incurred in the sale of taxpayer's primary residence are not deductible. See, by contrast, *capital gain.*

capital structure – the proportion or mix of debt and equity of a capital investment. For example, a building currently worth $1,000,000 was purchased several years ago for $800,000 with a down payment of $100,000, a first trust deed of $500,000, and a second trust deed of $200,000. The current capital structure, assuming no amortization on the loans, would be $300,000 attributable to equity, $500,000 debt (first trust deed), and $200,000 debt (second trust deed).

capitalization – (1) a method of estimating the present value of a future income stream or event. It is commonly used to arrive at appropriate "indicated" (estimated) values for investment properties and other income-producing assets. The formula is generally [*annual net income ÷ the appropriate market-derived or desired rate of return for the type of asset and risk*]. For example, for an apartment building with an annual net income of $100,000, assuming that the average rate of return for such buildings in this market is 8%, the indicated current capitalized value of the income from the building is [$100,000 ÷ 8%] or $1,250,000.

(2) the components of wealth. For example, the capitalization of a business might include shareholder equity, plant and equipment, cash and investments, accounts receivable, and the value of current inventory.

capitalization (cap) rate – the rate of interest that is considered a reasonable return on an investment; also, the rate that is used to determine investment value based on net income. The cap rate is a measure of an investment's risk—the higher the cap rate, the higher the risk, and lower the rate, the lower the risk.

capture rate – a measure of particular seller's competitive position in a specific real estate market. For example, builder Abel sells 100 houses in a six-month period. The total sales for the area during the same period are 400 houses. Abel's capture rate is 25%.

caravan – an organized group tour of several properties for sale by local brokers. It may be organized by a local board of Realtors®, by a real es-

tate company, or through a multiple listing service.

carport – a parking structure having at least a roof and open on at least one side.

carryback financing – any form of seller financing in which the seller takes a note from the buyer as part of the purchase price.

carrying charges – (1) the ordinary costs of owning a property, such as principal, interest, taxes, insurance, association dues, and utilities; (2) the costs associated with holding unimproved land for investment.

carryover basis – a tax term describing the basis of a property acquired from a decedent. The basis is generally the fair market value of the property at the time of death.

casement window – a window hinged to open from the side.

cash equivalent value – (1) value of a property when purchased; (2) an appraisal term describing value that includes adjustments that should be made to the selling price of a comparable property because of nonstandard financing. For example, Abel sells his property to Baker for $1,500,000 but carries a first trust deed of $400,000 at no interest with a balloon payment in five years. Assuming that comparable loans on the open market would cost 10% simple interest, Abel has effectively received $200,000 less than the nominal price paid. The cash equivalent price that Abel might have accepted to achieve the same result would be $1,300,000.

cash flow – (1) measure of actual cash received minus operating expenses for a particular period (inflow minus outflow); (2) positive or negative dollar amount derived from an income-producing asset such as an apartment building after subtracting operating expenses and mortgage payments from rents.

cash method – an accounting method that recognizes income in the year it is actually received and deducts expenses in the year they are actually paid. See also *accrual method*.

cashier's check – a check drawn by a bank on its own account rather than on the account of a depositor. Cashier's checks or wired funds are required in many states to close a real estate sale.

cash-on-cash return – a rate-of-return measure equal to the yearly gross (before tax) cash flow divided by the dollar amount of the capital investment.

casing – (1) the visible trim around a door or window; (2) a frame.

casualty loss – a loss in value to property caused by a sudden and unforeseeable event, such as a storm, theft, or a fire. Deterioration due to age is not a casualty loss.

cause of action – a legal claim

with enough merit to warrant a lawsuit.

caveat emptor – a Latin phrase meaning "Let the buyer beware."

caveats – (1) warnings and cautions in a contract intended to shift responsibility to the party being cautioned; (2) explanations designed to prevent any misinterpretation.

CBA – See *controlled business arrangement*.

CC&Rs – See *covenants, conditions, and restrictions*.

CE – See *certificate of eligibility*.

ceiling joist – horizontal board to which a finished ceiling is attached.

cellar – a storage area under a structure. See also *basement* and *crawl space*.

cement – a powdered mixture of alumina, silica, lime, iron oxide, and magnesia, which, when mixed with water and allowed to cure, becomes very rigid. It is a component of both mortar and concrete. See also *concrete* and *mortar*.

cement block – a hollow building block composed of shaped cement. Also called *cinder block*.

census tract – a geographical area mapped by the federal government in which detailed demographic information, such as age, education, income, and family status, is compiled, maintained, and updated. The data are often useful to businesses seeking to determine the most profitable location for a new business enterprise and to certain interests in political representation.

CERCLA – See *Comprehensive Environmental Response, Compensating, and Liability Act of 1980.*

certificate of eligibility (CE) – a document issued by the Veterans Administration warranting that person named in the document is a veteran qualified to receive a VA loan. See also *certificate of reasonable value* and *VA loan.*

certificate of occupancy (CO) – a document issued by a local government agency certifying that a structure is substantially complete, is in compliance with relevant building and safety codes, and is fit to be occupied.

certificate of reasonable value (CRV) – a document issued by the Veterans Administration after a qualified appraisal of a dwelling warranting a particular value for that dwelling. The CRV is used to establish the upper limit of the VA loan.

certificate of title – an expert opinion, rendered by an attorney, an abstractor, or a title company after a diligent title search, concerning the marketability of the title of a particular property. It is not, in and of itself, title insurance, but it may form a basis for the issuance of title insurance.

certificate rate – the interest rate

that Freddie Mac pays to investors as specified on the participation certificate. See also *Freddie Mac.*

Certified Property Manager (CPM) – the professional designation issued by the Institute of Real Estate Management (IREM) to a real estate licensee after a specified course of study.

Certified Residential Broker (CRB) – the professional designation for real estate licensees who attend a course of special education in the brokerage of individual houses. Issued by the Residential Sales Council, an affiliate of the National Association of Realtors®.

Certified Residential Brokerage Manager (CRBM) – a professional designation certifying training in the area of managing a residential brokerage. Issued by the Realtors® National Marketing Institute (RNMI) to Realtors® after a specified course of study.

Certified Residential Specialist (CRS) – a professional designation for real estate licensees who attend a course of special education and demonstrate a certain level of experience in real estate sales. Issued by the Residential Sales Council, an affiliate of the National Association of Realtors®. Applicants must first hold the GRI designation. See also *Graduate, Realtor® Institute.*

certiorari – a writ of common law origin in which a superior court orders a complete review of the record of a lower court case.

cession deed – a form of deed used to dedicate some portion of a property to a government agency.

cesspool – an underground pit lined with a porous material and designed to collect and hold sewage or other liquid waste. See also *septic tank*.

chain – a measure of length used in the government survey method. A chain consists of 100 links totaling 66 feet. Ten square chains equal 1 acre. See also *link*.

chain of title – a chronological summary of all recorded grants, legal actions, wills, instruments, and proceedings affecting title to a particular piece of real property. The summary begins with the first known owner of the property, often the recipient of a land grant, and seeks to link all subsequent owners without any gaps. If a gap is found, a legal action to "quiet title" may be required to reestablish the legitimacy of the chain. See also *quiet title action*.

change order – an instruction to an architect or builder authorizing changes in design, materials, or construction details to a structure under construction. Change orders usually result in changes in the price of design or construction.

Chapter 7 (bankruptcy) – the federal legal proceeding that allows

insolvent business debtors to escape further liability on the debts incurred up through the time of the filing of the bankruptcy petition.

Chapter 11 (bankruptcy) – the federal legal proceeding that allows insolvent individual debtors to reorganize and restructure debts and obligations incurred up through the time of the filing of the bankruptcy petition under the supervision of a bankruptcy judge or referee.

Chapter 13 (bankruptcy) – the federal legal proceeding that allows insolvent individual debtors to escape further liability on debts incurred up through the time of the filing of the bankruptcy petition. Certain individual assets, such as a homestead, clothes, and personal items, are protected and retained by the bankruptcy petitioner, while other assets are liquidated and distributed among the creditors by the bankruptcy judge or referee.

chattel – an item of personal property (as opposed to real property).

chattel mortgage – a security agreement in which a lender takes a security interest in personal property. Generally superseded by other types of security arrangements under the Uniform Commercial Code. See also *Uniform Commercial Code*.

chimney – a pipe or flue through which smoke from a fire is intended to pass.

cinder block — See *cement block*.

cistern — a tank for storing rainwater, often under ground.

city — any large incorporated municipal area. See also *county, town,* and *village*.

clapboard — boards used as siding that have one edge thicker than another, allowing them to be installed horizontally in a manner similar to shingles. The thick edge of the top board overlaps the thin edge of the bottom board. See also *shingle*.

clear lumber — lumber having a straight grain with no knots, generally used for furniture, cabinets, and visible trim.

clear title — title to real property that is free of unacceptable defects, liens, and encumbrances. Very few properties are free of all encumbrances; clear title describes a normal state of marketable title. See also *cloud on title*.

clerestory window — a window above a door or above the level of the door.

client — (1) one who has engaged the professional services of another; (2) in real estate practice, the party to whom an agent owes a fiduciary duty.

CLO — See *computerized loan origination*.

closed period — the portion of a mortgage term during which the loan cannot be repaid, most often found in ARMs and some commercial property loans.

closed-end mortgage — a mortgage that prohibits the borrower from using the mortgaged property as security for additional loans.

closing — the final transfer of ownership of real property from one party to another; the delivery of the deed to the purchaser. Closings take many forms. In some states, closings occur in an attorney's office; in others, they take place in an escrow office, in a real estate broker's office, or in an office of the county recorder.

closing costs — expenses to both buyer and seller of consummating a real estate transaction which are separate from the actual price of the property. Closing costs vary by jurisdiction, but may include loan fees and points, escrow and title costs, termite and radon inspections and corrective measures, attorney's fees, home warranties, association transfer fees, appraisal charges, and brokers' commissions. See also *Real Estate Settlement Procedures Act*.

closing date — the day on which title in a real estate transfer is actually delivered or recorded. This may be a day or more after the loan has funded (financial closing).

closing statement — (also called a *settlement statement*) a detailed accounting of all cash credits and debits in a real estate transaction provided to the parties. The closing statement is usually prepared by an escrow officer, an accountant, an attorney, or a broker involved in the transaction. See also *settlement statement* and *Real Estate Settlement Procedures Act.*

cloud on title — a presumably invalid encumbrance injuring the marketability of title to real property. Typical examples include recorded but expired options, prior owners whose names continue to appear on title, and paid liens that have not been released. Buyers and title insurers usually require the seller to take action to remove the cloud before title can be transferred. See also *exceptions to title, title,* and *title insurance.*

CMA — See *comparative market analysis.*

CO — See *certificate of occupancy.*

code of ethics — a written description of the ethical duties and standards required of real estate licensees. The National Association of Realtors® requires its members to adhere to a strict written code of ethics, which governs the Realtor's® conduct toward clients and other parties in a real estate transaction. Several states have adopted portions of the code as part of their own real estate licensing rules.

codicil — a document that adds to or modifies a will. See also *will.*

COFI — See *Cost of Funds Index.*

co-insurance — (1) a sharing of insurance risk by insurer and owner; (2) an insurance contract provision specifying the minimum percentage of total building value that must be insured to collect full value in the event of a loss. For example, a $100,000 building typically must be insured for at least 80%, or $80,000. If a fully insured policyholder experiences a $40,000 casualty loss, he or she will receive $40,000 minus any deductible. If the policyholder purchased only $40,000 in casualty coverage, either through inadvertence or because the replacement of the property had risen since the policy was purchased, the co-insurance clause would limit the payment to $20,000 (40% ÷ 80%) minus any deductible. The policyholder will never collect more than the lesser of the actual loss, the policy limit, or the co-insurance limit. Note that many policies with co-insurance clauses also have inflation riders designed to increase coverage automatically as replacement costs rise.

cold call — a phone call made by a real estate salesperson to a prospect without any prequalification of the prospect.

cold canvas — door-to-door solicitation of listings in a residential neighborhood by a real estate salesperson.

COLI — See *Cost of Living Index.*

collar beam — a horizontal structural member connecting the roof rafters at a point above the level of the top of the walls designed to add rigidity and strength to the roof structure.

collateral – a thing of value pledged as security for a debt. In a typical residential mortgage, the thing of value is the property itself. In the event of default, the lender may seize the collateral.

collection account – an institutional intermediary between a party making periodic payments and the ultimate recipient of the payment. Collection accounts are typically established for the protection of buyers in transactions in which the seller remains liable for the mortgage loan. The administrator of the account collects mortgage payments, insurance payments, and taxes from the buyer and passes them directly to the appropriate entities, thus assuring both the buyer and the seller that payments are actually being made.

collusion – the opposite of an arm's-length relationship; a circumstance in which two or more participants in a transaction maintain a secret agreement in order to commit fraud or some other illegal act. An example is a real estate broker who agrees with a buyer to overstate the actual purchase price of property in order to obtain a higher appraisal and more favorable financing.

color of title – the mistaken belief in the appearance of clear title. For example, Abel sells a home to Baker using a forged deed. Baker takes possession of the property under color of title.

column – a vertical pillar, usually supporting a structure.

commercial bank – a financial institution traditionally offering checking accounts and specializing in short-term business loans. In recent years, financial deregulation has blurred the lines between credit unions, banks, and savings and loan associations.

commercial lease – a rental agreement involving office or retail facilities. Commercial leases can be complex and are often drafted by attorneys acting for the principals. See also *lease*.

commercial property – real property used for such business purposes as retail sales, offices, and hotels. See also *industrial property*.

commingling of funds – the illegal mixing of client funds, such as deposits and rents, with a real estate broker's own funds. Most states require a separate trust account for client funds.

commission – compensation paid for a real estate broker's services in arranging a real estate transaction. To earn a commission, the broker must have both a valid real estate license in the state where the property is located and a signed listing agreement or buyer–broker agreement authorizing the payment of the commission.

Commissions are usually stated as a percentage of the purchase or lease price. They are negotiable and are typically paid only upon the successful close of a transaction. Attempts to set or regulate commissions by brokers acting in cooperation with one another may violate federal antitrust laws. See also *advance fees.*

commission split – (1) the common practice of sharing a commission between two brokers in a transaction. For example, broker Abel represents the seller and has a commission agreement with the seller for 7% of the total purchase price. Broker Baker obtains a buyer for the property. Abel may agree to give half of the total commission (3.5%) to Baker in exchange for Baker's procurement and representation of the buyer. (2) the percentage division of the commission between a broker and a salesperson or broker-associate under his or her supervision. Typical splits start at 50% and range up to 95% in favor of the salesperson or broker-associate.

commitment – a lending term meaning a pledge or promise to make a loan. A commitment falls short of formal loan approval, but is often employed by buyers in a commercial and industrial context as a method of establishing financial credibility.

common area – portion of properties, such as planned unit developments, condominiums, or co-ops, designated for nonexclusive use by owners, residents, and guests. Examples include association pools, tennis courts, greenbelts, and elevators.

common area charges – fees charged to individual property owners or tenants for the maintenance of shared areas.

common law – a body of principles, rules, and practices derived from the statutory and case law of England prior to the American Revolution and the establishment of the U. S. Constitution.

common wall – a wall shared by and between two separate dwellings or two separate units in a condominium development.

community association – See *homeowners' association.*

community property – a form of property ownership in some states. Arizona, California, Idaho, Louisiana, Nevada, New Mexico, Texas, and Washington provide for two classes of property: (a) separate property, which is property owned by a husband or wife prior to the marriage or property acquired during the marriage by gift or inheritance; and (b) community property, which is all property acquired during the marriage by means other than gift or inheritance and is deemed to be the fruit of the efforts of both parties. In community property, both parties are entitled to a one-half share of all such real and personal property, which each may sell, devise, or will. See also *joint tenancy* and *tenancy in common*.

co-mortgagors – two or more signatories to a single mortgage, sharing financial responsibility but not necessarily ownership rights. For example, a parent who co-signs a mortgage for a child is obligated under the loan, but might not be a title holder to the property. See also *accommodation party* and *cosigner*.

comparable sales ("comps") – recent sales of local properties that are substantially similar to the subject property.

comparative market analysis (CMA) – (sometimes called the *direct sales comparison approach*) a method of determining the value of real property used by appraisers and real estate brokers that compares actual recent sales of similar local properties to arrive at an indicated value. Small differences in the properties are assigned positive or negative dollar values to allow for direct comparison.

compensating balance – funds deposited by a commercial borrower in an interest-bearing account at a savings institution as an inducement to the institution to approve a loan. Line-of-credit agreements will often tie the maximum amount of the loan to a percentage of compensating balance. Compensating balances are not commonly required in residential mortgage lending.

compensatory damages – See *damages*.

competent party – a party to a contract who has the legal capacity to enter into a contract. See also *capacity to contract*.

completion bond – a type of insurance designed to guarantee that a particular improvement will be built to contract specifications within the contract period. It is typically required in a public works project, such as a freeway, or the construction of a new city hall. See also *bond* and *surety bond*.

compound interest – a method of calculating interest payments in which interest is paid on accrued interest as well as on the remaining principal. The compounding period may be short (one day), or long (quarterly or yearly). Compounding has the effect of increasing the yield of an interest-bearing account. See also *simple interest*.

Comprehensive Environmental Response, Compensation, and Liability Act of 1980 (CERCLA) – (commonly known as Superfund) the Act giving the Environmental Protection Agency (EPA) authority to respond directly to releases or threatened releases of hazardous substances that may endanger human health or the environment.

computerized loan origination (CLO) — a streamlined point-of-sale loan process in which the borrower applies for the loan via a networked computer at a location remote from the lender's office.

concession — a discount or other benefit offered to a prospective commercial tenant as an inducement to sign a lease. Typical concessions include "free rent" (often late in the lease term) and credits for tenant-required improvements to the structure.

concrete — a compound consisting of a mixture of water, cement, and uniformly small pieces of stone used for creating hard flat surfaces or grouting material. A common material for foundations, concrete can also be used to build walls and patios and is even found in modern roof tiles. See also *cement*.

concrete block — a manufactured hollow brick commonly 8 by 8 by 16 inches, used to build walls and raised foundations.

concurrent ownership — ownership of a single parcel of real property by more than one party. See also *community property, joint tenancy,* and *tenancy in common.*

condemnation — an administra-

tive governmental proceeding in which private property is "taken" for public use. Fair compensation to the property owner is generally required. See also *eminent domain.*

conditional commitment — an agreement by a lender to make a loan or loans to an unspecified qualified borrower(s). Conditional commitments are primarily used as a marketing device by residential builders who wish to have attractive financing to offer prospective buyers.

conditional offer — an offer to buy a property that may be withdrawn if certain contingencies or conditions are not met. For example, Abel's offer to purchase Baker's vacant agricultural land only if the city agrees to rezone the land for commercial use is a conditional offer.

conditional sales contract — (also called a *contract for deed* and a *contract of sale*) a sales contract in which the seller retains title to the property until all of the sale conditions are met, usually until the buyer has completed paying for the property. The buyer is said to have an equitable interest in the property until title is transferred.

conditions — provisions in a real estate sales contract that certain events must occur before the parties must fully perform. Examples include a buyer's approval of the inspection report and the preliminary title report, and the lender's approval of

both the buyer and the property. Failure of a condition may excuse the party from performance.

condo — See *condominium*.

condominium — a form of collective ownership of real property. In a condominium, the individual property owners typically own the airspace within their own walls. The structures themselves, the land and the amenities built on the land, are owned in common with the other members of the association.

condominium owners association — a parliamentary organization comprised of all the owners in a condominium complex that makes decisions concerning joint expenditures and enterprises, and enforces the bylaws and the CC&Rs. See also *homeowners' association*.

conduit — (1) a metal covering through which electrical wires are threaded; (2) any pass-through arrangement. For example, partnerships typically receive "conduit tax treatment," in which money flows through the partnership tax-free. The income is taxable to the partners themselves.

confirmation of sale — a judicial approval of a court-ordered or court-supervised sale of real property. Commonly encountered in probate sales. See also *probate sale*.

confiscation — (1) public seizure of private property without just com-

pensation. See by contrast *eminent domain*. (2) public seizure of property used for certain illegal purposes. For example, government agencies may take without compensation property used in illicit drug dealing.

conforming loan — a residential mortgage loan limited to an amount specified in accordance with rules established by the Federal National Mortgage Association (FNMA or Fannie Mae) or the Federal Home Loan Mortgage Corporation (FHLMC or Freddie Mac) for the purchase of such loans. Dollar limits vary over time and between states. Because conforming loans are readily bought and sold, they generally carry a lower interest rate than that of nonconforming loans. See also *jumbo loan, nonconforming loan*, and *super-jumbo loan*.

conforming use — in zoning, a land use or structure that complies with current local land use laws and regulations. See also *non-conforming use* and *zoning*.

consequential damages — damages suffered by one party as an indirect and unforeseen result of an act of another party. For example, in a real estate contract for the sale of a property, a breach by the buyer leaves the seller unable to raise the cash necessary to complete construction on another home and *as a consequence* forced to borrow money at a high rate of interest. The cost of borrowing the money might be considered consequential damages. See also *damages* and *punitive damages*.

conservator — a person appointed by a court to manage property held by another. Conservators are usually appointed to protect the financial interests of legally incompetent persons.

consideration — anything of value exchanged as part of a contract. It may be money, property, or a promise to do something or refrain from doing something. To be enforceable, a contract requires adequate consideration.

construction loan — an interim loan designed to provide funds for the actual construction of improvements on land. See also *acquisition loan* and *takeout loan*.

constructive eviction — a doctrine adopted by courts that allows tenants to break leases because the property has been allowed to become uninhabitable or unfit by the actions or omissions of the landlord for the use specified in the lease. The tenant is said to have been constructively evicted by the landlord.

constructive notice — (also called *legal notice*) a judicial device that imputes knowledge of certain facts to certain parties based on a legal presumption that a reasonable person would have discovered the facts. Examples include recorded liens and notices of default on real property that are public documents by virtue of having been recorded or published in a newspaper of general circulation. See also *actual notice*.

constructive receipt — an income tax rule which holds that having the immediate right to receive money or some item of value, such as in a demand promissory note, is the same for tax purposes as the actual receipt of the money or item of value. For example, if Abel wins a lawsuit for $10,000 in damages against Baker in the year 2000, Abel may be taxed on the $10,000 in the year 2000 even if Baker does not pay the award until the year 2001.

Consumer Price Index (CPI) — a statistical compilation of economic indices maintained by the Department of Labor, Bureau of Labor Statistics that measure the consumer level inflation and deflation over time and that are used by landlords to make adjustments in commercial leases. The index is established at a value of 100 for the base period, which is 1982–1984.

contiguous— sharing a common boundary; touching. See also *adjacent*.

contingency — an event that must take place before the contract is enforceable. A common example is a clause providing that a property must appraise at the full purchase price before the buyer is obligated to complete the purchase. A failure of a contingency is not a breach.

contingency clause — a provision in a contract providing for a contingency. See also *contingency* and *contingent sale.*

contingent sale — a sale in which some contingency remains to be satisfied before the sale contract is enforceable. A common example is a contingency in which the purchaser of a property must first sell another property in order to qualify for a new loan. See also *contingency* and *contingency clause.*

contour map — a topographic map showing elevations with lines connecting points of equal elevation.

contract — a multilateral agreement between two or more parties in which each party agrees to perform or refrain from some act or deliver some property in exchange for a reciprocal promise or delivery from the other party. A valid contract requires competent parties, legal consideration, and mutuality of agreement and obligation. Although contracts generally need not be in writing, real estate contracts for more than a one-year lease must be evidenced by a writing to be enforceable. See also *competent party, consideration,* and *Statute of Frauds.*

contract for deed — (also called *land contract* or *conditional sales contract*) an agreement for the sale of real property in which (a) the buyer makes periodic payments to the seller; and (b) the seller retains legal title to the property and remains primarily liable under any existing mortgages, until the buyer has paid the entire purchase price. The seller retains legal title, while the buyer has the right to possession and use of the property and is said to have equitable title. Note that a contract for deed may trigger a due-on-sale clause in an existing mortgage. See also *conditional sales contract* and *land contract.*

contract of sale — See *agreement of sale.*

contractor — a tradesperson or vendor who offers to perform the work required in constructing improvements to land, such as buildings, in exchange for a fee. General contractors are those tradespeople or vendors who supervise two or more tradespeople in different specialties (called subcontractors) in the construction of a single improvement or during the course of a larger project. In the construction of a house, a general contractor might supervise and coordinate the work of a foundation specialist, a framer, a plumber, an electrician, a finish carpenter, a drywall subcontractor, a tile subcontractor, a landscaper, and a roofer. Contractors typically must have state-issued licenses to enforce payment for their services. See also *subcontractor.*

contribution — an appraisal concept reflecting the pragmatic conclusion that an improvement is worth what it adds to the property's total value, regardless of the cost of the improvement. For example, a second-story addition costing $100,000 might add (contribute) $125,000 to the value of a home, whereas a swimming pool costing $50,000 might add only $20,000 in value. See also *appraisal*.

controlled business arrangement (CBA) — a creation of RESPA, the Real Estate Settlement Procedures Act, meaning ownership by one individual or real estate business entity of more than 1% of another business entity to which business is referred. A common example is a real estate company that also owns an escrow or title company. A CBA is permitted as long as the ownership is disclosed to the consumer, fees are estimated accurately, no referral fees are exchanged between the companies, and the consumer is free to choose other service providers. See also *Real Estate Settlement Procedures Act (RESPA)*.

conversion — (1) any taking, whether legal or illegal, of another's property; (2) the practice of legally changing the status of a residential income property, such as an apartment building, to individual units, such as a condominium; (3) the change in status for tax purposes of a primary residence to a rental property.

convertible ARM — an adjustable rate mortgage with a provision allowing the borrower to elect a fixed interest rate after a certain period of time. See also *adjustable rate mortgage (ARM)*.

convey — to transfer ownership and title to another.

conveyance — (1) the manner in which real or personal property is transferred; (2) the instrument by which the transfer is accomplished.

co-op — cooperative ownership of real property typically used in multi-family dwellings. Property owners purchase shares in a business entity that actually owns the building. As a stockholder, the property owner generally receives a leasehold right to occupy a particular dwelling unit. See also *condominium*.

cooperating broker — a real estate broker who assists the listing broker in a sale. Generally this will be the broker representing the buyer.

corbel — a projecting stone or timber at the bottom of an exterior wall. Corbels are typically used to support bay windows or other structural projections. See also *bay window* and *bow window*.

cord — a measure of volume usually applied to firewood, equivalent to a stack 4 feet high, 4 feet wide, and 8 feet long; 128 cubic feet.

corner — (1) in surveying, a point at which a property line changes direction; (2) real property bounded by two intersecting roads.

corner bead — a strip of perforated

metal applied at the outside junction of two sheets of drywall meeting at a 90° angle and designed to form a durable and rigid corner.

corner influence — in an appraisal, the added value of a corner or near-corner location. See also *appraisal* and *corner*.

cornice — a projecting horizontal design element at the top of an exterior or interior wall.

corporation — a legal entity registered with and regulated by the state. Corporations are generally considered persons for legal purposes and are authorized to buy and sell property, enter into contracts, and pay taxes. Corporations take several forms. The common elements include limited liability for shareholders, unlimited lifespan, and easily transferable ownership interests.

corporeal — capable of being touched; having physical reality. A parcel of real estate is corporeal; the view from the parcel is not.

correction deed — a deed recorded to correct an error in a prior deed. Such corrections typically address misspellings of names or minor errors in a property description.

cosigner — one who signs a note along with another party. A cosigner essentially guarantees payment of the note in the event of default by the primary borrower. See also *accommodation party* and *co-mortgagers*.

cost approach — an appraisal term describing the method of determining the current replacement cost of recreating an improvement as of the valuation date, as an approach to determining value.

Cost of Funds Index (COFI) — a benchmark floating interest rate, derived from a mixture of savings account interest, FHLB advances to member banks, and other borrowed funds. Used primarily as an index to which the interest rates of certain adjustable rate mortgages (ARMs) are linked. See also *Cost of Living Index, LIBOR*, and *prime rate*.

Cost of Living Index (COLI) — a general index of inflation compiled by the federal government. It is used as an index for certain commercial leases and adjustable loans. See also *inflation*.

cost-plus contract — an agreement that the total payment due on a building project will equal the actual cost plus a fixed profit (or fixed percentage override) to the builder. Contrast with a fixed price contract, in which the total cost is known in advance.

co-tenancy — a general term describing an arrangement in which two or more parties have a concurrent ownership interest in real estate. Co-tenancy encompasses tenants in common, joint tenancy, and community property.

Counselor of Real Estate (CRE) — a real estate licensee who is a member of the American Society of Real Estate Counselors (ASREC).

counteroffer — (1) a response other than a rejection or acceptance by a seller to an initial offer; (2) any subsequent response by either buyer or seller. Counteroffers usually incorporate and accept some of the original terms, countering only those deemed objectionable. Any ultimate contract will be defined by the mutually agreed-upon terms contained in the original offer and all counteroffers.

counterparts — duplicate documents intended to be signed separately by parties to a contract. Counterparts provide a way to obtain original signatures on contract documents without shipping the same piece of paper to all the parties in turn. Properly executed counterparts are generally treated as a single agreement.

county — a geographically bounded agency of government within a state. Counties often contain several cities. See also *parish*.

covenant — a promise or agreement to perform, or refrain from performing, some act.

covenants, conditions, and restrictions (CC&Rs) — a set of rules that define the relationships among property owners in a subdivision or condominium. They are typically recorded along with the deed and cover such issues as the responsibility for property maintenance, architectural rules, and use restrictions.

covenants running with the land — written agreement or provision by a property owner that is annexed to the land and that binds successive titleholders. For example, Abel donates a parcel of land to a city with the covenant that it will always be used only as a public park.

CPI — See *Consumer Price Index*.

CPM — See *Certified Property Manager*.

crawl space — any area within a building large enough to permit entry or passage by a person but not large enough for the person to stand up. Crawl spaces may be located below the first floor, between floors, or between a roof and the top floor.

CRB — See *Certified Residential Broker*.

CRBM — See *Certified Residential Broker Manager*.

CRE — See *Counselor of Real Estate*.

creative financing — any method of financing a real property purchase other than a conventional institutional mortgage. Creative financing is usually employed in high interest rate environments or in circumstances where the borrower is not deemed sufficiently credit-worthy for a loan from conventional lenders that meets secondary mortgage market requirements. See also *agreement* *of sale, all inclusive deed of trust, equity sharing,* and *seller financing.*

credit — (1) a loan; (2) an agreement to extend a loan; (3) funds paid to or deemed to have been paid to a party in a real estate transaction. For example, the down payment from the buyer is a credit to the buyer, as are closing costs paid on the buyer's behalf by the seller. (4) a dollar-for-dollar reduction in taxes, as in the investment tax credit.

credit rating — an evaluation of the creditworthiness of a borrower based on a credit report. See also *credit report.*

credit report — a summary evaluation of the credit history of an individual or business. Individual reports are available through several different companies, such as Equifax, Trans Union, and Experian. Individuals have the right under the Consumer Credit Protection Act to review and correct any errors in their credit reports. Business credit reports are available through Dun and Bradstreet.

credit scoring — a numerical method of evaluating an individual's creditworthiness using weighted factors such as job type, job history, credit history, and income history. See also *FICO.*

creditor — an individual or entity that is owed money.

crown molding — trim covering the joint between walls and a ceiling, applied at a 45° angle to the walls and ceiling.

CRS — See *Certified Residential Specialist.*

CRV — See *certificate of reasonable value.*

cul-de-sac — a dead-end street with a circular vehicle turning area at the closed end.

curb — an edging built along a street to form the raised portion of a gutter.

current yield — a method of measuring investment return at a particular point in time. The formula is generally [*current net income* ÷ *investment cost*]. For example, if Abel purchases an apartment building for $1,000,000 and derives income of $80,000 after expenses, his current yield would be ($80,000 ÷ $1,000,000) = 8%.

curtesy — a common law concept giving a husband a life estate interest in a portion of his wife's property after her death. Many states have abolished curtesy or have adopted community property rules that preempt it.

custom builder — a builder who specializes in custom homes. See *custom home.*

custom home — a house built at the order of a particular buyer to their specifications. See, by contrast, *tract home.*

cut and fill — excavation of a hillside or sloped lot in which some of the removed soil (cut) is added to another portion of the lot (fill) to create a flat or buildable lot.

D

dado — a square or rectangular groove made in a piece of wood, into which another piece of wood is fitted and glued. See also *tongue and groove.*

damage deposit — an advance payment made by a tenant to a landlord to cover any excessive wear and tear on the property during the tenancy.

damages — the recoverable monetary loss suffered by a party to a lawsuit or by a party covered by a liquidated damages clause in a contract. See also *liquidated damages.*

damper — an adjustable opening at the top of a fireplace firebox designed to regulate the flow of combustion gases.

date — a particular day in a particular month in a particular year.

DBA — (also called "fictitious business name") "doing business as," a legal alias for a business.

de facto — Latin term meaning "in fact," used when the appearance of something leads to the belief that it is real. For example, a *de facto* corporation might be a business entity that operates like a corporation and appears to the public to be a corporation, yet has failed to file the proper papers with the state.

dealer — for tax purposes, a person who regularly offers for sale property that he or she owns. The test for dealer status is complex and inexact, relying on such variables as the number of properties bought and sold, the length of time the properties are held, and the extent of other income attributable to the taxpayer.

debit — funds paid or deemed to have been paid by a party in a real estate transaction. For example, property taxes due and not yet paid would be a debit to the seller in a real estate transaction and would typically be prorated by an escrow company. See also *credit.*

debt — (1) the actual amount of money owed to another; (2) an obligation to pay money to another.

debt service — the dollar amount required to satisfy periodic or annual loan payments on real property. Refers only to the actual loan payments, not to total expenses or other carrying charges.

debtor — one who owes money to another. See also *creditor.*

debt-to-income ratio — a formula describing the relationship between either total debt or housing debt and total income. The formula is [*debt ÷ gross income*]. For example, if Abel has total monthly debt obligations, including car payments, credit card payments, and real estate loan payments, of $3,000, and gross monthly income of $7,000, his debt-to-income ratio would be ($3,000 ÷ $7,000), or 42.8%. See also *front-end ratio* and *back-end ratio.*

decedent – a person who has died, either with or without a will; most commonly, someone who has died recently.

decibel – a scale for measuring the loudness of a noise, ranging from 0 (inaudible) to 130 (threshold of pain).

deck – (1) an outside floor area constructed of wood. See also *patio.* (2) any flat, artificially surfaced, outside floor area (pool deck, roof deck, etc.).

declaration – (1) a formal statement of a legal pleading; (2) an out-of-court, unsworn statement by a party to a lawsuit; (3) a legal document filed by a developer to create a condominium.

declaration of trust – a written statement by a trustee that certain property, real or personal, is being held in trust for the benefit of another. See also *trust, trustee,* and *trustor.*

declaratory judgment – a determination by a court of the rights and status of the parties to a lawsuit prior to the granting of any actual relief.

For example, a judgment by a court that Abel had "standing" to sue Baker would be a declaratory judgment.

dedication – the gift of land by a private party to a public agency for a public purpose. See also *appropriation* and *cession deed.*

deed – a written document conveying title in real property from a grantor to a grantee. Various types of deeds serve many different purposes. See also *grant deed, grantee, grantor, quitclaim deed, sheriff's deed, trust deed,* and *warranty deed .*

deed in lieu of foreclosure – a deed given by a property owner in default under a trust deed or a mortgage to the lender as an alternative to a formal foreclosure proceeding. Acceptance by the lender generally extinguishes any further obligation to the lender on the part of the borrower. Junior liens, however, are not extinguished. See also *foreclosure* and *short sale.*

deed of confirmation – (also called "correction deed") type of deed employed to correct errors in a previous deed, such as a misspelling of a name or a mistaken property description.

deed of reconveyance – a common form of deed used to transfer legal title from a trustee to a borrower after the loan has been paid in full. See also *trustee.*

deed of release — See *quitclaim deed*.

deed of trust — See *trust deed*.

deed restriction — provision incorporated into a deed that limits and defines the uses of the property. The restriction runs with the land and is binding on successive owners. By imposing restrictions, the grantor has deeded less than a fee simple absolute estate. See also *fee simple absolute estate, remainder,* and *running with the land.*

default — an unexcused failure to perform a contract obligation. A default may also be a breach of contract and can lead to an award by a court of damages or of specific performance. See also *breach of contract, damages,* and *specific performance.*

default judgment — a court-ordered judgment against a defendant who fails to appear in court or answer a complaint.

defeasance — an instrument that destroys or nullifies the force of some other instrument. Examples include a clause typically found in mortgages providing that, when the debt is paid in full, the mortgage is canceled, and clauses providing for rights of redemption by a borrower after a default. See also *redemption.*

defect in title — any recorded instrument encumbering and preventing the transfer of clear title to real property, for example, an unpaid mechanic's lien. Defects in title, which are not uncommon, render a title ineffective. They are not the same as a defective title. See also *defective title.*

defective title — title with a flaw (defect) that renders it ineffective and unenforceable. For example, title obtained through a fraudulent signature is defective title.

defendant — the party from whom relief is sought in a court of law. See also *plaintiff.*

deferred interest mortgage — (also called *negative amortization loan*) a mortgage in which the periodic payment is less than the fully amortized payment. Payment of the accumulated interest is deferred until the mortgage is refinanced or paid off. See also *negative amortization* and *adjustable rate mortgage.*

deferred maintenance — (1) an appraisal term referring to excessive deterioration of an improvement due to lack of normal maintenance. For example, if Abel fails to re-roof his apartment building when required, the building may suffer water damage (a type of deferred maintenance) that reduces its market value. (2) lack of normal maintenance.

deferred payments — payments on a loan obligation that are postponed by agreement to a later date.

deficiency — the dollar shortfall incurred by a lender after a foreclosure and sale. For example, if Abel defaulted on a $300,000 loan on his home, and the lender foreclosed and later sold the home for $250,000 net of all foreclosure costs, the $50,000 shortfall would be called a deficiency. See, however, *antideficiency laws*.

deficiency judgment — a court order stating that a debtor owes the lender the amount of a deficiency after a foreclosure. Some states have enacted antideficiency laws prohibiting deficiency judgments against a homeowner who loses his or her residence in a foreclosure on a purchase money loan. See *antideficiency laws*, *deficiency*, and *purchase money mortgage*.

delayed exchange — (also called *Starker exchange*) a version of an IRC Section 1031 tax-free exchange of real property held for investment. In a delayed exchange, an accommodator holds the sale proceeds while the seller searches for a suitable exchange property. Currently, the seller has 45 days after the close of escrow to identify a new property and 180 days to close the escrow. See also *accommodator*, *Section 1031 exchange*, *Starker exchange*, and *tax-free exchange*.

delinquency — unexcused lateness in the performance of an obligation, such as payment on a mortgage.

delivery — (1) a transfer of possession from one party to another; (2) the transmission, by appropriate means, of the acceptance of an offer.

Delivery is an essential element of acceptance. The law concerning delivery is complex, but generally, delivery of acceptance must be made in a form similar to that of the negotiation. For example, if all offers and counteroffers have been conducted through hand-delivered documents, acceptance should also be hand-delivered. If negotiations have been conducted primarily by fax, Portable Document File (PDF), or other electronic means, an acceptance delivered in like fashion may be sufficient.

demand — (1) the written request by a lender for the amount owed under a note or mortgage, typically submitted to escrow in the sale of real property. (2) in economics, the effective desire (desire backed by ability to pay) for a particular good at a particular time and place. When demand exceeds supply, prices tend to rise. See also *supply*.

demand note — a promissory note giving the lender the unrestricted right to call the note due and payable at will. See also *note*.

demise — a conveyance of a limited estate in real property to another for a period of years or at will. Most commonly used to describe a lease. See also *demised premises* and *estate at will*.

demised premises — property subject to a lease or other limited transfer. See also *demise*.

demography – the study of human population variations, such as age, employment, education, gender, and income. Demographic studies are a key element of real estate market research.

demolition – the physical destruction of a structure or improvement.

density – in urban planning, the relative intensity of land use, the number of dwelling units allowed per unit of land.

department of real estate (DRE) – a state agency charged with the licensing and regulation of real estate professionals.

depletion allowance – a tax credit given in compensation for the loss of value to land caused by the exhaustion (depletion) of a natural resource, such as coal or oil.

deponent – one who gives sworn testimony in a deposition. See also *deposition*.

deposit – (also called *earnest money*) money paid by a buyer as evidence of good faith and as part of the consideration for a contract.

deposit receipt – (1) written record of the deposit paid as part of a contract for the sale of real property; (2) in some states, a term describing the offer itself. See also *offer*.

deposition – sworn testimony by a witness or a party to a lawsuit given in an out-of-court proceeding, gener-

ally before the trial. See also *deponent*.

depreciable life – tax term meaning the maximum number of years over which a particular asset may be depreciated. See also *depreciation*.

depreciated cost – See *adjusted tax basis*.

depreciation – (1) a tax term meaning the allowable tax deduction for wear to and aging of a particular improvement to real property. For example, residential real estate is now generally "27½-year property," meaning that approximately 3.64% of the cost or basis of the improvement may be deducted each year. Depreciation deductions are allowed even if the asset as a whole is appreciating. Depreciation of investment property, if not taken by the taxpayer, will be imputed by the IRS. (2) an appraisal term meaning actual loss in value to an improvement. Depreciation may be attributed to physical depreciation (wear and tear), functional obsolescence (the improvement becomes outdated and less desirable), or economic obsolescence (loss of value caused by factors outside the property, such as changing neighborhood needs or demographics). See also *basis*.

derogatory – colloquial expression for a negative item (an item indicating a slow payment or a default) on a credit report. See also *credit report*.

descent – the acquisition of property by individuals through the operation of law when a decedent leaves no valid will. See also *decedent* and *escheat*.

description — a written definition of the precise location and extent of a parcel of real property. Sometimes also called *legal description*, it identifies the property for purposes of transfer, recordation, and title insurance. See also *government survey method; legal description; lot, block, and tract (subdivision); metes and bounds;* and *plat map.*

designated broker — a licensed real estate broker who is responsible under state law for the operations of one or more real estate offices. See also *broker.*

detached housing — a residential dwelling built on a separate lot and sharing no common walls with neighboring dwellings. Although this phrase most commonly describes a single-family house, it can also refer to a freestanding condominium unit.

developer — an individual or business entity responsible for the creation of improvements to real property, such as shopping centers, housing, and office buildings. A developer is distinguished from a contractor in such a project by the higher levels of responsibility, financial risk, and planning and supervision.

development — (1) the process of planning and constructing substantial improvements to real property; (2) the completed improvements themselves. For example, a completed housing tract is sometimes referred to as a development.

development rights — an agreement by a landowner to allow the construction of improvements on the land. This right is typically sold by the landowner to a developer. Often, the development rights are purchased in conjunction with a master lease that allows the developer to construct improvements on the land and derive enhanced rents from them for a specified period of time. See also *entitlement* and *master lease.*

devise — the transfer of real property by operation of a valid will. See also *bequeath.*

devisee — one who receives real property under the terms of a will. See also *devise, devisor, testator/testatrix,* and *will.*

devisor — a person, specifically, a *testator*, who leaves real property to another through means of a will. See also *devise, devisor, testator/testatrix,* and *will.*

diluvion — the gradual removal by water action of land along a shoreline or watercourse. See also *alluvium/alluvion.*

dimensional lumber — standard sizes of milled lumber used in residential and commercial construction. Sizes are typically expressed in the form "inches x inches x feet." For example, a "2 x 4 x 8" is a board nominally 2 inches deep by 4 inches wide and 8 feet long. See also *board* and *board foot*.

direct capitalization — See *capitalization*.

direct costs — (also called *hard costs*) expenses associated with the actual construction of an improvement to land, such as site preparation, grading, lumber, and construction labor costs. Indirect costs or soft costs include expenses such as building permit fees, architect's fees, insurance, and broker commissions. See also *indirect costs*.

direct endorsement — an FHA program designed to streamline the loan process for borrowers that authorizes certain approved lenders to underwrite FHA loans directly. See also *FHA loan*.

direct reduction mortgage — the most common home loan; a fully amortized real estate loan in which the periodic payment includes both interest and some principal reduction. Over time, with a level payment, the amount applied to principal reduction increases and the amount for interest decreases. See also *amortized loan*.

direct sales comparison approach — See *comparative market analysis*.

disability — a physical or mental impairment. See also *Americans with Disabilities Act*.

disaffirm — to repudiate or cancel a contract. A party to a contract may elect to disaffirm a voidable contract. For example, a minor who purchases a car without an adult cosigner may disaffirm the contract.

disbursement — money paid out.

discharge — (1) to satisfy an obligation through full payment or performance; (2) satisfaction of a debt through full payment.

discharge of bankruptcy — a court order legally releasing the petitioner (debtor) from specific debt obligations. Discharge of bankruptcy is the final step in a bankruptcy proceeding. See also *bankruptcy*.

discharge of contract — cancellation or termination of a contract. Discharge may occur through full performance, mutual rescission, or by operation of law, such as bankruptcy or the Statute of Frauds. A breach is not a discharge. See also *contract*.

discharge of lien — an order removing a property lien, which may be issued because the lien has been satisfied, or for some other reason, such as illegality or fraud. See also *lien*.

disclaimer — (1) a statement denying knowledge of some fact(s) or disavowing legal responsibility. Disclaimers are common in real estate contracts. For example, a listing broker may disclaim knowledge of the actual square footage of a property, placing the buyer on notice that the buyer should make his or her own measurements. (2) a renunciation of any ownership interest in a parcel of real property.

disclosure – in real estate practice, the transmission of facts by a seller or a broker to a buyer with regard to a particular parcel of real property.

disclosure statement – (1) a document given to a buyer of real property by a seller and/or broker that includes facts known to the seller and/or broker concerning the physical condition and legal status of the property. For example, roof leaks and unpermitted room additions would typically be disclosed in this document. Required by law in an increasing number of states as part of the residential real estate sales process. (2) any factual statement or statements required by law in a transaction involving real estate. For example, the federal Truth in Lending Law (Regulation Z) requires that a lender provide a detailed statement of the estimated costs of a loan to borrower before the borrower agrees to accept the loan.

discount – the difference between the face value of an instrument and its sale price. For example, if a seller carried back a one-year $100,000 note from a buyer with no interest and immediately decided to sell the note, he or she would need to discount the note to make it attractive

to an investor. If the investor in the example required a 15% return, the price the investor would be willing to pay for the $100,000 note would be $79,755.98 (the amount you would need to invest today at 15% interest to have $100,000 in one year). The discount would be ($100,000 – $79,755.98), or $20,244.02.

discount broker – a licensed real estate broker who offers real estate services for less than the typical rate in a given area. Often, but not always, the services are less extensive than those provided by a conventional broker.

discount points – a percentage (percentage points) of the loan amount paid by a seller or buyer to a lender to compensate for any difference between the allowable VA or FHA loan interest rate and the current market interest rate. One discount point is equal to 1% of the loan amount. See also *points*.

discount rate – a rate at which the Federal Reserve makes short-term funds available to member banks. Controlling the discount rate is one way the Federal Reserve attempts to influence market interest rates. It is closely watched.

discounted cash flow – a method of determining the present value of a future income stream. The income is discounted, using an appropriate rate of return to arrive at a present value. The present value can be calculated using a financial calculator or estimated using a present value table. See also *internal rate of return* and *net present value.*

discovery – a pre-trial process in which the litigants can compel one another to produce evidence and the testimony of witnesses that may be used at trial.

discrimination – as defined in the federal Fair Housing Act of 1968, unequal treatment of potential buyers or renters based on the buyer's or renter's race, color, religion, gender, or age constitutes unlawful discrimination. Other federal and state laws prohibit discrimination in residential lending. Also, other laws prohibit discrimination for other physical characteristics, such as physical disability. Landlords, sellers, real estate brokers, and agents are all bound by these laws.

disposal field – an underground drainage area designed to disperse waste from a septic tank. See also *septic tank.*

distress sale – a sale of real property in which buyers are aware of the seller's urgent need to dispose of the property quickly. Reasons can include divorce, tax liens, and imminent foreclosure. Appraisers may treat distress sales as below-market or liquidation sales.

divided interest – an estate in real property in which two or more persons hold separate title. Tenants in

common hold a divided interest in the same property. See also *estate.* See by contrast *fractional interest.*

divorce – a legal dissolution of a marriage, which often requires a division of property, including any real estate held by husband, wife, or husband and wife together. See also *community property.*

documentary evidence – evidence in written form used in a legal proceeding.

documentary tax stamps – a term covering both the original stamps used as evidence that a real estate transfer tax had been paid and the tax itself. See also *tax stamps.*

dock – a structure extending from land into a river, lake, or other water, for purposes of tying up water craft, fishing, or diving.

domicile – the state in which a person maintains a permanent residence. A domicile may be established largely through intention; that is, a person who has lived 20 years in New York may legitimately claim California as a domicile if he or she has maintained some type of residence in California and has an intention to return there. Generally, a person may have only one domicile.

dominant tenement – the estate (property interest) that benefits from an easement on another property. For example, Abel owns a farm to which the only access is by an easement road over Baker's property. Abel's farm is the dominant tenement. Baker's property is said to be the servient tenement. See also *easement* and *easement in gross*.

donee – a recipient of a gift or bequest.

donor – a person or entity making a gift or bequest.

dormer, dormer window – a vertical window projecting through an existing roof and having its own distinct roofline.

double entry – an accounting term describing a system of accounting in which dollar entries appear as both a credit and a debit. Escrow closing statements use double entry. Each amount appears as a credit to one party and a debit to the other. See also *credit* and *debit*.

double escrow – (also called "back-to-back escrow") set of escrows in which party A agrees to purchase property owned by party B using one escrow and simultaneously agrees to sell the property to party C at a higher price using a separate escrow. Double escrows present opportunities for fraud, and real estate licensees are generally under an affirmative obligation to disclose the existence of a double escrow to all parties when they are aware of it.

dower – (also called "dower right") in some states, the right of a widow to a share of her deceased husband's estate. States with community property laws have abolished dower. See also *curtesy*.

down payment – the portion of the purchase price for real property paid directly by or on behalf of a purchaser at the time of purchase, as opposed to the portion paid from the proceeds of a new mortgage loan or loans. The down payment does not include closing costs such as escrow and title fees. For example, Abel purchases a property for $200,000. He obtains a new loan for $160,000. His closing costs are $5,000. His down payment would be $200,000 less $160,000, or $40,000. He still must pay the $5,000 closing costs.

downspout – a vertical pipe designed to carry rainwater from an eaves trough along the lower edge of the roof or upper part of a structure to the ground. See also *gutter*.

downzoning – change in zoning to reduce density or intensity of land use. A common example is an increase in the minimum lot size required to build a house, which results in fewer houses per acre. Downzoning does not generally require that compensation be paid to affected property owners, although it often has a negative effect on certain individual property values. See also *eminent domain*.

dragnet clause – a provision in a mortgage loan in which the borrower pledges other properties as collateral on the loan. Any default on any of the pledged properties may trigger a foreclosure by the holder of the mortgage on the property with the dragnet clause. See also *spreading agreement.*

draw – a provision in a construction loan allowing for periodic disbursements of a portion of the loan proceeds as certain expenses are incurred and tasks are completed. The draw is typically administered by a bank officer, who is charged with monitoring the progress of construction to ensure that the loan is being used properly.

DRE – See *department of real estate.*

dry mortgage – a real estate loan in which the property itself provides the lender's only security; a non-recourse loan in which there is no personal obligation to pay any deficiency after a foreclosure.

dry rot – damage to wood caused by a fungus.

dressed lumber – lumber having one or more smooth sides. See also *lumber.*

drywall – an alternative to (wet) plaster. An interior wall and ceiling material composed of a sheet of gypsum bonded to heavy paper. Drywall is available in various sizes ranging upward from the common 4 by 8 feet and is typically ½ inch thick. Drywall is fastened to wood or metal studs with nails or screws. The seams between sheets are covered with a thin paper or plastic mesh tape. The seams and nail or screw holes are then covered with a thin layer of drywall compound, sanded, and primed. The entire wall or ceiling may then be painted. See also *drywall compound* and *gypsum.*

drywall compound – a paste designed to cover and conceal seams in drywall. See also *drywall.*

dual agency – a circumstance in which a single real estate broker represents both buyer and seller in a single transaction. Dual agency exists even when different agents associated with the same real estate company represent the buyer and the seller. Because of the potential for conflicts of interest and the difficulty of maintaining a fiduciary relationship with two parties whose interests are not the same, most states require that the dual agency relationship be disclosed to the parties and further require that the parties consent in advance to the arrangement.

dual contract – a fraudulent real estate purchase agreement submitted to a lender for the purpose of obtaining a higher loan-to-value ratio than would otherwise be allowed. For example, Abel agrees to purchase Baker's property for $500,000 with a 20% down payment. Abel then submits a modified (and fraudulent) purchase agreement to his lender, showing a purchase price of

$625,000, in an effort to obtain a loan for 80%, or $500,000, the actual full purchase price.

duct – a cable, pipe, tube, or pathway designed to contain and enclose wiring, plumbing, and conditioned or exhaust air within a structure.

due date – a date after which a payment specified in a note or contract is delinquent. See also *grace period*.

due diligence – (1) a reasonable effort made to determine relevant facts concerning a transaction or undertaking; (2) an obligation by the parties in a transaction to make a reasonable effort to fulfill the contingencies of the transaction. A common example is the duty of a buyer of real property to complete and submit a loan application promptly to an appropriate institutional lender. A failure to exercise due diligence may constitute a breach of contract.

due-on-sale clause – See *acceleration clause*.

dummy – one who substitutes for another in a transaction in order to conceal the principal's identity. Examples include shell corporations set up to obtain real estate loans and a "straw man," an individual who purchases a property on behalf of another party, intending to transfer it immediately to that party. See also *straw man*

duplex – a dwelling comprised of two separate, complete living units.

duress – (1) illegal coercion of one party by another by threats or actual bodily harm; (2) undue influence of one party over another. An example is the sale of a property by an elderly person to a younger (influential) guardian at a below-market price. Courts may void a contract signed under either form of duress.

duties of care – affirmative obligations of an agent to act responsibly on behalf of not only the principal, but often also on behalf of other participants in a transaction or negotiation. In real estate practice, the duties of care of each agent are specified by applicable state law, and vary by jurisdiction. Generally, an agent owes a fiduciary duty of utmost care, integrity, honesty, and loyalty toward his or her principal. An agent also may owe a somewhat lower good faith and fair dealing duty of care toward other participants in a transaction or negotiation. These duties might include an obligation to act diligently and responsibly, a obligation to act honestly and in good faith, and an obligation to disclose facts that materially relate to the value of the property to all parties to the transaction. In the case of dual agency, a single agent may owe a fiduciary duty to both the buyer and the seller. See *also agency, dual agency, fiduciary duty*, and *good faith and fair dealing*.

dwelling — any structure used or designed for human habitation. See also *home, residence,* and *domicile.*

E & O insurance — See *errors and omissions insurance.*

early occupancy — (1) possession of a property by a buyer prior to the close of an escrow. Usually established by agreement in the purchase contract, early occupancy is considered a form of tenancy until escrow actually closes. (2) may also apply to entry into leased premises by the lessee for purposes of improving the premises prior to the rent payment start date. The usual pre-conditions of such early occupancy are the payment of security deposits, executing the lease, providing required insurance policies and utilizing only lessor-approved plans and specifications for such improvements.

earnest money — (1) a deposit offered by a prospective purchaser of real property as evidence of good faith and capacity to purchase, usually credited toward the purchase price at the close of escrow; (2) the measure of liquidated damages in the event the buyer breaches the real estate purchase contract. See also *good faith deposit* and *liquidated damages.*

easement — a limited property interest held by one person in the real property owned by another. Unlike leasehold, an easement is not a possessory interest and generally consists of the right to pass over or use another's property for purposes of enjoying one's own property. See also *dominant tenement, easement appurtenant, easement by necessity, easement by prescription, easement in gross, negative easement,* and *servient tenement.*

easement appurtenant — an easement attaching to a parcel of property, the servient tenement or servient estate, and benefiting a parcel of property owned by another, the dominant tenement or dominant estate. Easement appurtenant is said to "run with the land," meaning that it is in the nature of a covenant and survives transfers in ownership of either property. Common examples are the right to pass over another's property to reach a public roadway, and the use of shared driveways on flag lots.

easement by necessity — an easement created by operation of law when a single grantor has transferred a parcel of property to another that equitably requires some use of some other parcel of land owned (or once owned) by the grantor for its effective enjoyment. The most common example is a landlocked property where the only possible access is over another property owned by or transferred by the grantor.

easement by prescription – a method of acquiring a property interest personally through long-standing usage or custom adverse to the actual property owner's interest and under claim of right or color of title. The continued usage is restricted to the original claimant and his or her ancestors or grantees. One example is the use over a statutory number of years by owner Abel of a path to the beach over owner Baker's land, even though Abel has alternative access to the beach over a less convenient public road.

easement in gross – an easement typically acquired by grant allowing the grantee personally to use or travel over the property of another. It does not involve a second property, is not transferable, and usually ends with the death of the grantee or the transfer of the property. One example is a right that property owner Abel grants to friend Baker to hike over Abel's land during camping trips to an adjacent wilderness area.

eave – the portion of a roof that projects beyond the side walls of a building.

ECOA – See *Equal Credit Opportunity Act.*

economic base – the industries and businesses within a geographic area that generate employment and taxes for the area.

economic life – (1) the time period over which an improvement to land will generate revenues in excess of operating expenses; (2) the time period over which an improvement to land will generate revenues in excess of those attributable to the land itself; (3) the time period over which an improvement to land has value in excess of its salvage value; (4) the time period over which an improvement is forecast to produce income at a competitive rate of return. The economic life of an improvement is usually less than its physical life and forms the basis of the income tax concept of depreciation. See also *depreciation.*

economic obsolescence – a loss in value to a property caused by factors external to the property. Common examples include a local recession that depresses property values and a new landfill or airport constructed near a residential property.

economic rent – the rent a property could command on the open market, which may be more or less than the current contract rent. See also *market rent.*

effective age – an appraisal concept meaning the apparent age of improvements to real property based on wear and tear rather than the chronological age of the property. Poorly maintained properties will have a greater effective age (and a lower value) than actual age would indicate. See also *actual age.*

effective gross income – potential gross income at 100% occupancy minus a vacancy allowance plus any miscellaneous income. For example, consider a 10-unit apartment building in which each unit rents for $1,000 per month and coin laundry income of $200 per month produces a potential gross income of $10,200 per month. Assuming a 5% vacancy factor, the effective gross income would be [$10,000 - (5% of $10,000) + $200], or $9,700 per month.

effective interest rate — the actual rate of interest on a loan taking into account all financing costs. For example, Abel takes out a $100,000 real estate loan at 7% simple interest for one year. He pays three points plus loan fees of $1,000. His total financing costs are, therefore, $11,000 ($7,000 + $3,000 + $1,000) and the effective interest rate is 11%. See also *annual percentage rate* and *effective yield*.

effective tax rate — the combined local, state, and federal income tax rates for a taxpayer. A simplified formula is [effective tax rate = federal rate + state rate + local rate - (any deductions for local and state taxes at the federal level and any deductions for local taxes at the state level)].

effective yield — the actual return on a loan taking into account all charges and fees. See *effective interest rate* for an example.

efficiency apartment — a small individual dwelling without a separate bedroom within a larger multi-family structure. Efficiency units typically have one room that serves as a living, dining, sleeping, and kitchen space, with an attached small bath. See also *studio apartment*.

egress — (1) exit; (2) a passage serving as an exit. See, by contrast, *ingress*.

EIR — See *Environmental Impact Report*.

EIS — See *Environmental Impact Statement*.

ejectment — a legal action by a property owner to regain possession of property not subject to a lease; an action brought to regain possession of property subject to a contractual agreement such as a conditional sales contract. An example is an action by a landowner to remove squatters from his or her property. Some states permit the use of ejectment as an alternative to foreclosure in certain circumstances.

election of remedies — a choice made by a party injured by a breach of contract concerning the relief to be sought. The choice of one method of recovery will usually preclude any alternative. For example, in a breach of a real estate contract by a buyer, the seller will usually be required to choose between an action for money (damages) or an action for specific performance (forcing the buyer to purchase the property on the contract terms).

elevation – (1) height above sea level; (2) in architectural drawing, a view projected to a vertical plane, such as the front, rear, or side view.

emblement – crops grown on a landlord's property but produced through the labor of a tenant. They are generally considered the personal property of the tenant and may be removed by the tenant even after the expiration or cancellation of the tenant's lease agreement.

eminent domain – the right to take private property against the wishes of a property owner for public uses. While the power generally rests with public agencies, such as city and state governments, it may be delegated to private parties authorized to act for the public interest. The exercise of eminent domain requires fair compensation to the property owner. See also *condemnation*.

encroachment – an improvement, or portion of an improvement, to one property built on, or partially on, the property of another. Common examples include fences and walls.

encumbrance – any claim attaching to a property that affects or may affect its value or hinder its transfer. Examples include mortgages, tax liens, encroachments, and covenants, conditions, and restrictions (CC&Rs).

end loan – the final, or "takeout," loan on a parcel of real property. For example, the individual mortgages used by buyers of a condominium project from a builder with a construction loan would be end loans. See also *permanent financing* and *takeout loan*.

endorsement – (1) the signature on the back of a check or other note, which effectively transfers the check or note or guarantees payment to another party; (2) a contract provision modifying the terms of an insurance policy.

energy efficient – a term applied to buildings and appliances within buildings, such as heaters, air conditioners, and refrigerators, indicating that some effort was made in their design to minimize the gas, electricity, or other energy resources needed or used.

enjoin – to forbid or require some act. A court order to enjoin is called an injunction. See also *injunction*.

enterprise zone – an urban renewal device in which businesses are given tax incentives to locate in areas considered to be depressed or in need of redevelopment.

entitlement – something owed. In real estate, entitlements refer to the rights obtained through government approvals required to construct an improvement to land.

environmental audit – a formal

investigation of a property by a professional inspector to identify the presence of any hazards, such as asbestos, radon, PCBs, and groundwater contamination. Lenders often require environmental audits as a condition of a loan on commercial or industrial property.

Environmental Impact Report (EIR) — a state or locally mandated report concerning the effect on the environment of a proposed construction project. See also *Environmental Impact Statement.*

Environmental Impact Statement (EIS) — a federally mandated report concerning the effect on the environment of a proposed construction project required by the National Environmental Policy Act (NEPA) for all federal government projects and for many other projects requiring federal approvals or licenses. See also *Environmental Impact Report* (the nonfederal equivalent).

Environmental Protection Agency (EPA) — a federal agency responsible for setting standards, performing research, and mandating remedial action in the areas of pollution, air and water quality, and solid and hazardous materials disposal. The EPA is also responsible for the enforcement of various federal civil and criminal laws in the area of the environment.

EPA — See *Environmental Protection Agency.*

Equal Credit Opportunity Act (ECOA) — a package of federal legislation enacted in 1974 designed to complement and extend the Consumer Credit Protection Act of 1969. The ECOA provides that credit must be extended without regard to race, color, religion, national origin, gender, marital status, or source of income (such as alimony and social security payments).

equalization board — See *board of equalization.*

equitable conversion — a legal doctrine most commonly applied when the seller of a property dies before a transaction has been completed. The seller's estate may be forced to complete the sale on the theory that the seller's interest in the property had been converted into an interest in the buyer's consideration (usually money) at the time the contract became binding on the parties.

equitable title — an ownership interest held by one who does not have legal title to a property. The doctrine also applies in other circumstances where fairness requires that the "true" owner of the property be protected against adverse action by the holder of bare legal title. See also *contract for deed, contract of sale,* and *legal title.*

equitable titleholder — the person for whom legal title is held. Most commonly, this is a beneficiary under a trust.

equity – the difference between an owner's debt and lien obligations on a property and its current market value. For example, if Abel owns a home with a mortgage of $100,000, a tax lien of $25,000, and a market value of $350,000, his equity is $225,000 [$350,000 – ($100,000 + $25,000)]. Equity can be negative if the debt exceeds the value of the property.

equity build-up – the increase in equity over time due to appreciation of a property and the gradual retirement of debt.

equity of redemption – the right of an owner of property in foreclosure to pay the principal, interest, legal, and court fees necessary to extinguish the foreclosure and retain *or* regain his or her property. In some states, a right of redemption exists for a period of up to one year after a judicial foreclosure. See also *judicial foreclosure.*

equity participation – an arrangement by which an investor/lender provides part or all of the down payment or financing on a parcel of property in exchange for a share of the appreciation when the property is sold.

equity sharing – a form of co-ownership in which only one party is entitled to occupy the property. Typically, an individual investor provides the down payment for a home purchase while the buyer lives in the property and makes payments for an agreed upon term, usually three to five years. Both the investor and the buyer are "on title." At the end of the term, the property is sold or refinanced, and the investor receives a portion of the appreciation, less the costs of any capital improvements made by the buyer. See also *on title.*

erosion – the gradual removal of land by action of water or wind. See also *diluvion.*

errors and omissions (E&O) insurance – professional liability insurance designed to protect real estate brokers and agents against claims of malpractice or negligent misrepresentation.

escalation (escalator) clause – a provision in a lease contract specifying that lease payments will increase upon the increase in some other expense or set of expenses. A common example is a lease tied to the lessor's actual operating costs, including such items as debt service, taxes, and maintenance. When these costs increase, the lessor is entitled under the contract to pass along the increase to the tenant.

escape clause – a provision in a contract allowing a party to cancel the contract if some specified contingency is not satisfied. Typical examples in real estate contracts are financing contingencies, inspection contingencies, and clear title contingencies. Properly exercised, the use of an escape clause is not a breach of contract. See also *contingency*.

escheat – the reversion of title to a decedent's real property to the state or local government in a circumstance in which no other persons are entitled to receive the property under a will or the laws of succession.

escheator – the government officer in charge of an escheat. See also *escheat*.

escrow – a process, performed by a third party, of collecting and distributing the funds and documents necessary to complete a real estate transaction between principals. Escrow "closes" when all parties have fulfilled their contractual obligations, delivered all necessary documents and money, and satisfied or removed all contractual contingencies. See also *escrow account, escrow company, escrow fees, escrow instructions, escrow officer*, and *escrow statement*.

escrow account – (also called *impound account* or *trust account*) an account set up so that deposits are made to a neutral party, who is then responsible for passing along the payments to the appropriate payees. Escrow accounts are typically used to satisfy parties that certain critical payments, such as property taxes, are made in a timely fashion.

escrow agent – See *escrow officer*.

escrow company – a business entity responsible for processing transactions in which valuable consideration is exchanged by the parties through the company rather than directly between the parties. There are several types of escrow companies. Some are licensed and regulated by state departments of real estate or insurance or by corporations, while others are essentially unregulated. See also *escrow*.

escrow fees – the charges imposed on the parties to an escrow by the escrow company for the processing of a transaction. In a typical residential sales transaction, escrow fees are split equally between buyer and seller.

escrow instructions – a document executed by all parties to a transaction in which escrow is authorized to collect money and documents from the parties, and perform other acts as agreed by the parties. In residential sales transactions, escrow instructions are usually derived from the terms of the purchase contract.

escrow officer – (also called *escrow agent*) an employee of an escrow company with the primary responsibility of ensuring that the parties have delivered all documents and money necessary to complete a transaction and have complied with all other terms of the escrow instructions.

escrow statement – (also called *closing statement* or *settlement statement*) a detailed accounting provided to the parties after the consummation of a real estate transaction listing all cash credits and debits to the parties, and all sums paid through escrow to third parties, such as lenders, appraisers, real estate brokers and taxing agencies. The escrow officer involved in the transaction prepares it. See also *closing statement* and *Real Estate Settlement Procedures Act.*

estate – (1) the legally recognized interest a person has in real or personal property. For purposes of a real estate transaction, *estate* is synonymous with the concept of *title.* (2) the property and claims or entitlements of a decedent. See also *title.*

estate at sufferance – the interest of a tenant in rightful possession of a landlord's property after expiration of the term of the agreement under which the tenant occupied the property. The tenant is allowed to continue to occupy the property as long as the owner continues to give permission. A withdrawal of permission ends the lawful tenancy.

estate at will – a leasehold estate of undefined term that may be terminated at any time by either the landlord or the tenant.

estate for life – (also called a *life estate*) an estate whose duration is limited to the life of the estate holder or the life of some other person who was alive at the time the estate was created (*estate pur autre vie*). Upon the death of the named person, the estate may revert to the original owner or pass to some other person.

estate for years – a leasehold interest with a definite start and end date. It need not be for more than a year; a month-to-month lease is an estate for years.

estate in reversion – the residue of an estate that will return at some future time by operation of law to the grantor or his or her successors. The most common example is a landlord's reversionary interest in a leased property. When the lease expires or is terminated, the landlord once again enjoys the fullest ownership interest in the affected property. See also *remainder.*

estate in severalty – an estate held by a single individual without connection to any other person; sole ownership.

estate on condition – an interest in land that may be created, enlarged, or destroyed upon some event occurring or not occurring. An example is a gift of land to a school for as long as the land is used for educational purposes. If the school stops using the land for those purposes, the estate is defeated, and the land passes to some other party as specified in the gift.

estate *pur autre vie* – estate for the life of another. See also *estate for life* and *pur autre vie.*

estate tax – a federal levy on the total value of the assets in a decedent's estate. The tax is imposed on the estate, not on the heirs. Currently, the first $600,000 in value is exempt from estate tax.

estimate – (1) to give an approximate value; (2) an approximate value. An appraisal is an estimate of the value of a parcel of real property.

estoppel – a legal doctrine based on fairness which holds that a person should not be able to disavow his or her own acts or admissions to the detriment of another person who has relied on the acts or admissions. For example, Abel tells Baker that his apartment building generates $100,000/year in income. Baker buys the building based on the representation but later learns that the income is only $50,000/year. In a lawsuit against Abel by Baker, Abel would be estopped from claiming that Baker should not have relied on the representation of the higher income level.

estoppel certificate – any signed statement certifying that certain facts are true, prepared for the purpose of preventing the signatory from asserting a contrary claim at a later time. Estoppel certificates are typically used in income property transactions in which tenants are asked to confirm the terms of their leases and describe any deposit agreements.

estovers – the common law right of a tenant to take that which is necessary for basic survival from the land that he or she occupies. For example, a tenant on land in a wooded area may remove a quantity of timber necessary to heat his or her house. See, by contrast, *waste.*

et al. – abbreviation of the Latin phrase *et alia* meaning "and others," used in legal documents such as pleadings. For example, a large number of parties in a lawsuit may be referenced as "John Smith, *et al.*"

ethics – (1) a general system of moral principles; (2) in real estate, often refers to the *Realtors® Code of Ethics*, a set of principles by which all members of the National Association of Realtors® agree to abide. This Code defines proper behavior toward parties to a transaction, other licensees, and the general public. Many states have adopted all or part of the *Realtors® Code of Ethics* in their real estate licensing laws.

eviction – a legal proceeding forcing a tenant to vacate premises unlawfully occupied. It may also be applied to any party in possession of the property upon some claim of right. For example, a homeowner who has lost title to a property in foreclosure, but who has retained possession of the property may be evicted.

eviction, actual – the act of legally removing a tenant from leased premises.

eviction, constructive – a material change caused by the landlord in leased premises that renders the property uninhabitable. An example is the termination of utility services such as electricity or water to a building. Constructive eviction is a common tenant's defense to such a breach of lease.

eviction, partial — the effective removal of a tenant by a landlord from a portion of a leased property. For example, if a commercial tenant is barred from using the ground floor of an office building because of ongoing structural remodeling scheduled by the landlord, the tenant may have been partially evicted from the affected portion of the premises. A partial eviction may require rent abatement. See also *rent abatement*.

evidence of title — documents, such as a deed or a certificate of title, which tend to establish ownership of real property.

examination of title — the process of researching the chain of title to a parcel of real estate for the purpose of establishing marketable title. It may be less extensive than a full title search. See also *certificate of title, chain of title, title insurance,* and *title search.*

exception — a portion of real property that is excluded from the conveyance of a larger contiguous parcel and retained by the grantor. For example, Abel deeds Greenacres to Baker "excepting the north 40 acres." See also *reservation.*

exception to title — an encumbrance affecting title for which a title company is not willing to provide insurance. Such exceptions may include matters of record, such as tax liens or existing real estate loans, as well as matters discovered by a title insurance company during a title search, such as a mechanic's lien or an unrecorded option to purchase.

exchange — most commonly, a tax-free exchange of like-kind property under the provisions of Section 1031 of the Internal Revenue Code. A Section 1031 exchange allows an investor or business owner to convey an income or business property in exchange for a similar property. In general, the new property must be of a value the same as or greater than the exchanged property. When Section 1031 rules are followed precisely, the exchange does not trigger a taxable capital gain for the current tax year.

exclusive agency — a real estate employment contract in which a seller hires a broker to list his or her property for sale, with the understanding that the seller retains the right to sell the property directly to a buyer not produced by the broker without paying a commission. The listing broker may publish the listing in the MLS and cooperate with other brokers to sell the property. The nature of the listing must generally be disclosed, because it places cooperating brokers at risk of losing a client to the seller. See also *exclusive listing,* *exclusive right to sell, net listing,* and *nonexclusive listing.*

exclusive listing – (1) most commonly, a term for *exclusive right to sell* (see below); (2) in some areas, a real estate employment contract with a broker by which only that broker may sell the property and the cooperation of other brokers is not solicited. In other words, the listing broker himself or herself must locate and represent the buyer. See also *exclusive agency, exclusive right to sell, net listing,* and *nonexclusive listing.*

exclusive right to sell – (also called "exclusive listing") a real estate employment contract in which a seller hires a single broker to list his or her property for sale. The broker may publish the listing in the MLS and cooperate with other brokers in the sale. The broker is entitled to receive a commission regardless of who actually sells the property. For example, if the sellers decide to sell to a relative, the broker would still be entitled to a commission. See also *exclusive agency, exclusive listing, net listing,* and *nonexclusive listing.*

exculpatory clause – (1) a provision in a mortgage relieving the borrower of personal liability on the loan in the event that the borrower voluntarily surrenders the property to the lender. See also *antideficiency laws.* (2) any contract provision relieving a party to the contract of some personal liability.

execute – to render a document complete by signing or acknowledging it and delivering it to the appropriate party. For example, in a real estate transaction, the seller executes a new deed in favor of the buyer by signing the deed in the presence of witnesses.

executed contract – a contract that has been performed. If all parties have completed all obligations, the contract is wholly executed or fully executed. If one party has performed, but not the other, or if any contract obligation remains outstanding, the contract is partially executed or executory.

execution – (1) the signing and delivering of a contract; (2) the completion of a contract obligation.

executor/executrix – a person chosen by a testator/testatrix to implement the terms of his or her will, including the sale or disposition of any real estate assets. A real estate license is not required. The suffix "or" refers to a male; the suffix "ix" refers to a female.

executor's deed – a deed signed by an executor transferring title to a decedent's real property. If not specifically authorized by a testator, the deed may require probate court approval.

executory – something that has not yet been performed. A contract for the sale of real property is executory until all contract provisions have been satisfied and the consideration has been exchanged.

executory contract – a contract that has been signed but not yet fully performed. See, by contrast, *executed contract*.

executory interest – a general term describing a variety of future interests or estates in land or personal property. An executory interest transfers title to property from one transferee to another upon the occurrence or nonoccurrence of some event in the future. An executory interest cannot qualify as a remainder or a reversion. For example, Abel deeds Greenacre to Baker "unless Baker marries, then to Smith." Smith has an executory interest in Greenacre. See also *remainder* and *reversion*.

expansion joint – an engineered open space between elements of a structure designed to allow for some movement. For example, a bridge may have expansion joints between sections of the roadway to allow for thermal expansion and contraction and to prevent buckling.

exposure – risk; possible loss that an investor faces on an investment. See also *at-risk rules*.

expropriation – the taking of private land for public use. See also *condemnation* and *eminent domain*.

express agency – an agreement by one person (the agent) to act on behalf of another (the principal) that

is intentionally entered into by both the principal and the agent. Express agency is often evidenced by a written agreement. In modern real estate practice and under most state laws, a real estate broker or agent obtains a signed agency agreement from a principal before performing any acts on his or her behalf. See also *agency, duties of care, and implied agency*.

extended coverage – (1) an enhanced title insurance policy generally covering additional items not disclosed in public records. Examples include unrecorded easements, encroachments, and mechanic's liens. See also *American Land Title Association*. (2) any enhanced insurance policy, such as a fire insurance policy that also covers acts of vandalism and water damage.

extension – an additional period of time allowed to perform a contract obligation beyond that specified in a contract. Extensions must be approved by the parties and are considered mutual modifications of the contract.

external obsolescence – an appraisal term referring to the loss in value attributable to factors outside the property itself, such as changed economic conditions, changes in zoning, and construction of nearby nuisances.

F

façade – (1) the front of a structure; (2) the material covering the front of a structure, such as wood, brick, or stucco.

face – the direction toward which a structure, structural component, room, etc., is positioned. "The kitchen window faces east." See also *façade*.

face value – the dollar value printed on a financial instrument such as a note, mortgage, or bond. Face value is usually, but not always, the amount borrowed. For example, a $100,000 mortgage amortized over 30 years at 8% would have a face value of $100,000.

facilitator – a real estate licensee who assists in arranging real estate transactions. The distinction, if any, between traditional real estate brokers and facilitators is that facilitators tend to charge hourly fees for their services, rather than charging a commission rate.

facsimile ("fax") – (1) an electronic form of document transmission. Many states now consider faxed signatures on most real estate contract documents as binding on the signatory. (2) any exact copy of an original.

Fair Credit Reporting Act (FCRA) – a federal statute designed to assure borrowers that credit reports maintained by credit reporting agencies do not contain inaccurate information concerning the borrower's credit history. The Act allows individuals to inspect their own credit reports, add explanations, and demand the removal of incorrect information.

Fair Housing Act – See *Federal Fair Housing Act.*

Fair, Isaac Company – See *FICO.*

fair market rent – the rent that a property could command in an open, competitive, and unrestricted market, whether or not the property is currently rented. Appraisers use fair market rent as a component in the income method of appraisal. See also *appraisal.*

fair market value (FMV) – an appraisal term meaning the probable selling price of a property if it were placed on the market at a particular time. Assumes that a competitive market exists for properties of this particular type, that no coercive relationship exists between buyer and seller, and that neither buyer nor seller is under undue pressure to buy or sell. See also *comparative market analysis* and *market value.*

false advertising – real estate advertising containing information the advertiser knows or should know is incorrect or misleading. For example, if a broker advertises a home as "3,500 square feet" without making any effort to determine the actual size, he or she may be subject to discipline for false advertising if the property is not exactly 3,500 square feet.

familial status – a protected category under the Federal Fair Housing Act and under many state laws that refers to whether a person is single, married, or divorced, and whether the individual is a parent or legal guardian to children living with him or her.

Fannie Mae (FNMA) – Federal National Mortgage Association. Created in 1938, FNMA is a quasi-governmental agency that purchases real estate loans after they are originated by a lender. FNMA requires that the loans be underwritten to certain guidelines. It raises funds to purchase the loans through the issuance of bonds. See also *back-end ratio, Freddie Mac, front-end ratio,* and *loan-to-value ratio.*

farm – (1) land devoted to agricultural use; (2) a geographic area or social group targeted by a real estate agent as a source of business. "Farming" may consist of phone calls, direct mail, and door-knocking.

Farmer's Home Administration (FmHA) – a federal agency charged with making farm-related housing available in smaller rural communities.

fascia – a long horizontal board or band, applied to cover the ends of rafters or along a cornice.

FCRA – See *Fair Credit Reporting Act.*

FDIC – See *Federal Deposit Insurance Corporation.*

Federal Deposit Insurance Corporation (FDIC) – a quasi-independent public corporation, established in 1933, that insures depositors in commercial banks against losses up to $100,000 per separate account in the event of a bank failure. The member banks pay the premiums. In practice, during a wave of bank failures in the 1980s, the FDIC covered nearly all depositor loss, regardless of the size of the deposit. See also *Federal Savings and Loan Insurance Corporation.*

federal discount rate – the interest rate that is charged depository institutions when they borrow from their District Federal Reserve Banks.

federal estate tax – See *estate tax.*

Federal Fair Housing Act – a 1968 federal law, enacted as Title VIII of the Civil Rights Act, to prohibit discrimination on the basis of race, color, gender, national origin, familial origin, familial status, handicap, or religion in the sale or lease of most dwellings and vacant land intended to be used for dwellings. The Act prohibits a wide range of behavior linked to these categories, such as refusal to sell to a person, refusal by real estate agents to show a property, denial of loans by a lender, and advertising that indicates a discriminatory preference. The Act does not prohibit discrimination in other types of real estate transactions, such as commercial and industrial properties, although other civil rights laws may generally cover discrimination in these settings.

federal flood insurance – coverage made available to individuals and business in communities qualified for coverage under the National Flood Insurance Act. Prior to passage of the Act in 1968, flood coverage was very difficult to obtain.

Federal Home Loan Bank Board (FHLBB) – the board that once chartered federal savings and loan associations and controlled the Federal Home Loan Banks. FIRREA transferred the chartering and regulating of all such thrift institutions to the Office of Thrift Supervision (OTS) in 1989. See also *Financial Institutions Reform, Recovery, and Enforcement Act,* and *Office of Thrift Supervision.*

Federal Home Loan Banks – a series of 12 regional banks, established during the depression of the 1930s, designed to support the new federally chartered savings and loan associations and to provide needed liquidity. They are regulated by the Federal Housing Finance Board, formerly the Federal Home Loan Bank Board (FHLBB), under the Office of

fice of Thrift Supervision (OTS), Department of the Treasury.

Federal Home Loan Mortgage Corporation (FHLMC) – See *Freddie Mac.*

Federal Housing Administration (FHA) – a federal administrative agency, established in 1934, and now operated under the auspices of the Department of Housing and Urban Development. Congressional intent was to make home loans more readily available to borrowers with limited down payments, to exert pressure on the building industry to create more standardized good-quality housing, and to regulate the mortgage industry. Maximum FHA loan limits are relatively low and vary according to the cost of housing within a particular region. In an FHA loan, the FHA insures lenders against loss on low down payment loans provided that both the borrower and the property comply with FHA underwriting guidelines. The funding mechanism is a mortgage insurance premium (MIP) paid by the borrower. If the borrower defaults, the mortgage insurance program will pay the bulk of the lender's loss. See also *FHA loan.*

Federal National Mortgage Association – See *Fannie Mae.*

Federal Reserve System ("the Fed") – the regulatory backbone of the nation's banking system. Established in 1913, the Fed consists of a presidentially appointed Board of Governors with a highly visible chairman and 12 Federal Reserve District Banks. The Fed is charged with regulation of the nation's money supply. It uses a variety of financial tools to exert upward or downward pressure on interest rates as the economy expands and contracts. Federal Reserve policy has a direct effect on mortgage interest rates.

Federal Savings and Loan (S&L) Association — an institution chartered by the U. S. Department of Treasury, Office of Thrift Supervision, for home mortgages. There are also state-chartered savings and loans. Savings and loans tend to make consumer loans, whereas commercial banks traditionally made business loans, although deregulation of banks and S&Ls has blurred the historical distinctions.

Federal Savings and Loan Insurance Corporation (FSLIC) — abolished by FIRREA in 1989. The functions of the FSLIC were split between the FDIC and the OTS. Similar to the FDIC, the FSLIC insured depositors in federally chartered savings and loan institutions against losses up to $100,000 per separate account in the event of a savings and loan failure. Member S&Ls paid the premiums. As with the FDIC, during a wave of S&L failures in the 1980s, the FSLIC covered nearly all depositor loss, regardless of the size of the

deposit. See also *Federal Deposit Insurance Corporation, Federal Savings and Loan Association Office of Thrift Supervision,* and the *Savings Association Insurance Fund.*

federal tax lien — a legally enforceable claim for unpaid taxes placed by a branch of the federal government against privately owned real property. The tax may be unrelated to the property itself, and may be a personal obligation of an owner of the property. Generally, the lien must be paid when the property is transferred. See also *lien.*

Federal Trade Commission (FTC) — a federal agency charged with the regulation of interstate commerce. The FTC affects the real estate industry primarily through oversight of misleading advertising practices and shared responsibility with the Justice Department for antitrust enforcement.

fee — (1) a charge for a service, such as a loan processing fee; (2) an ancient term for ownership.

fee ownership — an estate without condition, freely transferable, inheritable, and potentially unlimited in duration.

fee simple — See *fee simple absolute estate.*

fee simple absolute estate — (also called "fee simple estate") the most comprehensive possible ownership interest in real property. Fee simple absolute ownership is freely transferable, inheritable, and potentially infinite in duration. All other ownership interests may be created from it.

fee simple conditional — a potential fee estate that requires the occurrence of some condition before the transfer is completed. An example is a grant by Abel to Abel's daughter Abigail, provided that she marry before the age of 30. If Abigail has not married by that time, the estate is defeated, and is transferred to another party named by Abel in the granting instrument.

fee simple defeasible — a fee estate that can be defeated if a certain condition occurs. For example, Abel grants property to Abigail provided that Abigail not marry Baker's son, Bosco. In the event that Abigail and Bosco marry, the estate reverts to Abel.

fee simple determinable — a grant of a fee estate that contains language ending the estate upon the occurrence of a particular stated event.

fee tail — (1) an estate that is limited to the lineal descendants of the grantee. While potentially unlimited in duration, the estate will end if the line of direct blood descendants ends. (2) an estate limited to certain classes of particular heirs, for example, eldest sons of eldest sons.

felt paper — (also called "tar paper"

or "building paper") a thick paper sold in wide rolls and impregnated with a waterproofing substance. It is often used to sheath roofs and walls before the final outer covering is installed.

fence — a lightweight vertical barrier designed to mark a property boundary, to establish privacy, or to keep domestic animals from straying. See also *wall.*

fenestration — the arrangement of doors and windows in a building.

FHA — See *Federal Housing Administration.*

FHA escape clause — See *escape clause.*

FHA loan — a mortgage loan insured by the FHA. See also *Federal Housing Administration.*

FHLBB — See *Federal Loan Bank Board.*

FHLMC — Federal Home Loan Mortgage Corporation. See *Freddie Mac.*

fiberglass insulation — blanket or rigid insulation composed of glass fibers bound together with a binder, typically sold in compressed rolls sized to fit between wall studs. It may be faced (attached to a thin vapor barrier) or unfaced and is used to insulate roofs and walls. See also *insulation.*

FICO — a credit scoring method developed by the Fair, Isaac Company.

FICO considers such factors as an individual's length of residence at a particular location, length of employment, type of job, financial obligations, amount of total available credit, amount of credit used, history of payments, and the length of time that credit has been established. The score is dynamically generated each time a credit report is generated. Higher scores are equated with a lower risk to a lender. See also *credit report* and *credit scoring*.

fictitious business name — See *DBA*.

fidelity bond — insurance policy designed to protect against losses caused by the intentional dishonesty of an employee. Fidelity bonds are common for services involving access to valuables or personal property of others, such as security guards or house cleaning services.

fidelity exclusion — a provision of a fidelity bond that excludes coverage for losses caused by the intentional dishonesty of the insured.

fiduciary — a person or institution charged with the highest standard of care in administering the property of another party. Examples include trustees and executors. See also *fiduciary duty*.

fiduciary duty — the highest legal standard of care that one individual or institution can owe to another. One who owes a fiduciary duty must exercise the utmost fidelity toward the subject of the duty and must do everything reasonably required to protect the interests of the subject. In real estate, an agent typically owes a fiduciary duty toward his or her principal. See also *good faith*..

fifteen-year mortgage — a mortgage amortized over 15 years instead of the more conventional 30 years. Because the principal is paid down sooner, the total cost of a 15-year mortgage is substantially less than that of a 30-year loan, although the periodic payment will be more than that of a 30-year loan. Typically, the interest rate on a 15-year loan is slightly less than on a 30-year loan.

fill — dirt or other solid material added to a building site to form a new grade. Contrast with "cut," in which material is removed to form a new grade. Fill must generally be compacted before it can properly support a structure.

filtering down — the occupation of a residential neighborhood by progressively lower income individuals over time.

final decree — a court decision regarding a matter in which all the evidence has been heard. See, by contrast, *interlocutory decree*.

final value estimate — an appraisal term referring to the reconciliation of all appraisal methods used to arrive at a value estimate.

finance charge — (1) costs associated with a loan, including interest, points, and fees. See *Truth in Lending Law (Regulation Z)*. (2) a disclosure required by the Federal Truth in Lending Law. The total of all costs paid to the lender by the borrower directly or indirectly as an incident to the extension of credit, including, but not limited to, interest charges, finder fees, origination fees, discount points, service charges, application and processing fees, and credit report fees.

financial calculator – a hand-held calculator with financial functions such as amortization and the time value of money. They replaced financial tables and are now widely used by real estate and loan professionals.

financial institution – any of a variety of banks, savings and loans, thrifts, credit unions and other institutions that engage in lending activities.

Financial Institutions Reform, Recovery, and Enforcement Act (FIRREA) – a 1990 federal law designed to manage and mitigate the failure of numerous savings and loans during the 1980s. FIRREA created the Resolution Trust Corporation (RTC) to liquidate the assets of the failed institutions and adopted numerous regulatory reform measures to prevent a recurrence of systemwide failures. RTC functions were transferred to the FDIC in 1997.

financial leverage – the principle of using borrowed money over time to acquire an asset that generates returns higher than the cost of the borrowed funds.

financial statement – a report, often prepared by an accountant or financial officer, of the assets, liabilities, income, and expenses of an individual or business.

financing – (1) the use of borrowed money to acquire an asset; (2) the structure of the credit arrangement itself. For example, "90% financing" is an arrangement in which the borrower makes a down payment of 10% of the cost of the real estate. The lender provides the remaining 90%.

financing contingency – a clause in a real estate contract providing that the buyer's obtaining of financing to acquire the property is a requirement for the contract to be enforceable against the buyer. If the buyer is unable to obtain financing, the buyer may cancel the contract.

finder's fee – a sum of money paid to a person who is not a real estate licensee as a reward for locating a property or a buyer for a property. Finder's fees are regulated by state and federal law and are illegal in many circumstances. Some jurisdictions prohibit them altogether. See also *referral fee*.

finish flooring – the final flooring material, such as carpet, wood, or tile, which is applied to the subfloor.

fire door – a door designed to withstand a fire for a specified period of time. Fire doors are typically found in multifamily residential structures and between garages and living areas in single-family structures.

fire insurance – property insurance covering damage to structures caused by fire. It is often a component of a multipart fire, casualty, and liability policy that covers against fire, personal injury lawsuits, and other hazards. Real estate lenders often require fire insurance as a condition of a loan.

fire sprinkler system – a series of ceiling or wall-mounted water spray devices activated by heat or smoke.

fire stop – a horizontal block fitted between wall studs designed to slow the spread of a fire in the walls of a structure.

fire wall – a wall constructed with fire-resistant materials, designed to withstand a fire of a specified temperature for a specified period of time. Building codes often require fire walls between condominium units and between a dwelling and a garage.

firm commitment – a binding expression of intent by a lender to make a specific loan to a specific borrower.

firm price – a price set by a seller with the understanding that no lower price will be accepted. See also *asking price*.

FIRPTA – See *Foreign Investment in Real Property Tax Act*.

FIRREA – See *Financial Institutions Reform, Recovery, and Enforcement Act*.

first mortgage – a real estate loan with priority over any other loans on the property. Ordinarily, the first loan recorded against the property has priority, but certain operations of law, or agreements called subordination agreements, can alter the order of priority. For example, Abel's farm has a first mortgage of $500,000, recorded in July 1999, a second mortgage of $300,000, recorded in July 2000, and a third mortgage of $100,000, recorded in July 2001. If Abel sells his property in 2002 for $750,000, the first mortgage holder would receive the full $500,000 owed. The second mortgage holder would receive $250,000, and the third mortgage holder would receive nothing. In some states Abel may face a deficiency liability on the unsatisfied debts. See also *antideficiency laws, deficiency judgment, mortgage, second trust deed, subordination,* and *trust deed*.

first right of refusal – (also called *right of first refusal*) a contractual option to purchase a property at the price and terms offered by another party. For example, Abel gives Baker a first right of refusal on a parcel of property adjoining Baker's property. If Portnoy offers Abel $100,000 for the property, Abel must first give Baker the chance to match the price and terms offered by Portnoy. If Baker is unable or unwilling to do so, Abel may sell the property to Portnoy.

first trust deed — See *first mortgage*.

fiscal year — a 12-month period used for financial reporting or tax purposes. One commonly used fiscal year is July 1 to June 30 of the following calendar year.

fixed expenses — for income-producing properties, those costs that are incurred whether or not the property is occupied or producing income. Examples include debt service, real estate taxes, and hazard insurance. See also *operating expenses*.

fixed premium — any payment for insurance coverage that remains the same for the entire length of the premium-paying period.

fixed rate loan — a loan in which the interest rate and payment remain the same for the life of the loan. For example, $100,000 borrowed at a 7% fixed rate over 30 years would require 360 monthly payments of $665.00 each. See also *adjustable rate mortgage* and *variable rate*.

fixer-upper — an advertising or colloquial term denoting habitable real property in need of considerable re-pair. See also *teardown*.

fixture — an movable article of personal property that has been attached or affixed to real property in such a way as to convert it to real property. Fixtures are generally conveyed with the real property. Examples include attached lighting fixtures, built-in ranges, water heaters and furnaces, plants in the ground, fireplace mantles, and attached bookcases. Freestanding lamps, refrigerators, potted plants, and free-standing bookcases would generally be considered personal property, although interpretation varies by state and region.

flag lot — a parcel of land with access from the public right of way through a narrow, extended portion of the parcel. A typical shape resembles a flag with a pole.

flashing — a strip of waterproof material such as metal or plastic used to cover a joint between dissimilar materials, such as brick and wood, or an opening in the structure such as a window, door, or skylight. The purpose of the flashing is to divert water away from the joint or opening.

flat — a colloquial term for an single-level apartment, condominium, or co-op in a multistory building.

flat roof — a roof that forms a 90° angle to the walls. Flat roofs rely on roof drains and waterproof membranes rather than slope or pitch to shed water.

flexible payment mortgage – a real estate loan in which payments are tailored to anticipated changes in a borrower's financial outlook. For example, a young professional person at the beginning of his or her career might choose a loan in which the payments are lower than required to amortize the loan for the first five years. For the remaining 25 years of the loan, the deferred interest would be added to the regular payment so that the loan is fully amortized after 30 years.

flexible rate mortgage – See *adjustable rate mortgage*.

flight pattern – the aerial path and gradient altitude that aircraft must follow when approaching or taking off from an airport.

flip – a real estate transaction in which the buyer expects to resell the property immediately at a profit. See also *double escrow*.

float – (1) the time value of money during the period after a check is written but before it is cashed; (2) (also called *margin*) the spread between a variable rate loan index and the actual rate charged; (3) in construction, to level a subfloor with a leveling compound.

floating floor – a sound-insulated or isolated floor used most commonly in industrial buildings to minimize the sound transmission of machinery.

floating interest rate – (also called "floating rate") an interest rate that varies over time based on changes in an index. See also *adjustable rate mortgage*, *variable interest rate*, and *variable rate mortgage*.

floating lien – a provision of an existing real estate loan which provides that the existing mortgage lien will attach to properties acquired by the borrower later in time. See also *anaconda mortgage*.

flood insurance – federal flood insurance coverage, authorized by the National Flood Insurance Act of 1968, is provided by private insurers at a federally subsidized and regulated rate for properties located in federally designated flood-prone areas. If a property is located in a flood hazard area, private mortgage lenders will generally require the borrower to purchase flood insurance. Prior to passage of the Act, it was virtually impossible to obtain affordable flood insurance.

flood map – topographic map showing the relative flood hazards of properties in flood-prone areas. Used by lenders to determine whether a particular property will require flood insurance.

flood plain – flat areas of land bordering rivers and other watercourses that may be inundated as the water rises.

floor area ratio – the mathematical relationship of the total square footage of a structure to the total square footage of the parcel of land it occupies. The formula is [*total building square feet* ÷ *total parcel size*]. Used as one measure of density in local building codes.

floor duty – in real estate sales offices, the practice of rotating the responsibility of responding to walk-in and call-in buyer and seller questions. Real estate agents obtain leads from these contacts.

floor joists – structural beams providing support for the finished floor.

floor loan – a minimum commitment by a lender on a commercial property construction loan. As the property is occupied by tenants, the lender releases additional sums until the full permanent loan has been funded. For example, a lender agrees to a $10,000,000 permanent loan for a new office building with a floor loan amount of $7,000,000. The lender releases the $7,000,000 as construction progresses. As tenants sign leases and occupy the property, the lender releases the remaining $3,000,000 until the loan is fully funded.

floor plan – (1) the configuration of rooms or other divided areas in a structure; (2) a two-dimensional architectural drawing of the configuration of rooms or other divided areas in a single level of a structure as seen from above.

floor register – floor opening in an air duct, usually with a grill cover.

flue – an enclosed conduit designed to carry hot gases or smoke. Flues are typically made of fire-resistant materials, such as masonry or clay, and are usually found in chimneys or attached to furnaces.

FmHA – See *Farmer's Home Administration.*

fmv – See *fair market value.*

FNMA – Federal National Mortgage Association. See *Fannie Mae.*

foot-candle – a measure of the amount of light generated by a lighting fixture or fixtures. Equal to the illumination present 1 foot from one candle.

footing – a structural component of a building designed to support the weight of the structure, usually constructed of poured concrete and partially buried in the ground to resist damage due to frost. See also *foundation.*

footprint – the area of the portion of a parcel of land that is covered by a structure.

for sale by owner (FSBO) – a home or other real property offered for sale by the owner without the assistance of a real estate professional.

forbearance – refraining from pursuing an enforcement action or legal remedy that is available. A typical example is a lender delaying foreclosure action on a defaulted loan.

force and effect of law – a legal term meaning that administrative regulations properly adopted by government agencies are to be accorded the same status as laws passed directly by a legislature. Examples are IRS and DRE regulations.

force majeure – an irresistible and unforeseeable event or cause. Commonly seen in construction and insurance contracts, a *force majeure* clause excuses a party for nonperformance or late performance in the event of such unforeseen events as flood, fire, strikes, and war.

forced sale – an involuntary sale of real property, usually in anticipation of foreclosure.

forecast – a projection of future results, as in a corporation's estimate of the next quarter's profit or loss.

foreclosure – a legal process in which, against the wishes of the owner, real property is sold to satisfy a public or private debt for which the real property has been pledged as security. See also *foreclosure sale, judicial foreclosure, nonjudicial foreclosure,* and *strict foreclosure.*

foreclosure sale – the actual sale of real property at the conclusion of a foreclosure proceeding. The sale may be to a third party as a result of a high bid, or to the foreclosing creditor if there are no bids higher than the amount of the defaulted debt plus foreclosure costs. If the sale generates proceeds beyond the satisfaction of the debt and foreclosure costs, the balance generally must be refunded to the party who has lost title to the property.

foreign corporation – a corporation chartered in another state or country than that in which it is doing business. For example, a corporation chartered in Delaware but doing business in all 50 states would be a foreign corporation in 49 of the states.

Foreign Investment in Real Property Tax Act (FIRPTA) – a federal law which provides safeguards to ensure that "foreign persons" as defined by the Act pay U. S. income tax on the sale of real property located in the United States. Several states have adopted similar legislation to protect state tax revenues. The mechanism employed requires the buyer in the transaction to withhold a portion of the seller's proceeds. If the seller completes an affidavit that he or she is not subject to FIRPTA, the buyer need not withhold proceeds. See also *foreign person.*

foreign person – as defined in FIRPTA, an individual nonresident alien or a foreign corporation with direct or indirect real property holdings within the United States. See also *Foreign Investment in Real Property Tax Act.*

foreshore land – that portion of shoreline that is covered by water at high tide and uncovered by low tide.

forfeiture – the loss of something of value as a result of a breach of some obligation or failure of some condition in a contract. Forfeiture is generally considered by courts to be a harsh and potentially excessive remedy for a breach.

forgery – illegal falsification or alteration of signatures or documents. Forgery in a deed used in a real estate transaction will generally render the sale void. Title insurance may cover losses by a bona fide purchaser where there has been forgery in the chain of title.

Formica® – a trade name for a manufactured countertop material consisting of layers of paper bonded to plastic substrate. Formica® is one of the least expensive durable countertop materials.

forum – the jurisdiction in which a lawsuit, complaint, or claim is to be heard. Examples of forums are courts, administrative agencies, and arbitration panels.

foundation – the portion of a structure that rests on or in the ground and provides the primary structural support for the building. Modern foundations often consist of reinforced poured concrete. See also *footing*.

foyer – a separate area located immediately behind an entrance door that is intended to serve as a gathering or transition space between the exterior and interior of a structure.

Foyers are often found in public and commercial buildings and in larger private homes.

fractional interest – a property right, such as a sublease, which represents only a portion of the total bundle of rights attached to the property.

framing – the structural skeleton of a house or building, typically made of wood or steel.

franchise – a business arrangement in which the franchisee (small business owner) pays an initial fee to the franchiser (larger business) to use the business name, materials, and resources of the franchiser. Franchisees also often pay fees based on transaction or sales volume. Franchisees also usually purchase goods, supplies, and other material from the franchiser. Examples of franchises include certain real estate companies, such as Century 21 and RE/MAX, and fast-food restaurants such as McDonald's.

franchise fee – (1) the initial cost of purchasing a franchise; (2) the continuing fee paid by the franchisee to the franchiser based on sales volume or number of transactions.

fraud – a deliberate attempt to deceive or cheat another. Fraud in a real estate transaction may give rise to an action for rescission or damages. Fraud by a real estate licensee in a transaction can lead to loss of the real estate license.

Freddie Mac (FHLMC) – the Federal Home Loan Mortgage Corporation. A federally chartered corporation established for the purpose of increasing liquidity in the secondary mortgage market. Freddie Mac purchases loans underwritten and documented in conformance with FHLMC guidelines. These "conforming loans" are originated by private lenders, then packaged and sold to Freddie Mac. Freddie Mac, in turn, often amalgamates, repackages, and then resells the loans as mortgage-backed securities, for which it issues a guarantee. See also *conforming loan* and *Fannie Mae*.

free and clear title – title to real property that is not encumbered by liens, loans, or any other clouds on title. In practice, it usually refers to properties without a mortgage.

freehold – generally, an estate in real property that has no exactly defined end date. Examples include life estates and fee ownership.

freestanding – a structure that is not attached to any other structure.

freeway – a high-speed multilane road generally designed for long-distance driving. Freeways are also characterized by controlled access to and from surface streets through the use of on and off ramps. Also, freeways typically do not charge tolls, hence the "free." See also *highway*.

French drain – a perforated pipe designed to be buried in the ground for the purpose of diverting and draining underground water away from a structure. French drains are employed to prevent excess water from damaging a structure or undermining under and around a structure. Perforations on one side of the pipe allow water to enter from the surrounding soil. Once in the pipe, the water flows downhill to a drain or basin.

front – (1) the façade of a structure; (2) a person who secretly acts on behalf of another, pretending to be a principal. See also *face*.

front-end ratio – a lending term referring to the portion of a loan applicant's gross income that would be required to service the proposed debt. For example, a borrower with a monthly gross income of $10,000 applying for a loan with payments of $2,500/month would have a front-end ratio of 25%. Lenders use ratios as rules of thumb for underwriting the loan. Different loan programs may have different front-end underwriting guidelines. Currently, typical front-end ratios acceptable to major home lenders range from 28 to 45% or more. See also *back-end ratio*.

front-feet or **front footage** – the dimension of a property measured in feet along the street on which it is situated; used primarily to compare values of similar properties in urban settings, where the "street frontage" of a property is a good measure of its ability to generate income through ground floor retail business.

front-foot value — an appraisal rule of thumb that compares the values of properties bordering the same street or watercourse by dividing the price by the frontage. For example, if a property on Maple Street with a frontage of 150 feet sells for $300,000, it would have a front-foot value of $2,000 per square foot.

front money — (also called "seed money.") the initial equity (as opposed to borrowed money) required to begin a particular real estate development project. It can be in the form of cash or ownership of the underlying land

frontage — the dimension in feet of a side of a parcel of real property that borders a street or watercourse.

frost line — the maximum depth of ground freezing in a particular location. Structural foundations must extend below this line to prevent the structure from shifting as the ground freezes and thaws.

fructus industriales — Latin for "fruits of industry"; annual crops planted, cultivated, and harvested through the labor of the occupants of the land. Generally considered personal property. See also *emblement*.

fructus naturales — Latin for "fruits of nature." Plants, such as trees and grass, that do not require planting each year, and metals ob-

tained from the land. Generally considered real property.

FSBO — See *for sale by owner*.

FSLIC — See *Federal Savings and Loan Insurance Corporation*.

FTC — See *Federal Trade Commission*.

full disclosure — an account, given by a seller to a buyer of real property, that contains all material facts, conditions, and defects of the property being transferred. State disclosure laws are nearly universal and are designed to prevent fraud in the sale of real property. Real estate licensees are generally required to disclose fully all material facts known to them, whether or not their principals do so.

fully amortized mortgage — (also called "fully amortizing loan") a loan in which interest and principal payments are made on a schedule designed to fully liquidate the loan over a stated period of time. A $100,000 mortgage loan with equal monthly payments of $665.00 at 7% interest will be full amortized at the end of 30 years. A loan may also be partially amortized, with some principal reduction and a balloon payment at the end of the term. See also *balloon payment*.

fully indexed interest rate — a term referring to adjustable or variable rate loans meaning a rate equal to the current applicable index plus the margin. For example, a variable rate loan tied to an index such as the six-month Treasury bill (assume 5.5%) plus a margin of 3% would have a fully indexed rate of 8.5% (5.5% + 3%). Lenders often offer loans with "teaser" rates that are below the fully indexed rate for a short period of time. See also *adjustable rate mortgage, annual interest cap, annual payment cap, index, margin,* and *negative amortization.*

functional obsolescence – an appraisal term meaning loss of value to improved real property due to inadequate, outmoded, or inappropriate improvements. Examples include older apartment buildings without elevators, shopping centers with inadequate parking, and a one-bedroom house in an area of four-bedroom houses.

fund – to make the proceeds of a loan available to the borrower.

funding fee – a charge imposed on a borrower by some lenders as part of the *closing costs* for a new loan. For some lenders, such as the Veterans Administration (the VA), the fee is required and is linked to the loan commitment itself. For private lenders, it is simply another variable component of the cost of the loan. See also *closing costs* and *Trust in Lending Law (Regulation Z).*

fungible – goods in which each item or particle is identical to the others and may be freely interchanged with them. Fresh water, rice, and gasoline may be fungible goods. Real property is rarely considered fungible.

furring strip – a board attached to a flat surface to extend the surface or to provide a nailing or gluing foundation for some other material. A common example is 2- by 4-inch boards attached to a basement block wall to provide a nailing surface for finished wood paneling.

fuse box – a type of overload protection for electrical circuits found in older structures. It consists of a metal box containing engineered strips of metal enclosed in glass through which the electricity for various circuits in the structure flows. If the load on the circuit exceeds the engineered design, the strip of metal melts, breaking the circuit, and preventing a potential electrical fire within the structure.

future advance clause – a term in a loan agreement providing for additional sums to be borrowed on the same terms as the original loan amount, using the same collateral.

future interest – a legal interest in real or personal property in which possession and enjoyment are to be delayed until a later time. In real estate, future interests include remainders and reversions. See also *remainder* and *reversion.*

G

GAAP – See generally accepted accounting principles.

gable – the upper section of a wall that rises to an inverted V- shaped roof.

gable roof – an inverted V-shaped roof.

gain – a tax term meaning the profit realized upon the sale of a capital asset, such as a home or building. See also *capital gain*.

gambrel roof – best visualized as a barn-type roof. A gambrel roof has two slopes per side as opposed to the single slope of the gable roof. The lower slopes are steeper than the upper slopes.

gap financing – (1) (also "swing loan" or "bridge loan") interim real estate financing designed to allow a purchaser of a property to complete the purchase before selling another property, whose proceeds will ultimately be used to retire the gap loan; (2) in commercial real estate, the loan that makes up the difference between the floor loan and the actual amount needed. When the permanent loan is fully funded, the gap loan is retired. See also *floor loan, permanent loan,* and *takeout loan.*

gap in title – a break in the history or "chain" of title to a particular property. This can occur because of lost or damaged records, or because a transfer was not properly recorded. A gap can cloud title, making a property difficult to sell.

garden apartment – a first-floor condominium or apartment unit that faces on a yard or lawn.

garret – a room or unfinished part of a house just under the roof. See also *attic.*

gated community – a housing development surrounded by a security fence, with access through an automatic or attended gate. The interior streets are often owned and maintained by the homeowners' association for the development. Many communities prohibit the gating of public streets.

gazebo – a lightly built partially enclosed structure, usually found in a garden, which provides outdoor seating and adds visual interest to the garden. Gazebos are often built of a lattice of wood or metal.

GCR – See *guest-car ratio.*

GEM – See *growing equity mortgage.*

general benefits – enhanced value to adjacent properties caused by the condemnation of a particular property. For example, if a city condemns property to build a sports stadium, it is likely that the adjacent properties will become more valuable.

general contractor – a licensed

tradesperson who is authorized to hire, organize, and supervise the work of subcontractors on a construction project. The general contractor is responsible for paying subcontractors as the work is completed. See also *contractor* and *subcontractor*.

general lien — a lien against all property owned by a debtor, regardless of the initial source of the debt or judgment. Common examples are tax liens and judgment liens. Any or all of a debtor's property may be seized and sold to satisfy a general lien. However, see also *homestead*.

general partner — a co-owner of a business venture legally organized as a partnership who is authorized to enter into contracts binding the partnership. The general partner may be an individual ("natural person") or a corporation. There are two types of partnerships with general partners, general partnerships and limited partnerships. In both, general partners are personally liable for the acts and obligations of the business. See also *general partnership* and *limited partnership*.

general partnership — a business venture in which at least two co-owners operate a business for profit and in which each partner is authorized to act for and to bind the partnership. Each partner is liable for the debts of the partnership. See also *general partner*.

general plan — an official document describing and prescribing the long-term land use and management goals of a local community government. General plans are implemented through the further adoption of specific plans, zoning laws, and other ordinances. See also *specific plan* and *zoning*.

generally accepted accounting principles (GAAP) — a set of accounting rules and practices in common use by public and private accountants at a particular point in time. Substantial deviation from GAAP may be an indication of fraud.

gentrification — the result, assuming a free market, of the rehabilitation of a neighborhood of substandard housing. As the properties are repaired and renovated, their value rises, forcing many low-income residents out of the area, and encouraging more higher-income individuals to invest and live in the neighborhood. It is the opposite of filtering down. See *filtering down*.

geodetic survey system — the U. S. Coast and Geodetic Survey System. It is a based on a system of benchmarks linked to latitude and longitude, and covers the entire country. Originally designed to locate and survey federal government land precisely. See *government rectangular survey method* and *government survey method*.

GFI — See *ground-fault interrupter*.

GI loan — See *VA loan*.

gift deed — a deed to real property in which the no material consideration is exchanged in return for the deed. The recital of the consideration in the deed is traditionally "love and affection."

gift letter — a personal letter, usually addressed to a lender, in which the gift giver verifies that all or some of the down payment used by the borrower has indeed been a gift. It is designed to prevent purchasers from secretly borrowing their down payment. Gift letters are most credible when the giver is closely related to the borrower.

gift tax — a progressive federal tax on the value of a gift. The first $10,000 per donee is excluded from tax. Trusts are sometimes used to avoid the gift tax penalty for larger gifts.

GIM — See *gross income multiplier*.

gingerbread — elaborate ornamentation without any structural function applied to a house. Gingerbread work is characteristic of most Victorian homes.

Ginnie Mae (GNMA) — See *Government National Mortgage Association*.

girder — a heavy structural beam, usually made of steel or wood, which supports floor or ceiling joists. See also *joist*.

girt — a horizontal bracing applied between vertical columns or other structural members to increase the stiffness of the framing.

GLA — See *gross leasable area*.

glass block — a semitransparent hollow brick of glass often used as a decorative exterior or interior wall.

glass wool insulation — See *fiberglass insulation*.

glue-laminated beam — an engineered structural member consisting of several thin boards glued together to create a larger board.

GMC — See *guaranteed mortgage certificate*.

GNMA — (also called Ginnie Mae) See *Government National Mortgage Association*.

GNMA options — See *Government National Mortgage Association options*.

good faith — an honest act, even if negligently performed. See, by contrast, *bad faith*.

good faith and fair dealing — a shorthand description of the duties owed by an agent to the party or parties in a transaction who are not the agent's principal. For example, an agent representing the seller in a transaction will generally be obliged to tell the truth to the buyer, to disclose material defects in the property even if the seller chooses not to do so, and to avoid making misleading statements to the buyer. See *also agency, dual agency,* and *fiduciary duty*.

good faith deposit — the initial sum of money accompanying an offer on real property. See also *earnest money*.

good faith purchaser — a *bona fide* purchaser of real property who takes possession of the property unaware that there is a cloud on the title. Courts will generally protect good faith purchasers of property against later claims, even if there was a serious flaw in title, as long as the purchaser did not actually know of the flaw. Title insurance offers more certain protection against similar risks. See also *bona fide*.

good title — title free of reasonable doubt as to its validity. See also *marketable title*.

goods and chattels — generally, the personal property of an individual, as opposed to his or her real property.

goodwill — an intangible , but valuable, business asset. It includes such things as the expectation of continuing patronage, the reputation of a business for quality and honesty, and the value of the business name. It is an important factor in appraising an ongoing business concern.

gore — (also called *hiatus*) a small parcel of land created by an error in a legal description.

Government National Mortgage Association (GNMA) — (also called *Ginnie Mae*) a federal association established in 1968 as a corporation owned and managed by HUD. GNMA issues securities backed by a pool of federally insured mortgages. GNMA issues guaranty certificates backed by the full faith and credit of the U.S. government to enhance the marketability of the securitized loans. See also *guaranteed mortgage certificate*.

Government National Mortgage Association (GNMA) options — a method whereby investors buy and sell GNMA securities through the use of "puts" and "calls," as with other options. A "put" option allows the investor to sell a package of GNMA securities at a specified price within a specified period, while a "call" option entitles the investor to buy a package of GNMA securities at a specified price within a specified period. Sudden interest rate moves may make the options very valuable or worthless.

government patent — (also referred to simply as "patent") the initial grant of land by the U.S. government to the people of the United States. See also *patent*.

government rectangular survey method — a U.S. government method of surveying land in which land is divided into imaginary rectangular grids divided by north–south lines called meridians, and east–west lines called base lines. The entire country is divided into squares, 24 miles on each side. Each square is called a quadrangle. The quadrangles are further divided into 16 equal squares, each measuring 6 miles on each side, which are called townships. Within each township are 36 square miles. Each square mile, which is an area equivalent to 640 acres, is called a section. Sections may be further divided into half sections, quarter sections, etc. A line of townships extending north and south is called a range. Ranges are numbered east and west of the closest principal meridian. This method is primarily useful for describing relatively large parcels of land. See also *base line, government survey method, meridian, quadrangle, range, section,* and *township.*

government survey method – a method of describing the boundaries of a parcel of land based on the government rectangular survey. See also *government rectangular survey method.*

GPM – See *graduated payment mortgage.*

grace period – a mutually agreed upon or statutory period of time after a contract obligation is due to be performed within which performance may still be tendered without being considered a default. An example is a mortgage loan with a monthly payment date of the first of each month and a 10-day grace period. The loan would not be considered in default until the tenth of the month.

grade – the angle of the ground surface, relative to the horizon, of a lot or a portion of a lot, expressed in degrees.

grade level – the elevation of a lot above a fixed reference point, such as a street.

graded lease – See *graduated lease.*

graded tax – a local property tax intended to promote development by setting a higher tax rate on unimproved land and a lower tax rate on improvements.

gradient – the slope of a pipe, surface, or road over a horizontal distance, usually expressed as the number of inches rising or falling per foot of horizontal distance. In the special case of a sloped roof, the gradient is called pitch and is expressed as the drop in feet per each 12 feet of roof length. For example, a roof can be said to have a "4 in 12" pitch, meaning that the surface of the roof drops 4 feet vertically for each 12 feet it extends horizontally.

grading – the act of moving earth to change the natural slope and contour of a lot. Rough grading raises or lowers the level of the site and corrects the pitch. Finish grading fine-tunes the rough grade, adjusts for drainage, and prepares the site for any structures that will be built. If earth is removed from a site, leaving a natural surface, the lot is said to be "cut." If soil or other material is added to the site, the lot is said to be "fill." See also *cut and fill.*

Graduate, Realtor® Institute (GRI)

— professional designation offered by the National Association of Realtors®. Once a Realtor® member complies with the educational requirements and takes a series of tests, he or she is awarded the designation.

graduated lease — (also called *graded lease* or *step-up lease*) a commercial lease in which the lease payments rise according to a predetermined schedule or by reflecting changes in an index (such as the rate of inflation) over the term of the lease. An example is an office lease with first-year payments of $4,000/month and an inflation clause. If inflation in year 1 were 3%, the lease payment in year 2 would be ($4,000 + 3%), or $4,120/month.

graduated payment mortgage (GPM) — real estate loan with low initial monthly payments which rise each year until they reach a level sufficient to amortize the loan at the stated interest rate over the loan period. While the payments over the first several years are lower than they would be with a standard fixed rate loan, they will cross over and be higher than the standard loan over the bulk of the loan term. For example with a $150,000 30-year loan at 7%, a standard loan would have 360 equal payments of $997.96. A typical GPM would have payments as follows: year 1, $820.51; year 2, $861.54; year three, $904.61; year 4,

$949.84; year 5, $997.84 ; years 6 through 30, $1047.20. The FHA offers several popular GPMs.

grain elevator — a structure designed for the storage and processing of grain.

grandfather clause — a provision in a government law or regulation allowing a continuance of past practices or uses that had been allowed before that passage of the law or adoption of the regulation prohibited the practice or use. A typical example is a zoning change increasing the lot size needed for a duplex. Under a grandfather clause, duplexes on substandard lots that were in existence at the time of the change would still be considered legal.

granny flat — (also called "in-law unit") a colloquial term denoting a second separate living unit within or attached to a single-family residence. Such units are illegal under many zoning regulations.

grant — (1) to bestow or confer; (2) the act required for legal transfer of title to real property.

grant deed — a common form of deed in which the grantor warrants that he or she has legal and marketable title to the property and that there are no encumbrances except as noted on the deed. While the grantor makes only limited representations as to the state of the title, grant deeds are usually accompanied by title insurance. See also *warranty deed.*

grantee – the recipient of a grant. A grantee must be a legally competent person (either a natural person or a corporation) and alive or in existence at the time of conveyance. See also *grantor*.

granting clause – the specific language in a deed specifying the type of estate being transferred and to whom it is transferred.

grantor – a person, natural or corporate, who transfers title to, or an interest in, real property to another party. See also *grantee*.

grantor-grantee index – a list maintained by public recorders of all parties to real estate transactions within the jurisdiction of the recorder. The lists are indexed by the names of the parties. Parties are identified as grantor or grantee. They are used when title searches are performed.

gratuitous agent – a real estate licensee who performs real estate services for another without compensation. The agent is held to the same standard of care as if he or she had been compensated.

grazing rights – the right to allow domestic livestock to graze on the property of another. Grazing rights can be established by contract, usage, or operation of law.

green lumber – construction timbers that have not dried to the optimum level. The use of green lumber in construction can lead to warped walls and finish material cracks as the lumber eventually dries in place.

greenbelt – a strip of landscaped ground in a condominium project or planned unit development (PUD). Greenbelts are owned in common with the other homeowners in the project and are typically maintained by the homeowners' association. See also *common area*.

GRI – See *Graduate, Realtor® Institute*.

gridiron plan – a layout of streets in a rectangular, intersecting pattern.

grievance – within a local association of Realtors®, a grievance is a complaint by either a Realtor® or a member of the public against a member Realtor®. The complaint is heard by a grievance panel, which acts as a quasi-judicial forum. Realtor® members agree to be bound by the findings and recommendations of the panel.

grievance period – a period of time during which the public may officially express complaints concerning administrative matters such as tax assessments and zoning variances.

GRM – See *gross rent multiplier*.

groin – (1) the point at which curved walls, ceiling, or rooflines meet each other; (2) a structure built of pilings or rocks extending out from a shore into water and designed to prevent the movement of sand or to protect the shore from erosion.

gross acre — an actual acre (43,560 square feet), as distinguished from a "net acre" or the usable or cultivatable portion of an acre of land. See also *net acre*.

gross area — a measure of the total enclosed floor area of a building measured from the outside walls of the building. Usable area is the gross area minus interior projections, obstructions, and areas such as utility rooms, elevators, and staircases. See also *usable area*.

gross income — (1) for income tax purposes, the total income that an individual derives from all sources, before allowing for deductions, adjustments, and credits; (2) for income-producing real estate, all income attributable to the real estate, including such items as rent, income from coin-operated laundries, and parking revenues.

gross income multiplier (GIM) — a method of comparing the desirability of different income-producing properties of different prices and income streams. The formula is [*selling price ÷ gross annual income*]. For example, if Building A is priced at $500,000 and has gross income of $50,000/year, the gross income multiplier is ($500,000 ÷ $50,000), or 10. Building B is priced at $600,000, but has income of $75,000/year, for a gross income multiplier of 8. If other factors, such as the ages of the buildings and the maintenance costs are comparable, building B may be

more attractive to an investor. See also *gross rent multiplier*.

gross leasable area (GLA) — the portion of the total floor area of a building that is available for tenant leasing. For example, a building with a 100,000 square foot gross area might have 10,000 square feet in stairways, elevators, and utility or service rooms, and another 5,000 square feet in projections and structural supports, leaving a GLA of 85,000 square feet.

gross lease — a simple commercial lease in which the lessor pays all building-related expenses, such as taxes, utilities, insurance, and maintenance. The tenant pays a fixed monthly rent. Gross leases are usually associated with the rental of smaller spaces for short periods of time. For longer leases of larger spaces, other forms are usually employed which shift some or all of these costs to the tenant. See *triple net lease*.

gross profit — total profit before any deductions.

gross rent multiplier (GRM) — another name for the gross income multiplier when it is applied to residential rental property. See *gross income multiplier* for the formula.

gross sales — total revenue from the operation of a business. Commercial leases often tie a portion of the lease payment to a business's gross sales. As the business generates

|

more sales, the lease payments increase.

ground beam — a strong horizontal structural member designed to support the weight of the building at ground level.

ground cover — low plantings intended to hold soil in place.

ground-fault interrupter (GFI) — an electrical device designed to sense grounding situations that may present a risk of electrical shock to humans and quickly shut off the flow of electricity to the circuit. GFIs are required by modern electrical codes for outlets near water sources, such as kitchens and baths. They may also be installed at the source of a circuit to protect the entire circuit.

ground floor — the first floor that is at or only slightly above the building grade of a structure. The lower floor of a two-story house without a basement would be a ground floor. A basement itself is not a ground floor. A building, such as an apartment, in which the entire first floor is occupied by garage space would not be said to have a ground floor.

ground lease — a lease of raw land, often secured by an improvement to the land constructed by and for the lessee. These leases typically run for a period of years, with 30-, 75-, and 99-year leases being common. Due to the difficulty of forecasting future economic developments, lease payments are usually fixed in advance for a number of years, with a provision for renegotiating the payment according to a formula at some point or points during the middle of the lease period. The tenant may own the improvements as personal property. Ground leases are most common in commercial projects, in which businesses wish to preserve capital by not owning the land, but have been used for residential developments as well.

ground rent — the rent paid for the land under a ground lease.

grounds — the land not directly under a structure, but adjacent to and around the structure, if under the same ownership as the structure and fairly substantial in extent. See also *yard*.

groundwater — water present under the surface of the earth. Groundwater can present construction problems if not dealt with properly. See also *water table*.

grout — a mixture of cement and sand used to fill the gaps between bricks, pieces of tile, etc.

growing crops —once a seed is planted in the ground, it becomes a part of the land and is generally conveyed with the land. However, see also *emblement*.

growing equity mortgage (GEM) — a conventionally amortized mortgage with increasing payments over a period of years. The effect of the increased payments is to pay the principal down sooner and reduce the total cost of the loan.

guaranteed mortgage certificate (GMC) — a financial instrument issued by the Federal Home Loan Mortgage Corporation in which mortgages are pooled and sold to investors with the FHLMC guaranteeing the principal and interest.

guarantor —one who makes a guaranty. See also *guaranty*.

guaranty — a promise by one person (the guarantor) to secure the performance of another person in a matter such as a contract. A cosigner of a mortgage loan is a guarantor.

guardian — a person chosen by operation of a will or by court appointment, to care for another person (a "ward"), another person's property, or both. There are many reasons for appointing a guardian. The ward may be a minor, legally incompetent, or a spendthrift. A guardian need not possess a real estate license to buy or sell property, acting as an agent for the ward. Buyers of such property generally receive what is called a "guardian's deed."

guardian *ad litem* — a guardian appointed by a court to prosecute or defend a legal action on behalf of a minor or a person judged legally incompetent.

guest-car ratio (GCR) — in a condominium project or PUD, the number of parking spaces assigned per unit for guest parking.

guide meridians — a component of the government rectangular survey. Both the prime and guide meridians run north and south. Guide meridians correct for the convergence of the principal meridians introduced by the curvature of the earth.

Gunite™ — a trade name for a form of sprayed concrete used to line in-ground pools. It is sprayed over a mesh of reinforcing steel.

gutter — (1) an open channel running parallel to and immediately below the eaves of a roof, designed to collect and divert rainwater away from the base of the structure; (2) an open channel where curb and street meet, designed to divert water into a storm drain.

gypsum — a powder composed primarily of hydrous calcium sulfate. When mixed with water, it hardens. It is used as the base for drywall. See also *drywall*.

gypsum board — See *drywall*.

H

habendum clause — a clause in a deed beginning with the words "to have and to hold" that defines and limits the extent of ownership being granted. It is generally considered to be a term of limitation in which the grantor intends to grant less than a full fee simple estate.

habitable – a condition suitable for human beings to live in. Landlords are generally required to maintain their property in a habitable condition. If they fail to do so, tenants may terminate the rental agreement or withhold rent. In many states, builders are also held to an implied warranty of habitability in the sale of new homes.

habitable room – a room in a dwelling used for general living purposes, such as a living room, bedroom, and kitchen, as opposed to a hallway, bath, or laundry room. In areas where houses are compared by room count, only the habitable rooms are counted.

habitancy – a legal term for the place where a person lives.

hacienda – an estate or farm; originally, a Spanish royal estate.

half-bath – a bathroom with a sink and a toilet but without a shower or tub. A full bath includes at least a sink, toilet, and tub; a three-quarter bath includes a sink, toilet, and shower stall.

half-timbered – a construction technique in which the timber frame is exposed on the interior. The areas between framing members are generally filled with lathe and plaster.

hall – (1) a narrow passageway between rooms; (2) a building with at least one large, open room used as a meeting place or concert venue.

hamlet – a small town.

handicap – defined in the Fair Housing Act and in the Americans with Disabilities Act (ADA) as a physical or mental impairment that substantially interferes with at least one major life activity. Federal and state laws prohibit discrimination against persons with a designated handicap in the sale or lease of residential property. The definition has been expanded to include mental handicaps, such as drug addiction, physical diseases such as AIDS, and mental illnesses such as schizophrenia.

handicap access – a 1992 federal law, the Americans with Disabilities Act (ADA) mandates equal access for persons with handicaps as defined in the Act to public accommodations, which are broadly defined to include most private businesses. Access modifications can include wheelchair ramps, special parking spaces and rest rooms.

handicap parking – larger than usual designated parking spaces especially set aside for persons with physical handicaps. The spaces tend to be those closest to the entrance of a structure.

handyman – a tradesperson who specializes in a variety of small re-

pairs and minor construction projects. A handyman (or woman) typically offers limited electrical, plumbing, and carpenter work.

handyman special — an advertising term referring to a property for
sale in need of substantial repair or
rehabilitation. See also *fixer-upper*.

hangout — that portion of a loan
term which exceeds the term of the
lease on the property. For example, if
a lender makes a $10,000,000 15-
year loan on an office building in
which the sole tenant has signed a
10-year lease, the remaining five years
of the loan would be a hangout.

harbor — a man-made or natural
shelter in which ships may be an-
chored safely.

hard costs — the monetary costs of
acquiring land for development,
physically preparing the site, and
building a structure. Sometimes
called "sticks and bricks." Although
definitions vary by region, hard costs
generally do not include the costs associated with architects, attorneys,
and marketing. See by contrast *soft
costs*.

hard money loan — a real estate
loan in which the borrower receives
cash in hand, as opposed to a purchase money loan in which the borrower receives ownership of the collateral. Second trust deeds are the
most common form of hard money
loan, with the homeowner borrowing against the equity in a house for

some purpose other than the purchase of the home.

hardpan — tightly compacted clay
soil. It is difficult to excavate.

hardware — the metal-finish fittings
inside and outside a structure. Examples include doorknobs, hinges,
latches, and locks.

hardwood — any of a variety of
woods used for finishing with stain
as opposed to paint. Hardwoods are
denser than the less expensive soft-
woods, and are usually reserved for
finished surfaces such as cabinets,
furniture, and decorative moldings.

harmonious — an architectural mix
of similar or complementary styles.

hatchway — an opening in a floor
or ceiling allowing access to another
level of a structure.

hazard insurance — a real property insurance policy which covers
the insured against several kinds of
loss or damage. Typical coverage protects against fire, windstorm, and
casualty losses. Residential mortgage
lenders usually require the borrower
to obtain this coverage in an amount
sufficient to protect the mortgage
holder's interest.

hazardous substance — a material that poses a health threat to individuals or the environment. The
Environmental Protection Agency
publishes lists of hundreds of hazardous substances. Federal and state
laws mandate specific forms of dis-

closure to buyers in the sale of various kinds of property. Hazardous substances sometimes found in homes include lead-based paint, asbestos, radon gas, and certain plastic pipes.

hazardous waste — materials that are dangerous and/or difficult to dispose of safely. The Environmental Protection Agency regulates the disposal of such waste, including radioactive substances, biological waste from hospitals, and chemical waste, such as used oil from cars. Property owners are held to strict standards of accountability concerning the presence of unauthorized hazardous waste on their property.

head of household — tax term meaning an individual who maintains a home for, and is primarily responsible for, the support of one or more individuals who are connected to him by a close relationship such as blood, marriage, or adoption. Tax law gives preferential treatment to individuals who qualify as a head of household.

header — a horizontal structural support extending between two joists and spanning an opening such as a door or window.

hearing — a quasi-judicial procedure in which a hearing officer or officers collect facts and public opinions regarding some public issue and recommend a decision by a governing agency. Sometimes the hearing

agency itself is empowered to render a decision. A typical example involves zoning variance requests, which are heard by a zoning variance board, which then renders a decision in the matter. Administrative decisions of this sort may be appealed judicially.

hearth — the inside bottom of a fireplace. Local building codes specify the fire-resistant materials that may be used in a hearth.

heat pump — a device designed to both heat and cool a structure by taking advantage of the difference between outside and inside air temperatures. See also *heating system*.

heater — a device intended to heat a small area. See also *heating duct* and *heating system*.

heating duct — passage, often tubular, through which air is distributed throughout a building. See also *heating system*.

heating system — a building-wide device or combination of devices intended to heat the entire structure. See also *furnace, heat pump,* and *heater*.

hectare — a metric measurement of land area. One hectare is equal to 100 ares. An "are" is 100 square meters. One hectare is also equal to 2.471 acres, or 107,637 square feet.

heir — person entitled to receive property, either by operation of law or by will, when another person dies.

heirs and assigns – words of limitation in a grant. They are most commonly used to designate a fee simple estate, such as "to Abel, his heirs and assigns." Abel could then will the property, sell it, or give it to someone else.

hereditaments – all things capable of being inherited, including real and personal property. Corporeal hereditaments are substantial and physical, including land, livestock, and furniture. Incorporeal hereditaments are those property rights appurtenant or growing out of the corporeal. An example of an incorporeal hereditament would be a lifetime estate in a right to receive rents or royalties.

heterogeneous – an appraisal term meaning a variety of land uses or building styles in the area of the subject property. It is generally regarded as detrimental to values. See also *homogeneous*.

hiatus – (1) a missing element in the chain of title to real property. A hiatus, when discovered, may lead to a cloud on title, because it cannot be determined with certainty who the rightful owner of the property may be; (2) same as gore. See also *gore*.

high water line – the level on a shore that water typically reaches during high tides during periods of normal weather.

highest and best use – an appraisal term denoting the legally and physically possible use that, at the time of appraisal, is most likely to produce the greatest net return to the land and/or buildings over a given holding period.

high-rise – a residential or commercial building of more than approximately six stories with elevator access to the upper floors.

highway – high-speed multilane road generally designed for long-distance driving. Highways are also characterized by controlled access to and from surface streets through the use of on and off ramps. See *freeway*.

hip roof – a roof sloping up from all four sides of a structure, with a ridgeline at the top, usually parallel to the longest dimension of the building.

historic structure – a building recognized by a government or private agency as having special historic significance. The National Historic Register is one such agency. The purpose of the designation is to require or encourage the preservation of the structure in its original state.

historical cost – the cost of a building when it was first constructed.

historical district – an area that has been designated by a government agency as having special historical significance. Historical districts have building restrictions designed to preserve the physical character of the area, and often offer tax incentives to renovate or restore existing buildings.

HOA — See *homeowners' association.*

hold harmless clause — a contract provision in which one party agrees to indemnify and defend another party for certain risks associated with the transaction. A typical example is a hold harmless clause in a commercial lease, in which the lessee agrees to pay any damages incurred by third parties in connection with the lessee's use of the leased premises.

holdback — (1) a portion of a construction loan retained by the lender until the lender is satisfied that all contracted work is complete, or that a certain percentage of a commercial property is leased; (2) in a construction or home improvement setting, the portion of the contractor's compensation that is withheld until proof is provided that all subcontractors have been paid and all mechanic's liens have been released. See also *mechanic's lien.* (3) in an escrow, a portion of the seller's proceeds that is retained by escrow to secure performance of some task after the close of escrow. A typical example is money held to perform pest control work on the property after the close of escrow. Escrow companies will generally hold 1½ times the estimated cost of the work.

holder — the legitimate possessor of a bill of exchange, check, note, loan, or other valuable commercial instrument. The holder is entitled to receive the benefit of the value of the instrument.

holder in due course — a holder who takes possession of an instrument in good faith, without notice that is defective, invalid or has been dishonored. Generally, a holder in due course is entitled to the benefit of the instrument, even if it had at some earlier point been stolen. See also *good faith.*

holding company — a company limited to owning stock in, and supervising the management of, other companies.

holding costs — the total price of maintaining ownership of real property for a specified period of time. These include mortgage interest, taxes, insurance, and maintenance.

holding escrow — See *conditional sales contract, contract for deed,* and *land contract.*

holding period — a tax term meaning the length of time an individual or company retains ownership of a capital asset.

holding period return (HPR) — the return on investment of a capital asset such as real property over the time it has been owned. The formula is *[(capital gain or loss + rental income) ÷ purchase price].* For example, an apartment building purchased for $500,000 that generated yearly rental income of $50,000 and sold exactly one year later for $550,000 would have a HPR of [($50,000 + $50,000) ÷ 500,000], or 20%.

holdout – a landowner who refuses initially to sell to a purchaser who intends to purchase a number of contiguous parcels in order to complete a development plan. Because the purchaser may need all the contiguous parcels in order to make the development work, the holdout property owner has considerable bargaining leverage.

holdover tenant – a tenant who retains possession of leased premises after the expiration of the lease term. He may be evicted or given a new lease. Generally, holdover tenants are deemed to continue to owe rent at the same level as their previous rent payments. See also *sufferance*.

holidays – federally recognized holidays are significant in real estate transactions in which time periods are calculated in terms of business days. Business days do not include weekends or federal holidays.

hollow wall – a wall enclosing an airspace, such as a typical wood stud wall with drywall inside and wood or stucco on the outside. Hollow walls also serve to conceal electrical wires, heating and cooling ducts, and plumbing pipes.

holographic will – a will handwritten by a testator, but not witnessed. Some states recognize holographic wills. Others do not. The potential

for fraud and forgery is always present in an unwitnessed document. See also *testator/testatrix* and *will*.

home – (1) a single-family residence; (2) any domicile. See also *domicile*.

home affordability index – a measure of the average American family's financial ability to purchase the median price home at a given point in time. The components of the index are median family income, median purchase price, and current interest rates. When the index is 100, a family with median incomes has exactly the income needed to buy the median-priced home. If the index is 80, a family with median incomes has only 80% of the income needed to buy the median-priced home. Published by the National Association of Realtors®.

home equity line of credit – an open-ended form of credit secured by equity in a home. A lender commits to lend up to a certain sum of money to the homeowner based on the homeowner's ability to repay and the equity in the home. The homeowner/borrower then is able to write checks that draw on the loan, up to the maximum limit. The advantage over a traditional second trust deed is that the homeowner need not pay interest on the money until it is actually needed.

home improvement loan – a second trust deed obtained for the

express purpose of making significant repairs or additions to the property that secures the loan.

home inspection – an increasingly
common practice in which either the
buyer or seller obtains a formal third-
party inspection of real property that
is the actual or contemplated subject
of a contract. In many states, the
buyer's approval of the inspection is
a contingency of the contract. See
also *home inspector.*

home inspector – a person employed by a buyer for purposes of investigating the condition of a home
for possible purchase. The inspector
will examine all the major systems of
the home and issue a written report.
Some states now require home inspectors to be licensed. See also *home
inspection.*

home inventory – a list of the personal property contained in a home
for insurance purposes.

home loan – a loan secured by a
residence. If the proceeds are used to
buy the home, it is a *purchase money
mortgage.* If cash is obtained using the
equity in the home, the loan is called
a "cash-out refinance."

home rule – the constitutional authority and power of a local government to make and enforce laws derived from a grant by the state government.

home warranty – a type of insurance policy available to purchasers of

resale homes in most states. It is designed to protect against the failure
of certain major systems of the home
for a period of one year.

Typical coverage includes plumbing
systems, such as water heaters and
garbage disposals, built-in appliances,
electrical failures, and heating and
air-conditioning systems. Home warranties are often negotiated as part of
the purchase contract.

**homeowners' association
(HOA)** – a formal nonprofit organization of member homeowners in a
particular housing development or
developments. HOAs have bylaws,
elected officers, dues, a budget, and
certain enforcement powers. HOAs
may administer and modify covenants, conditions, and restrictions
(CC&Rs) and maintain common areas for the enjoyment of the homeowners. In most states, HOAs are
regulated by statute. Homeowners'
associations are not restricted to
condominiums, and may also be
found in areas with single-family
residences, and in planned unit developments (PUDs). See also *homeowner's fee; condominium; covenants,
conditions, and restrictions;* and *planned
unit development.*

homeowner's fee – [also called
homeowners' association (HOA)
dues] a charge to homeowners who
belong to a homeowners' association.
The fee may be mandatory or voluntary. It generally covers the cost of
maintaining common areas and fa-

cilities and any other services the association provides. In many states, unpaid homeowner's fees are a lien on the property. See also *homeowners' association.*

homeowner's insurance policy
— a multiple hazard policy designed to protect against theft, vandalism, fire, and storm damage, as well as liability for lawsuits by persons injured on the premises.

Homeowner's Warranty Program (HOW) — an insurance policy
offered through the National Association of Home Builders to new home purchasers. It covers significant construction defects for a period of 10 years, even if the original builder is no longer in business. Some states have statutory provisions mandating that builders provide this type of coverage.

homeownership rate — the pro-
portion of dwelling units occupied by owners in a given area. Most recently, the nation's homeownership rate has been in the 62% to 66% range.

homestead — (1) a statutory pro-
tection against a lawsuit judgment up to certain dollar limits. If filed properly, the homestead protects the homeowner against the loss of his or her home as the result of an unsatisfied judgment. Dollar limits to the protection vary widely by state. Homestead laws do not protect homeowners against foreclosure by a mortgage holder, nor do they shelter the homeowner against tax liens. (2) in some states, filing homestead provides for an exemption from a portion of property tax levied.

homogeneous — an appraisal term
meaning a clustering of similar structures and property uses such as single-family homes of similar size and age. From an appraiser's point of view, homogeneity stabilizes and protects values. See also *heterogeneous.*

horizontal property laws — a gen-
eral term referring to a wide variety of laws concerning condominium construction, transfer, and ownership. Condominium owners own only the airspace within their walls— hence "horizontal ownership," as opposed to the traditional "center of the earth to the top of the sky" vertical property rights associated with fee simple land ownership.

host liability — the liability recog-
nized by many states of a homeowner who serves alcohol to a guest who later, as a result, causes injury to another.

hostile possession — occupation of
land by a person in opposition to the interest of the titleholder. Hostile possession need not be hostile in the ordinary sense of anger by the possessor; rather, it simply requires that the possessor repudiate the rights of the titleholder. Hostile possession is an essential element in an action for title called adverse possession. See

also *adverse possession*.

hot water heater – (or simply *water heater*) a device designed to heat and sometimes store water for household, commercial, or industrial use.

hotel – loosely, a collection of lodging units in which 50% or more of the units are rented on a daily or short-term basis. The distinction between hotels, apartments, and timeshares is not well defined.

house – a single-family residence.

household – a dwelling containing two or more people connected by blood, marriage, adoption, or other close relationship.

Housing and Urban Development, U.S. Department of (HUD) – the U.S. Department of Housing and Urban Development. It was created in 1965 and is charged with ensuring an adequate national supply of safe, affordable housing. It administers or oversees a number of programs designed to promote home ownership, prevent discriminatory housing practices, and encourage rehabilitation of blighted areas.

housing expense – all costs associated with maintaining a dwelling, whether rented or purchased. These include rent, mortgage payments, utilities, association dues, taxes, and maintenance.

housing expense ratio – (also called *front-end ratio*) expressed as a percentage, the fraction of an individual's total gross income represented by actual or proposed housing-related expenses, such as principal, interest, taxes, insurance, and association dues (PITIA). This ratio is used by lenders for purposes of qualifying a prospective buyer for a loan. For example, Abel earns $60,000/year or $5,000/month and wishes to purchase a home with principal and interest payments of $1,000/month, taxes of $125/month, insurance of $25/month, and association dues of $85/month. Abel's housing expense ratio is [($1,000 + $125 + $25 + $85) ÷ $5,000], or 24.7%.

housing starts – the number of new dwelling units for which construction has begun during a particular period in a particular location. Quarterly national housing start figures are important to economic forecasters because housing starts are considered to be a leading indicator of the direction of the nation's economy.

HOW – See *Homeowner's Warranty Program*.

HPR – See *holding period return*.

HUD – See *Housing and Urban Development, U.S. Department of*.

humidifier – a device that raises the relative humidity in a room or structure by emitting water vapor into the air. Humidifiers are generally used in conjunction with heating systems to counteract the drying effects of the heat.

humus – the organic component of soil, consisting of decomposed organic material such as leaves and kitchen waste.

hundred percent location – the best possible location for an appropriate retail business in the most desirable downtown business center; the location that will generate the most traffic and business and maximize revenues.

hypothecate – to pledge an item as security for a loan without relinquishing physical possession of it. In a typical purchase money mortgage, the borrower hypothecates the home, giving the lender an equitable interest, while retaining possession and legal title.

HVAC – heating, ventilation, and air conditioning.

I

I-beam – a steel or iron structural framing member that, when viewed in cross section, resembles the uppercase letter "I."

I-girder – See *I-beam*.

iden sonans – names that sound alike when spoken. The rule of *iden sonans* holds that a misspelled name

in a document does not void the document, as long as the names sound the same and no fraud was intended.

illiquidity – difficulty or delay in selling an asset quickly. The more specialized the asset, the greater the illiquidity. Commonly, publicly traded stocks are very liquid, while real estate tends to be relatively illiquid.

illuviation – transportation of suspended or dissolved materials through layers of soil by the action of water.

immediate family member – defined by most lenders as a spouse, parent, grandparent, sibling, child, stepparent, or legal guardian.

immobility – incapable of being moved. Most improvements to real estate (such as buildings) are immobile.

impact fees – a local government cash assessment against a new development project designed to mitigate some external effects of the development, such as increased traffic and utility usage.

impaired credit – less than perfect credit record of a prospective purchaser of real property. In recent years, specialty lenders have been offering higher-priced loans to these sub-prime borrowers.

Imperial gallon – measure of liquid volume equal to 277 cubic inches. A standard gallon is 231 cubic inches.

implied agency — conclusion by a court that an agency relationship was created by the actions and words of the parties, even in the absence of an agency agreement. The issue arises frequently for real estate licensees who offer to assist in a real estate transaction without being formally involved. See also *agency*.

implied contract — a conclusion by a court that a contract was created by the actions and general language of the parties, absent any formal agreement. Implied contracts are enforced by courts where a failure to act would unjustly enrich one of the parties to the detriment of another. See also *quasi-contract*.

implied easement — an easement arising by operation of equitable principles of law rather than by explicit agreement. For example, the purchaser of a lakefront lot would be reasonably entitled to use the only road to the property if the road was also owned by the seller of the lot.

implied listing — listing arising out of the conduct of a real estate broker and a seller of real property, rather than by explicit agreement. In most states, however, listings must be in writing to be enforceable. See also *exclusive listing* and *Statute of Frauds*.

implied notice — form of actual, not constructive, notice of some fact; a judicial conclusion that a reason-able person, having knowledge of certain facts, should have known that further inquiry would lead to other relevant facts. For example, if Abel buys a house from Baker knowing that Baker does not occupy the house, and later learns that Portnoy is occupying the house under a two-year lease, Abel would have implied knowledge that Portnoy might have some claim to the property, even if Abel never viewed the house. Abel has this implied knowledge because a reasonable person would have verified that the house was vacant before completing the purchase. See also *actual notice* and *constructive notice*.

implied warranty of habitability — a legal doctrine applying both to landlords and to sellers of new homes. The doctrine imposes minimum standards of comfort, health, and safety of the premises, regardless of any contract language to the contrary, such as "as-is" or "without warranty." The theory is that public policy requires leased premises to be livable, and new homes to be reasonably well built. Resale homes are not held to this standard.

impound account — trust account designed to collect and disburse sums of money to satisfy obligations related to a parcel of real estate. A common example is a property tax impound account required by certain real estate lenders: The lender wishes to ensure that the taxes are paid on time and will require the borrowers to make monthly payments into the trust account. The trustee is responsible for paying the taxes when due.

improved land – real property that has been modified for higher value by human activity. See *improvement* for examples.

improved value – the total value of land and improvements taken together.

improvement – additions or modifications to property that are designed to add capital value. Examples include grading, landscaping, sewers and utilities, structures, fences and walls, streets, and room additions to existing houses. Improvements are more substantial than mere repairs.

improvement ratio – the proportion of the value of the improvement to the value of the land. The formula is [(*value of improvement ÷ value of land*)/1]. For example, if a house costing $300,000 to build is constructed on a lot costing $100,000 to buy, the improvement ratio would be [($300,000 ÷ $100,000)/1] or 3 to 1.

improvements and betterments insurance – in an insurance policy with contents coverage, up to 10% of the policy limit may cover improvements made by tenants for their own use, even if the tenant is uninsured. For example, if an apartment owner carried $50,000 of contents insurance on each apartment in the building, up to $5,000 would be available to cover tenant improvements such

as built-in bookshelves and desks.

improvements off-land – See *off-site improvements.*

improvements on-land – See *on-site improvements.*

imputed interest – a tax term meaning interest implied by law, even though not actually paid or received in the form of interest. It is intended largely to prevent sellers of capital assets form treating all installment payments as capital gain. The interest rate applied is imputed and published in the *Internal Revenue Bulletin,* a publication of the Internal Revenue Service.

imputed notice – actual knowledge by an agent that is deemed by a court to have been given to a principal, because of the agency relationship. The doctrine prevents principals from denying knowledge of material facts transmitted to their agents. See also *actual notice, agency, constructive notice,* and *implied notice.*

in escrow – time between the acceptance of an offer for the purchase of real property and the consummation of the sale. During this time, the escrow company collects funds and verifies documents in preparation for completion of the sale and the closing of the escrow. See also *escrow.*

in gross – See *easement in gross.*

in perpetuity – of potentially infinite duration.

in personam — legal proceeding against a person, as opposed to a proceeding against a thing. An action for damages is an *in personam* action. See also *in rem*.

in re — legal term meaning "in the matter of."

in rem — legal proceeding against a thing such as real property, as opposed to a proceeding against a person. A foreclosure is typically an *in rem* action. See also *in personam*.

inactive license — valid real estate license that has been placed on inactive status by the licensee, usually in exchange for reduced license fees. The licensee may not perform tasks requiring a license during this period.

inadequate improvement — See *underimprovement*.

inchoate — without final form; begun but not complete. An inchoate right is a right, such as a wife's dower interest, that will not take effect or be precisely determinable until after the death of her husband.

inchoate instrument — an unrecorded document, (such as a deed) which is valid between the parties to the document and others having actual notice of it. It will not generally be enforced against the world at large, as it would if it had been properly recorded.

incinerator — a device for burning trash and refuse for disposal.

income — (1) money received; (2) revenues from investment property or properties.

income approach to valuation — (also called the "capitalization approach" and "income capitalization approach") an approach to valuation that employs a desired rate of return (capitalization rate) and an anticipated net income stream to determine the value of income-producing real property. The formula is [*annualized net income ÷ cap rate*]. For example, a property with a net annual income of $100,000 and a *cap rate* (desired or market rate of return) of 9.5% would have a value of ($100,000 ÷ 9.5%), or $1,052,631.58. See also *capitalization (cap) rate*.

income multiplier — See *gross income multiplier*.

income property — any type of real property that is held for the production of income. It may be commercial, residential, industrial, or agricultural. Raw land that produces no revenues is not income property.

income statement — (also called *profit and loss statement*) a periodic financial statement prepared by a business showing the amounts and sources of income and the amounts and categories of expenses. See *profit and loss statement*.

income stream — net cash produced over some period of time by an income property. The simplest form is [*gross revenues - total expenses for the period*].

income tax lien — lien on real property, earnings, or other assets to secure payment of an unpaid income tax obligation.

income taxes — taxes calculated and paid on cash earnings or revenues. Income taxes may be federal, state, or local.

incompetent — a person who is judged not to have the legal capacity to contract. Minors, the seriously mentally ill, some drug addicts, comatose adults, and the mentally impaired elderly may be deemed incompetent. A court may appoint a guardian to contract for the incompetent person. See also *capacity to contract*.

incorporate — to form a business entity known as a corporation by preparing an filing articles of incorporation and paying the required fees to an appropriate state agency. Most states now have a dedicated department of corporations.

incorporation by reference — a contract term that includes in the contract the terms of another document by identifying and attaching it. Addendums and previous counteroffers are often incorporated by reference.

incorporeal rights — a property right without physical form; nonpossessory rights. Examples of incorpo-

real rights include easements, the right to receive future rents, and insurance claims.

increase clause — See *escalation (escalator) clause*.

increment — any increase in size or intensity.

incumbrance — See *encumbrance*.

incurable depreciation — See *incurable obsolescence*.

incurable obsolescence — (also called *incurable depreciation* and *economic obsolescence*) an appraisal term meaning that the loss of value to an improvement due to functional or external obsolescence is impossible or too costly to correct. See also *economic obsolescence, external obsolescence,* and *functional obsolescence*.

indemnification — contractual agreement by one person to compensate another in the event that the other suffers a specified loss. See also *hold harmless clause*.

indemnity agreement — See *indemnification*.

indenture deed — deed in which the grantee agrees in writing to accept certain obligations in connection with the property. Both grantor and grantee must sign the deed. In most other forms of deed, only the grantor signs the deed.

independent appraisal — property appraisal performed by an appraiser with no previous connection to the buyer, seller, or lender. See also *in-house appraisal.*

independent contractor – a self-employed person hired to perform a task with an emphasis on the end result. If by contrast, the person is subject to a high level of supervision and control, the law will deem him or her to be an employee. The distinction is relevant for tax and liability purposes. Most real estate agents are considered to be independent contractors. However, the more control over the agent's activity the broker exerts (such as requiring floor time, office meetings, etc.), the more likely it is that the broker has created an employment relationship.

index – a moving benchmark typically used to adjust an interest rate or lease payment. Examples include the Consumer Price Index (CPI) and the LIBOR index. See also *LIBOR* and *Consumer Price Index.*

index lease – rental agreement in which the rent is adjusted periodically based on changes to an agreed-upon index, usually a general economic index such as the Consumer Price Index or the Wholesale Price Index. The lease provision that calls for the adjustment is an escalation clause. See also *escalation (escalator) clause.*

Index of Leading Economic Indicators (LEI) – the econometric measurements in key areas of the national economy that are thought to be most sensitive to changes in the economy at large. The index is intended to predict business trends.

indexed loan – loan in which the interest rate and/or payment amount changes over time based on changes in an index specified in the loan documents.

indirect costs – (also called *soft costs*) expenses associated with a construction project that are not directly attributable to the cost of the structure. Examples include real estate taxes, insurance, and professional fees. See also *hard costs.*

indirect lighting – artificial light that is designed to reflect and scatter rather than to illuminate directly.

Individual Retirement Account (IRA) – a federal tax-favored retirement savings program for individuals. Individuals are permitted to invest a specified amount each year until retirement. The amount invested is not taxed until withdrawn. Individuals benefit through compounding of what would have been tax dollars, and through their presumably lower tax rate at retirement age.

indoor air quality – a measure of the presence of persistent pollutants inside a structure. Modern construction materials and the sheer size of buildings with no natural ventilation have added to the problem. See also *sick building syndrome.*

industrial development bond – a bond issued by a government agency or other entity for the purpose of financing industrial or commercial development.

Industrial Multiple – a multiple listing service (MLS) for industrial property maintained by the American Industrial Real Estate Association (AIR) for its members. See also *American Industrial Real Estate Association* and *multiple listing service.*

industrial park – a large area zoned for industrial uses. Such developments are the result of a general plan in which clustering of industrial land uses is deemed desirable. They may contain many sites or units for various industries and/or companies, along with common services for the park tenants/owners.

industrial property – (1) real property zoned for research, manufacturing, factory, or warehouse space; (2) structures used for industrial purposes.

Industrial Real Estate Association (AIR) – American Industrial Real Estate Association. a real estate trade group whose members specialize in the sale of industrial property. See also *Industrial Multiple.*

industrial siding – railroad spur line designed to serve an industrial park or specific building.

industrial tax exemption – exemption from local property tax designed to encourage industrial development and expansion in a particular area.

infiltration – (1) changes in neighborhood uses and character over time due to shifting economic and social forces; (2) penetration of water through the earth and into a structure; (3) unwanted outside air penetration into an insulated structure.

inflation – increasing general price levels caused by an oversupply of money or excess demand for goods and services.

informed consent – agreement by a party to a contract or an element of the contract made after the party has been advised of all material facts. The issue arises commonly in the context of real estate agency disclosures. If an agent conceals dual agency or self-dealing from a principal, the consent given by the principal to the agency may be voided. See also *agency* and *fiduciary duty.*

infrastructure – the human-made physical elements of a community, such as roads, sewer systems, telephone lines, hospitals, and railways.

ingress – the access, entrance, or approach to a property; the opposite of egress. See, by contrast, *egress.*

inharmonious – property usage that is not in keeping with surrounding usage. For example, an apartment building in an industrial area would be inharmonious. See also *harmonious*.

inheritance – property that descends to an heir by operation of law or by will when another dies.

inheritance tax – tax on the value of an inheritance, levied by a state against the heir directly, as opposed to an estate tax, which is levied against the estate itself. See also *estate tax*.

in-house appraisal – appraisal for purposes of a loan that is performed by an appraiser employed directly by the lender. See also *independent appraisal*.

in-house sale – real estate sale in which the same broker represents both the buyer and the seller. Note that even if different agents working under the same broker represent the buyer and the seller, the transaction would still be considered an in-house sale. See also *dual agency*.

initial payment – See *down payment*.

initials – handwritten first letters of a person's first, last, and (optionally) middle names and used as a substitute for a signature in real estate contracts in which all parties initial changes, or where they must separately acknowledge specific terms, such as liquidated damages clauses.

injunction – formal court order issued to compel or prevent some act by a person.

inland waters – all bodies of water other than oceans and seas.

inlet – recess in the shore of a body of water.

inliquidity – See *illiquidity*.

inner city – an urban area within a community that has physically deteriorated and become blighted. Inner cities often become the target of redevelopment efforts by local governments.

innocent misrepresentation – misstatement of material fact made by a party without negligence or the intent to deceive.

innocent purchaser for value – See *bona fide purchaser*.

inquiry notice – a form of constructive notice in which a party to a transaction is deemed to be aware of material facts that a reasonable person would have discovered through a reasonable inquiry. For example, if Abel purchases a three-bedroom house from Baker assuming that it is a five-bedroom house, Abel may be deemed to have inquiry notice of the discrepancy because a reasonable person would simply have counted the bedrooms.

in-service loan – program in which the federal government pays the mortgage insurance for active service personnel with certain federally insured home loans.

inside lot – parcel of land bordered

on at least two sides by other parcels, as opposed to streets or alleyways. Not a corner lot.

insolvency – state of being insolvent. See also *insolvent.*

insolvent – inability to meet current financial obligations.

inspection – physical investigation of the condition of a particular parcel of real property and any improvements thereon. The inspection can include a review of all construction elements, heating, plumbing, foundation, roof, etc., as well as a consideration of off-site issues such as the proximity of the property to a landfill or new road construction. Modern real estate contracts strongly advise buyers to perform a complete inspection.

installment contract – (also called *agreement of sale, contract for deed, contract for sale,* and *land contract*) a contract for the sale of real estate in which the seller accepts periodic payments from the buyer. Only after all payments have been made will the seller deliver the deed to the buyer. In the interim, the buyer is allowed to occupy and enjoy the property per the terms of the installment contract. The buyer has "equitable title" to the property, while the seller retains "legal title." See also *agreement of sale, contract for deed, contract for sale, equitable title, land contract,* and *legal title.*

installment land sales contract – See *installment contract.*

installment note – a debt instrument calling for specified periodic payments.

installment sale – real estate purchase arrangement in which periodic payments are made by the buyer to the seller over a period of more than one tax year. Usually, the goal is to minimize the capital gains tax for the seller. See also *equitable title* and *legal title.*

installments – periodic payments.

Institute of Real Estate Management (IREM) –a trade association of professional property managers. IREM issues the professional designation of ARM, Accredited Real Estate Manager.

institutional lender – term loosely describing financial institutions that routinely engage in the practice of lending money for real estate purchases. They typically lend depositor funds (banks and S&Ls) or customer money held in trust (insurance companies). Their activities and investments are regulated by a variety of state and federal agencies.

institutional property – property which is not strictly commercial, industrial, agricultural, or residential, but which serves some public purpose, even if privately owned. Examples include schools, hospitals, and airports.

instrument – written document specifying the rights and obligations of the parties in some matter. Examples include contracts, wills, leases, and deeds.

insulation – material added to a structure for the purposes of regulating the temperature or noise level within the structure.

insurable interest – a legitimate relationship between one person and another, or between a person and a property, which is sufficiently close that a loss would be suffered if the person or property were injured. An insurable interest is required in order to collect on an insurance claim. Real estate lenders are deemed to have an insurable interest in the property that secures the loan.

insurable title – a state of title that will lead a title insurance company to offer title insurance on a particular parcel. If the title is badly clouded, it may be uninsurable. See also *cloud on title*.

insurable value – value of an insured item. For real estate casualty insurance, it is generally the value of the structure and contents. The land is considered indestructible, and is therefore not part of insurable value. For title insurance, the purchase price usually represents the insurable value.

insurance – a mechanism for managing risk; a contract in which one party agrees to indemnify another for loss due to a specified risk (such as fire, death, or loss of property rights)

in exchange for a payment or payments. See also *insurance coverage*.

insurance coverage – a contract that provides indemnification in the form of money from an insurance company to an insured party in the event that a certain loss is suffered. An example is fire insurance, in which a homeowner and lender may receive compensation if the home is destroyed by fire.

insured loan – real estate loan that is insured by a third party against default by the buyer. FHA loans are insured, as are many low-down-payment conventional mortgages. See also *private mortgage insurance).*

insurer – a party to an insurance contract who has agreed to indemnify another party in the event of a covered loss. See also *insurance.*

intangible asset – thing of value that in its strictly physical form has little or no value. Such things of value that may accrue to an ongoing business enterprise, such as goodwill, patents, trademarks, copyrights, franchises, etc.

intangible property – See *intangible asset.*

intangible value – dollar value of an intangible asset. See also *intangible asset.*

inter alia – Latin phrase meaning "among other things." It is used in a pleading, especially in the recitation of a statute, where quoting the statute in its entirety is not desirable.

inter alios — Latin phrase meaning "between (among) other persons"; between those who are strangers to the matter in question.

inter vivos — Latin phrase meaning "between the living"; from one living person to another.

inter vivos trust — a trust set up during the lifetime of the settlor and becoming active during his or her lifetime. A testamentary trust takes effect only after the death of the settlor. See also *settlor* and *testamentary trust* .

interchange — system of connecting intersecting roads or freeways through overpasses, underpasses, and ramps, which eliminates the need for stop signs and signals.

interest — (1) ownership right to real or personal property; (2) specified or promised periodic return on a cash advance, in exchange for use of the money. It is distinguished from an equity investment, in which the investor acquires an interest in a percentage of the profits, if any, from the investment. Real estate interest is usually paid in arrears, meaning that a February 1 mortgage payment covers the interest accrued during January. (3) amount paid or credited to the holder of a savings account.

interest deduction — federal tax provision allowing the subtraction of

certain types of paid interest from the gross income of the taxpayer. The most common is the mortgage interest deduction, in which interest paid on an acquisition or refinance loan for a principal residence is deductible, subject to certain limits.

interest extra note — loan with an equal periodic payment of principal plus an additional amount representing actual interest. As payments are made, the principal declines, the amount of interest on the reduced principal declines, and the total payment declines. See also *interest included note*.

interest in property — legal or equitable share in a real or personal property. The interest may be a present interest, such as a lease or fee simple ownership, or it may be in the future, such as a remainder. See also *remainder*.

interest-included note — note with equal periodic payments, including principal and interest. As payments are made, the principal declines, and more of the total payment applies toward principal. This is the typical mortgage loan. See also *amortization* and *interest extra note*.

interest rate — periodic charge, usually expressed as a yearly percentage of the amount borrowed, for the use of money.

interest rate cap — upper limit to the interest rate of an adjustable rate mortgage (ARM). It is usually based on the initial rate. For example, an ARM with a start rate of 5.25% and a margin of 3% over the LIBOR index might have an interest rate cap of 12.25%. Thus, even if in the future, the index plus the margin should be 20%, the interest rate on the loan cannot exceed 12.25%. See also *adjustable rate mortgage, index, LIBOR, margin, payment cap,* and *start rate* .

interest-only loan — loan in which only simple (not compound) interest is paid periodically. No principal is paid until the due date on the loan, when the entire principal amount is paid. An example is a five-year $100,000 loan at 12% simple interest with monthly payments. The borrower would make 60 payments of $1,000 each, and one balloon payment of $100,000 at the end of the fifth year. See also *balloon payment, compound interest* and *simple interest* .

interim financing — See *gap financing.*

interim loan — See *gap financing.*

interim use — (1) temporary use for land until the construction of improvements that allow the "highest and best" use. For example, a vacant city parcel might be used as a parking lot while a development plan is worked out. (2) illegal or nonconforming use of land pending a ruling by a court or zoning authority. See also *conforming use, nonconforming use,* and *zoning.*

interior trim — cosmetic design elements covering gaps between differing materials, such as molding between a wall and a window, or baseboard between a floor and a wall. Trim may be made of wood, metal, plastic, or other material.

interlocutory decree — provisional court order, usually issued to delay an action until some other proceeding can be completed. Commonly seen in divorce actions with pending property settlements.

internal rate of return (IRR) — the type of discount rate derived from present value of all anticipated future cash flows equated to the initial investment. It allows comparisons of diverse types of investments, such as stocks, real estate, and business ventures, assuming similar risk factors. It is most easily computed with a financial calculator or investment software.

Internal Revenue Code (IRC) — body of law and administrative regulation which, taken together, form the basic income tax law of the United States.

Internal Revenue Service (IRS) — branch of the federal government responsible for interpreting, implementing, and enforcing the provisions of the Internal Revenue Code. The IRS utilizes both civil and criminal penalties to assure compliance.

international style of architecture — (also called "Bauhaus") architectural movement associated with Mies van der Rohe and Europe of the 1920s. Buildings tended to be simple rectangular shapes, smooth, functional, and without ornamentation. It became the primary style of downtown America for most of the twentieth century.

interpleader — legal proceeding in which a third party to a dispute places the disputed material at the disposal of a court for a final judgment. Escrow companies often resort to interpleader when the parties to a transaction issue conflicting instructions concerning the disposition of an asset.

interrogatory — series of written questions given to a party or witness to a civil proceeding. The answers are often given under oath and may be used by the trier of fact.

intersection — crossing of roads or lines on a map or survey.

interstate — (1) between two or more states; (2) high-speed roadway between two or more states.

Interstate Land Sales Full Disclosure Act — 1968 federal law mandating that information be provided by sellers to buyers of property that is offered for sale across state lines or by using any of the traditional trappings of interstate commerce, including national advertising and use of the mails. Disclosure is in the form of a written property report, and must be given to a prospective purchaser before any offer is made. Buyers also have a seven-day "cooling-off" period in which they can rescind the offer.

interval ownership — (also called *time-share*) form of shared ownership of residential vacation property. Each owner typically purchases one or more weeks' use of the property. That owner is entitled to occupy the property for that same period of time each year in perpetuity. Interval ownerships may be sold or traded. See *time-share*.

intestate — dying without a valid will. Property passes by operation of law to the legal heirs, who may not be the persons the decedent wished to benefit. See also *heir*.

inure — to accrue to the benefit of an individual; to take effect. For example, the benefits associated with possession inure to the tenant of a leased property.

inventory — (1) list of real or personal property; (2) the stock of a business; (3) act of creating an inventory.

inverse condemnation — legal proceeding in which a property owner seeks compensation for the loss of use or nearly total loss of value to his or her property due to some government action. The owner is attempting to force the government to condemn the property. The owner must prove that the property was effectively "taken" by the state without fair compensation. For example, homeowners in the flight path of a new or expanded airport might argue that the increased noise has rendered their properties value-less. See also *condemnation* and *just compensation.*

invest – to advance money or other assets in expectation of a profit later.

investment – (1) amount of money invested; (2) the asset purchased with the money.

investment analysis – a variety of rigorous methods that attempt to predict or measure the profit out-come of a proposed investment. Each attempts to evaluate and quan-tify the risks and rewards of various investment alternatives. Examples include internal rate of return (IRR), net present value (NPV), and gross income multiplier (GIM). See also *gross income multiplier, internal rate of return,* and *net present value.*

investment property – any real property acquired with an expecta-tion of appreciation over time.

investment tax credit – a con-tinually changing element of the In-ternal Revenue Code (IRC). To en-courage certain types of investments, the government periodically offers substantial tax credits to those who invest in the favored activities or business. A current example is a tax credit for investment in the construc-tion of low-income housing. See also *tax credit.*

involuntary alienation – loss of property due to an adverse action such as a foreclosure or tax sale. See also *involuntary conveyance.*

involuntary conversion – loss of property due to destruction, theft, or condemnation. It is distinguished from a voluntary sale of a property. Any gain realized on the involuntary conversion (from insurance proceeds or compensation from the state) may be considered nonrecognizable for federal tax purposes if the owner re-invests the proceeds in a similar property within a specified period of time. See also *condemnation.*

involuntary conveyance – trans-fer of real property without consent of the owner. Examples include con-demnation and divorce sales. See also *involuntary alienation.*

involuntary lien – a lien created by operation of law, such as a tax or judgment lien, as opposed to one created by the property owner inten-tionally, such as a mortgage lien.

Inwood tables – set of financial tables in wide use by appraisers and lenders before the advent of financial calculators. The tables allow calcula-tion of the present value of an in-come stream at a specified interest rate and maturity. See also *net present value* and *present value.*

IRA — See *Individual Retirement Account.*

IRC — See *Internal Revenue Code.*

IREM — See *Institute of Real Estate Management.*

IRR — See *internal rate of return.*

irrevocable — unchangeable; often refers to a promise or agreement that cannot be broken. An example is an irrevocable trust, in which the settlor relinquishes forever any control of the property placed in trust.

irrigation — artificial method of supplying water to plants or crops by means of pipes, sprinklers, or channels.

irrigation district — a local agency with the power to tax property for the purpose of building and operating an irrigation system serving a designated area.

irrigation ditch — an open channel designed to carry water for the purpose of irrigating crops. See *irrigation.*

IRS — See *Internal Revenue Service.*

island — (1) land completely surrounded by a body of water; (2) a raised area between opposing lanes of traffic, designed to provide an area of safety for pedestrians crossing the road. See also *median strip.*

island zoning — See *spot zoning.*

isohyetal line — a line on a map or chart indicating areas with similar rainfall.

J

jack — (1) to raise a structure off its foundation by mechanical means; (2) large blocks of wood or metal used to raise a structure off its foundation.

jack rafter — (1) a short rafter in a hip or valley roof; (2) a short rafter used to give the appearance of a rafter extending beyond the exterior walls of a building.

jalousie door, shutter or window — a door, shutter, or window in which the slats of wood, glass, or other material are arranged as a series of horizontal louvers, either fixed or adjustable. Adjustable jalousies have slats that can be tilted by a lever or crank to open and close.

jamb — (1) the portion of a door or window frame that provides vertical structural support at the sides of the door opening. See also *header.* (2) the visible inside lining of the door or window frame.

jeopardy — danger, peril, or risk of loss. Jeopardy can be physical, such as the risk of storm damage, or legal and financial, such as the pledging of real property as security for a loan.

jerry-built — built of inferior materials with poor workmanship.

jetty — a human-made formation of rocks or concrete projecting into the ocean from the shoreline. Jetties are generally designed to prevent the migration of sand. See also *groin*.

joinder — a legal term referring to a variety of circumstances in which disparate elements or parties are brought together to facilitate a desired result. One example, joinder of claims, is the right of a party to a lawsuit to assert all legally possible claims against the other party, whether the claims are equitable or legal in nature. Another, compulsory joinder, requires the naming of an unnamed party to a lawsuit where the presence of that party in court is required for complete relief for the plaintiff.

joinder of claims — See *joinder*.

joint — (1) two or more together; (2) a connection between two pipes or conduits; (3) an area where two dissimilar materials meet, such as a joint between a brick fireplace and a stucco wall.

joint and several liability — the right of a creditor to receive repayment from any and all those persons who were a party to the credit agreement. Partners are generally jointly liable for the debts of a partnership. Thus, if three of a total of four general partners become bankrupt, the remaining partner would be liable for the entire debt of the partnership. Joint and several liability also applies in a variety of other settings, such as leases signed by more than one party and claims subject to

indemnification agreements. See also *right of contribution*.

joint appraisal — an appraisal by two or more appraisers that presents their shared conclusions regarding property value.

joint estate — See *joint tenancy*.

joint note — a written promise to pay a debt, executed by two or more persons, each accepting responsibility for the entire debt. See also *joint and several liability* and *surety bond*.

joint tenancy — one of several forms of shared ownership in which more than one person owns an interest in the same real property. The traditional test for joint tenancy is the application of the "four unities": (1) unity of title - all owners share one title; (2) unity of time - the joint tenancy must be created by grant or will, executed and delivered at one time; (3) unity of interest - each joint tenant must have an equal interest in the property; (4) unity of possession - each owner must have an equal right to possess and enjoy the entire property.

There is also a right of survivorship: if one joint tenant dies, the surviving joint tenant(s) automatically receive the decedent's interest as a matter of law. If a joint tenant sells or grants his or her interest to another, the new owner holds title as a tenant in common with the remaining joint tenants. See also *community property* and *tenancy in common*.

joint venture – a form of business that may be expressly created by agreement or may be implied by action. In a joint venture two or more persons act together to achieve a common business goal. Joint ventures differ from partnerships in that they tend to be created for a specific project or limited purpose. See also *partnership*.

jointure – a freehold estate in real property secured to a wife. Jointure takes effect at the death of the husband, and requires the agreement of the wife, unlike dower. It is at least a life estate, and may continue longer. See also *dower*.

joist – a horizontal structural timber that provides primary support for a floor or ceiling.

judgment – a binding declaration by a court as to the rights and liabilities of parties to a lawsuit

judgment creditor – a person who is entitled to receive money from another as a result of a judgment.

judgment debtor – one who owes money as a result of a judgment.

judgment *in personam* – a court order concerning a person rather than a thing, for example, money damages.

judgment *in rem* – a court order concerning a thing rather than a person. For example, in a dispute over the ownership of a parcel of land, the final decision would be a judg-

ment *in rem*. See also *judgment in personam*.

judgment lien – a legal document filed to enforce a judgment against the assets of a judgment creditor. The lien does not, in itself, compel sale of the asset. Rather, it places the world at large on notice that the asset is encumbered by the lien. If the asset is sold or otherwise transferred, the lien must be paid. See also *writ of execution*.

judgment-proof – all persons against whom court-ordered money awards are to no effect. The person may be insolvent, have no assets in the jurisdiction, or be protected by statute. See also *bankruptcy, homestead*, and *insolvent*.

judicial foreclosure – a legal action in which a lender compels the sale of the collateral real property to satisfy the debt. Debtors have a period of notice, called an equity of redemption, in which the debtor may pay all sums then due and halt the foreclosure. He or she may also have a statutory right of redemption in which the property may be returned to the debtor even after the foreclosure upon the full payment of the debt plus foreclosure and administrative costs. See also *nonjudicial foreclosure* and *sheriff's sale*.

judicial sale – a court-ordered, as opposed to a voluntary, sale.

jumbo loan – a real estate loan larger than the maximum "conforming" loan limit. The actual amount changes frequently, reflecting the willingness of the secondary market to purchase loans of ever-increasing amounts. See also *conforming loan, secondary market,* and *super jumbo loan.*

junction box – a covered metal or plastic box used to enclose and protect electrical splices. Referred to as a "J-box" on blueprints and in technical jargon.

junior lien – See *junior mortgage.*

junior mortgage – a real estate loan that is legally subordinate to another loan on the same property. Priority can be established by the time of recording of the mortgage (earliest in time is generally first in priority) or by an agreement called subordination. The effect of priority is that, if the property is sold for less than the amount of all liens, the senior lienholder is paid in full first. Any remaining proceeds are apportioned to junior lienholders in the order of their priority. A foreclosure by a senior lienholder will generally extinguish all junior liens. In some states, the junior lienholder may have personal recourse against the debtor after such a foreclosure. See also *nonrecourse debt, priority, recourse debt,* and *subordination.*

jurat – the certificate of the officer or other person who swears to a writing. In modern practice, this is usually the statement by a notary describing the time, location, and par-

ties to the writing that appears at the bottom of an affidavit.

jurisdiction – the legal power and authority of a court to decide an issue that is placed before it. Not all courts have jurisdiction over all matters. Generally, the pleading by a plaintiff states why the plaintiff believes that the court is the proper venue in which to air the complaint.

just compensation – money owed to a real property owner whose property has been partly or wholly taken by the state. Under the federal constitution, property may not be taken by the state without the payment of a fair price. See also *condemnation* and *eminent domain.*

K

Keogh plan – a tax-advantaged retirement plan created by Congress to permit the self-employed to contribute a percentage of gross income to a savings or investment account. Monies contributed are treated as a deduction to gross income as an ordinary business expense in the tax year of the contribution. No tax is due on funds so invested until the plan distributes, and then only to the extent of the amount withdrawn.

kerf – (1) a shallow saw cut; (2) the width of material removed by a saw blade.

key employee insurance — (also called *keyman insurance*) an insurance policy purchased to compensate an organization for the death or disability of an employee on whom the organization relies for substantial earnings, management expertise, research and the like. Such insurance policies are usually required by lenders or partners to help securitize a loan or provide a method of recovery of funds invested on reliance of the expertise of one individual.

key lot — (1) a lot that, by virtue of its location, completes an assemblage of property that permits a use and valuation of the assemblage at its highest and best use; (2) a key-shaped parcel of land, often at the end of a cul-de-sac street in a residential development, which has a long, narrow driveway from the street to the main area of the lot, and which permits the siting of a home. Same as *flag lot.*

key tenant — See *anchor tenant.*

keyman insurance — See *key employee insurance.*

kick plate — a strip of plastic or metal located at the bottom of the side of a door to protect it from damage from being kicked.

kiln — a high-temperature oven designed for firing brick, tiles, or ceramics.

kilo — (1) a prefix in metric measurement indicating 1,000; (2) a shortened form of kilogram.

kilogram — a measure of weight equal to 1,000 grams or 2.204 pounds.

kilometer — a measure of distance equal to 1,000 meters or 0.62 mile.

kilowatt — a measure of energy equal to 1,000 watts of electricity. Electricity charges are often calculated on the basis of kilowatt-hours. See also *watt* and *kilowatt-hour.*

kilowatt-hour — 1,000 watts of electricity used consistently over a 1-hour period. See also *kilowatt.*

kiosk — a small structure or stand from which small convenience purchases or transactions can be made, such as periodicals, film and film processing, automated teller, etc.

kitchen — a room designed for the cooking and preparation of food.

kitchenette — a very small kitchen, usually with less than standard-size appliances, often found in a studio apartment or small condominium.

kite winder — kite-shaped or triangular steps attached to a circular or winding stairway.

knockdown — parts of a building that can be installed or removed easily. Common examples are partitions that are installed to divide a large office space for temporary purposes.

knoll — a slightly rounded hill.

knot — a hard, roundish, usually dark spot in wood created by the juncture of a tree branch with its trunk.

L

labor — (1) work; (2) an area of land equal to 177 1/7 acres.

laches — a legal theory applied by courts in circumstances where a party was negligent in asserting a claim in a timely manner and therefore loses the right to assert that claim.

lally column — a structural member used in light construction comprised of a steel column filled with concrete.

laminate — (1) a thin material used to provide a decorative or protective covering to a surface; (2) the act of applying a thin decorative or protective layer of material to a surface.

lanai — that part of the living area of a home that is partially or entirely exposed to the elements. In non–South Pacific or Polynesian areas, the term may refer to a porch or patio area.

land — that portion of the earth's surface that is not water. For purposes of deeds and valuation matters, the meaning takes on spatial attributes that imply ownership from the core of the earth to the heavens. See also *real estate*.

land bank — to acquire land for speculation, future development, or protection from development.

land certificate — a certificate issued by the federal government allowing the acquisition of certain federal land upon making the proper application.

land contract — a form of purchase contract wherein the buyer is permitted to occupy the subject property while making installment payments to the seller, however, no deed is given and ownership is not transferred until the installment contract is satisfied. See also *contract for deed, holding escrow,* and *installment sale.*

land description — a description or definition of a parcel of land written in such a way that it could not apply to any other parcel of land. Land descriptions are used in deeds, contracts, leases, and mortgages to set forth in great detail the precise location, boundaries, and attributes of the parcel in question. Several forms of land description are in use today. See *government survey method, legal description, lot block and tract (subdivision),* and *metes and bounds.*

land grant — (also called *land patent*) the act of granting or the land described in a grant from the government for the purpose of serving the public good. Examples are the late nineteenth century grants of land to railroads for westward expansion of the United States, opening of "wilderness areas" for population, such as those characterized by the Oklahoma land rushes, or property given to establish a college or university.

land lease — a contract covering the use or occupancy of land for a period of time at an agreed-on consideration. Leased land is most common in commercial or agricultural settings, but it is occasionally seen in residential real estate as well. See also *ground lease*.

land patent — See *land grant*.

land poor — the situation of owning so much land that its cost of ownership drains the wealth of the owner.

land reclamation — the changing of the character of land to allow a higher economic use by draining, filling, grading, removing hazardous substances, or other remedial measures.

land residual technique — an appraisal methodology that divides income from an improved property into two parts, one portion attributable to the land and the other to the building. The value of the building is determined first, and the income stream imputed to it is deducted from the net operating income of the property. The remainder net operating income is attributable to the land and is capitalized at the appropriate discount rate to determine the land value. See also *appraisal* and *capitalization (cap) rate*.

land sale–leaseback — the sale of land coupled with the immediate leasing by the seller of the land just sold. The seller generally remains in possession of the land, realizes financial gain from the sale, and potentially reduces the cost of occupancy.

land use map — a map or plat that graphically represents a land use plan. See also, *land use plan*, *land use*

regulation and *zoning*.

land use plan — a plan of development submitted to a governmental agency having entitlement jurisdiction that describes the nature, location, and density of a proposed development together with the likely impacts on public infrastructure. See also *general plan*.

land use regulation — a body of rules or laws enacted to establish and control the development of land in all areas of a corporate jurisdiction. See also *zoning*.

landlocked parcel — a parcel of land surrounded by other parcels of land that prevent direct access from a public right-of-way.

landlord — (also called *lessor*) the owner of real property who is described in and subject to the terms and conditions of a lease. See also *tenant* and *lessee*.

landmark — (1) a fixed monument or object that is relied on as a boundary marker. See also *monument*. (2) a designation for a historically or architecturally significant building or place.

landscape — (1) the natural terrain of unimproved land; (2) the removal, rearrangement, or replanting of trees, shrubs, flowers, gardens, and fences, or a change in topography designed to further an aesthetic theme or effect a visual improvement to the land.

landscape architect — a professional who designs the plan for the placement of improvements and landscaping on a parcel.

landscape architecture – the application of the art and science of the design of exterior amenities such as the situation of the structures, ingress and egress, hardscape, and botanical amenities.

landscaping – the botanical additions and cultivation maintained on a parcel for decorative and site stability purposes.

land-service road – an access roadway connecting various parcels of land with an arterial road or highway.

lap joint – a connection formed by overlapping two edges of material and attaching them.

lap siding – an exterior wall covering of long strips of material, either metal, wood, or vinyl, applied horizontally in a manner whereby the upper band slightly overlaps the lower band.

larger parcel – in eminent domain law, the more extensive landholding of which the condemned parcel was a part. Severance of the parcel from the larger parcel may therefore give rise to damages in excess of the actual value of the parcel condemned, to the extent that it interferes with or reduces the utility of the remaining landholdings. The modern test for a larger parcel requires unity of ownership (the same owner or owners) and unity of use (all the land must be used for the same or related purposes). The lands considered need not be contiguous if this test is met.

late charge – a penalty for a delinquent payment assessed by a lending institution, landlord, or others who have the contractual right to do so. Late charges are often subject to state usury laws or limits based on reasonableness.

latent – hidden or concealed; not susceptible to casual view or observation.

latent defect – malfunctions, flaws, or faults that are undiscovered or concealed until a problem arises that exposes the defect. Latent defects in improvements to real property are the subject of considerable litigation. See also *as-is* and *patent defect*.

lateral – (1) pertaining to the side; (2) a branch from a main line such as a water or sewer line.

lateral and subjacent support – the support received for one parcel of land from another. Adjoining landowners have a duty to each other to do nothing to their own property that will cause damage to the adjoining property. This includes matters such as excavations that weaken a neighbor's building or hillside, removal of minerals (which causes subsidence), or overwatering one's landscape to such a degree that the adjoining parcel may flood or suffer subsurface erosion.

lath – narrow strips of wood used for lightweight decorative structures such as gazebos and trellises, as well as for a base for interior plaster walls. See also *gazebo*, and *lath and plaster*.

lath and plaster — a form of wall surface construction where a slatted wood (lath) or wire screen base is constructed to which plaster is applied in sufficient coats and colors to achieve the desired color and texture. See also *drywall* and *plaster*.

latitude — an angular distance north or south from the equator of a point on the earth's surface as measured on the meridian of the point. Measurements of latitude and longitude taken together can precisely locate any spot on the globe. See also *longitude* and *meridian*.

laundromat — a business that provides washing machines and dryers at a central location for the use of the public. Most laundromats employ coin-operated washers and dryers.

lavatory — (1) a sink for washing hands and face; (2) a room containing a sink for washing hands and face; (3) a bathroom. See also *bathroom*.

layout — the arrangement of space in a structure. See also *floor plan*.

leach field — a network of perforated underground pipes designed to allow waste material from a septic tank to percolate into the soil. See also *percolation test* and *septic tank* .

leaching — the percolation of fluids through soil.

lead-based paint — paint containing lead. Lead had been used for many years as an additive designed to enhance the durability of the paint or to color it. Medical research has demonstrated that the lead in such paint can be ingested or inhaled by children and may cause brain damage and other health problems. Lead-based paint is now considered to be a hazardous material and has been banned for residential use since 1978. Homes built and painted prior to 1978 may pose a danger of lead poisoning. The Residential Lead-Based Paint Reduction Act of 1992 requires sellers and landlords of homes built prior to 1978 to provide buyers and renters with a disclosure concerning lead-based paint hazards.

lean-to — a casual structure such as a shed with three sides and a sloping roof, usually affixed to the side of another structure.

lease — a contract between the owner of property (landlord or lessor) and another (tenant or lessee) enumerating the terms and conditions of occupancy by the tenant. Types of leases include the following:

commercial lease—a lease of property for retail or office use.

gross lease—a lease where the landlord pays all expenses of the property.

ground lease—a lease of land that does not include improvements;

net lease—a lease where the lessee pays all or a portion of landlord's expenses.

percentage lease—a lease of retail property where additional consideration includes a percentage of sales or profits as defined in the lease.

sandwich lease—a tenancy where one's lease is between the landlord and another tenant, not unlike the position of a subtenancy.

See also *commercial lease, gross lease, ground lease, lessee, lessor, net lease, percentage lease, sandwich lease, sublease,* and *triple net lease.*

lease with option to purchase — See *lease–option.*

leased fee — the estate or interest of the landlord or lessor remaining after the creation of the leasehold estate.

leased fee interest — See *leased fee.*

leasehold estate — the tenant or lessee's interest in real property as defined in a lease. The four major types of leasehold estate are the tenancy (estate) for years, tenancy (estate) at will, tenancy (estate) at sufferance, and periodic tenancy. See also *lease, periodic tenancy, tenancy at sufferance, tenancy at will, tenancy for years,* and *tenant.*

leasehold improvements — additions, fixtures, or structures constructed or installed on leased property. See also *tenant improvements.*

leasehold interest — See *leasehold estate.*

leasehold mortgage — a mortgage placed on a leasehold estate by the tenant with the landlord's consent for purposes of improving the leasehold. This type of financing is usually secondary to the leased fee interests.

leasehold value — the dollar value

to the tenant of a long-term lease where the lease payments are less than market rent for similar premises. The tenant may be compensated for loss of this value in the event of an eminent domain "taking" of the leased property. However, see *no-bonus clause.*

lease–option — a lease that contains the right to purchase a leased fee estate by the tenant under terms defined in the lease, or by separate agreement. A lease-option may require the tenant to pay a consideration (an option premium) in addition to the rent for the right to purchase the leased fee. Additionally, it is not uncommon for a portion of the rent paid to be credited to the purchase price of the leased fee. The exercise of the option to purchase by the tenant would cause a merger of the leasehold and lease fee estates and would extinguish the lease as to the purchasing tenant. The optionee/tenant would acquire the leased fee estate of the optionor/landlord subject to any other leases and matters of record. See also *merger of title.*

lease-purchase agreement — See *lease-option.*

legacy — a disposition of money or personal property by a will. See also *devise.*

legal age — age at which a person is no longer a minor and may enjoy certain rights of citizenship, such as freely entering into contracts, voting, marrying, and the like.

legal description — an identification of a parcel of land written in such a manner as not to apply or be confused with any other parcel. Some legal descriptions are made using lot, block, and tract (subdivision). Others are prepared by a surveyor using a metes and bounds system. Other descriptions may be appropriate as well as long as they are accurate and unambiguous. See also *land description.*

legal notice — (1) notice that is either implied or mandated as a result of acquiring an interest in property or the recordation of a document in the public records; (2) adequate notice.

legal owner — a descriptive term of technical ownership which generally signifies the named owner as having an interest by virtue of a lien. See, by contrast, *equitable title.*

legal rate of interest — (1) a rate of interest established by statute to be used in the event a rate of interest is not specified or in the event a rate of interest is not specified in a note or contract but is imputed by law; (2) the highest rate of interest permitted by law. See also *usury.*

legal residence — the primary domicile and permanent place of residence for an individual. See also *domicile.*

legal title — the complementary partner of equitable title; complete and enforceable title; the nature of title held by a trustee under a deed of trust. Legal title or ownership normally does not carry the right of possession or beneficial enjoyment. See also *equitable title.*

legatee — one who receives property (either real or personal) by operation of a will. See also *devisee.*

LEI — See *Index of Leading Economic Indicators.*

lender — an institution or person who loans money to another, expecting it to be returned at a later time.

lender's policy — a policy of title insurance purchased by a property owner specifically to insure the lender against defects in title. See also *loan policy, owner's policy,* and *title insurance.*

lessee — (also called *tenant*) a person or legal entity who uses or occupies a property under terms and conditions set forth in a lease or rental agreement. See also *tenant* and *lease.*

lessee's interest — See *leasehold estate.*

lessor — a person who owns or has contracted the property used or occupied by a lessee under the terms of a lease. See also *lease* and *lessee.*

lessor's interest — See *leased fee interest.*

let — a term used regionally to be synonymous with rent.

letter of attornment — a notice, required by statute in some jurisdictions, advising a tenant that the property subject to the lease has been sold and that rent should be paid to the new owner.

letter of commitment — a letter from a lender to a borrower that enumerates the amount, interest rate, term, and other terms and conditions of a loan and the date on which the loan is to be funded. Although normally required in comercial real estate transactions, letters of credit are rarely seen in residential purchases.

letter of credit — an agreement between a bank and its account holder of substantial creditworthiness that the bank will honor demands, orders, or drafts by named third parties up to the maximum amount of the letter of credit. A letter of credit is often used as a security device to ensure or compel future performance of a financial obligation.

letter of intent — (1) a written expression of interest short of an offer; (2) a nonbinding indication of interest in participating in a development, making an offer or a loan, or entering into any other contractual arrangement without the intent of either party relying on such a letter in a manner that would cause damages or injury if it were not performed.

letters of administration — a judicial notice evidencing the appointment of a representative of the estate of an intestate decedent.

letters patent — an written instrument given by a government to a patentee, granting exclusive rights to land or to the fruits of an invention. See also *land grant*.

letters testamentary — a judicial notice evidencing the appointment of a representative of the estate of a testate decedent.

levee — an engineered embankment of a stream or river.

level payment mortgage — a note or mortgage that requires an unchanging periodic payment, usually monthly. A portion of each payment is allocated to reduce the principal, and a portion to pay the interest. As the principal declines, the amount of interest charged also declines, and more of each payment is dedicated to reducing the principal even further. If the loan balance will reach zero at the end of the term of the loan, the loan is called fully amortizing. See also *balloon payment* and *fully amortized mortgage*.

leverage — the use of any amount of borrowed funds to purchase an investment property, especially the use of a very large percentage of borrowed funds to acquire property in order to preserve capital, achieve higher returns on funds invested, and risk the least amount of equity. Leverage is usually described as the ratio between borrowed funds (debt) and a borrower's own funds (equity). Loan-to-value ratios are the primary criteria for measuring leverage. See also *loan-to-value ratio*.

levy — to impose and collect a tax, assessment, or fee. A levy can originate by operation of law, such as property taxes, or by contract, such as the case of a homeowners' association. The levying authority often has power to sell the asset that is subject to the levy after a period of time for nonpayment. See also *power of sale*.

liability — (1) an amount owed to

another; (2) a responsibility to perform or to refrain from performing some act; (3) a duty to pay court-awarded damages.

liable – having the responsibility or accountability for an act or omission.

liber – Latin term for "book," used in some states when referring to the book and page of a recorded document.

LIBOR – an acronym for the London Interbank Offered Rate. This is an interest rate that financial institutions use when lending Eurodollars among themselves. In the United States and other countries, the LIBOR is used as an index rate for short-term loans such as construction loans or variable rate mortgages.

license – (1) personal grant of permission to enter on another's property for a relatively short period of time for a specific purpose such as parking a vehicle, hunting or fishing, attending a performance, and the like; (2) permit granted by a governmental agency, after demonstrating competency, to perform a certain trade or profession such as a physician, attorney, general contractor, real estate salesperson or broker, appraiser, or escrow company. See also *licensee.*

licensee – (1) one who holds a license. See also *license.* (2) in real estate, one who holds a real estate license. In most states, certain activities relating to real property sales and rentals may only be undertaken by a real estate licensee or the owner of the real property.

licensing acts – the corpus of legislation relating to a government's authority and methods of granting licenses. Examples are the establishment of educational, testing, personal character, professional, and continuing education standards for qualifying for and maintaining a license to practice medicine, law, appraisal, real estate, architecture, pharmacology, and the like.

lien – any of a variety of encumbrances attaching to real or personal property, either voluntarily, as in the case of securing a loan to acquire property, or involuntarily, as in the case of a money judgment awarded by a court that encumbers the judgment debtor's property until the judgment is satisfied. An encumbrance resulting from a taxing authority securing unpaid taxes or an encumbrance placed on property for nonpayment of workers or material suppliers in a construction project. See also *encumbrance* and *mechanic's lien.*

lien release – a statement prepared by a lienholder or potential lienholder (as in the case of a mechanic's lien) that the lien or potential lien is removed from a property. See also *mechanic's lien.*

lien waiver – a release of mechanic's lien claim rights from a subcontractor in order to allow release of funds from a construction loan. See also *mechanic's lien.*

lienholder – the party who caused a lien to be placed and who will benefit from its payment.

life beneficiary – a person entitled to receive a right for his or her life.

life estate – an ownership interest in real property that has a duration measured by the life of the grantee of the life estate (a life tenant) or the life of another person (tenancy *pur autre vie*). At the death of the life tenant (the person granted the ownership interest) or at the death of the person whose life serves as the limitation of the estate, the estate passes either to the reversioner (the person who granted the estate) or the remainderman (another person named by the grantor of the estate). See also *remainderman* and *reversioner*.

life interest – See *life estate*.

life tenant – holder of a life interest. See also *life estate*.

light and air easement – an easement granted for the purposes of permitting or not obstructing the exposure of a property to the rays of the sun or the benefits of natural airflow to or from a prescribed height, direction, elevation, or other spatial orientation.

light industry – (1) manufacturing or assembling facilities that do not generate large amounts of air or water pollution or noise. A small cabinetmaking business is an example of light industry, while a steel mill is a classic example of heavy industry. (2) a zoning designation permitting only light industrial uses.

light well – a vertical shaft that permits natural light to reach the interior of a building.

like-kind exchange – See *Section 1031 Exchange*.

like-kind property – a broad classification of property held for investment defined in the U.S. Tax Code for purposes of effecting a tax-deferred exchange of property. In general, income tax based on capital gain may be deferred upon the sale of an investment property as long as another property, also intended as investment property, is purchased within a specified period in a specified manner. In the past, matching the types of properties was thought to be important, hence the term "like-kind." Current tax law allows exchanges across categories, for example a gas station for an apartment building, as long as both are held for investment purposes. Exchanging a principal residence for a commercial building is not an exchange of like-kind property for deferral of taxes. See also *Section 1031 exchange*.

limestone – a sedimentary rock used in building construction.

limitations of actions – statutory time period for bringing a suit or legal action, after which no suit or action will be permitted. The nature of the action will determine the length of time that applies to each situation. See also *laches* and *Statute of Limitations*.

limited liability company (LLC) – a legal form of business entity that is governed by an operating agreement and characterized by a blend of elements of a partnership and a corporation. Although state law defines the exact characteristics, LLCs enjoy shareholder liability limitations similar to those of corporations. Taxation is similar to a partnership, at the shareholder level, rather than at the corporate level and again at the shareholder level. See also *corporation* and *partnership*.

limited partnership – a partnership regulated by state statutes, governed by a limited partnership agreement, and comprised of at least one general partner and at least one limited partner. Although the general partner component is similar to that of a general partner in other forms of partnerships, limited partners may be limited in number and limited in their liability. They are prohibited from having any direct management control or decision-making responsibility in the enterprise that is the subject of the limited partnership. They are usually financially liable only to the extent of their contribution or investment. A limited partnership is a tax-advantaged form of operation. However; distributions to the limited partners involve complex tax rules regarding passive income and loss considerations. See also *general partnership* and *passive loss*.

limited power of attorney – (also called *special power of attorney*) a power of attorney that is restricted to a narrowly defined scope or transaction. It is a document that allows one person to act on behalf of another, binding that person. The person acting under a power of attorney need not be a licensed attorney. In es-

sence, it is an enhanced form of agency, accompanied by a fiduciary duty toward the principal. See also *agency, attorney in fact, fiduciary duty, power of attorney,* and *special power of attorney.*

line fence – a fence erected on or along a property boundary.

line of credit – a preapproved loan amount that may be drawn on at the borrower's discretion. The loan may be secured by a lien on real property or business assets. The borrower's payment and credit history are subject to periodic review, essentially causing the borrower to requalify for the line of credit. See also *home equity line of credit.*

linear/lineal – of or pertaining to a straight line.

link – (1) unit of length used in surveying equal to 7.92 inches; (2) an active connection to a universal resource locator (URL) for an Internet Web site or page.

linoleum – an early sheet floor covering made of ground cork bound by processed linseed oil to a burlap or canvas backing. In modern usage, this term also refers to floor coverings made of vinyl.

lintel – a horizontal structural component of building construction used as a beam to span openings above doors, windows, hallways, or other such openings.

liquid assets – cash and other items of value that can be quickly converted to cash.

liquidated damages – an dollar amount or formula for determining a dollar amount that the parties to a contract agree in advance will constitute the entirety of the damages to the injured party resulting from the failure to perform certain provisions of the contract. Liquidated damages clauses in real estate purchase contracts limit the amount that can be collected by the seller in the event of a breach by the buyer to the predetermined amount. See also *damages*.

liquidation – the conversion of assets into cash. Liquidation is usually done in situations reflecting duress or an unusual haste cashing out of a business enterprise.

liquidation price – (1) price or value reflected by a sale of property or other assets made under some unusual duress; (2) a price reflecting a value less than current market value.

liquidation value – See *liquidation price*.

liquidity – the ability to convert assets into cash in a reasonably short period of time. Publicly traded securities are more liquid than real estate and antiques. See also *illiquidity*.

lis pendens – a pending lawsuit. A notice of *lis pendens* is a notice filed on public records of a lawsuit pending affecting the title or possession of a parcel of land described therein. It serves as a warning to prospective purchasers that there is a dispute concerning the property. An adverse ruling may bind the purchaser. As a practical matter, it is difficult to sell a property subject to such a notice.

listing – an agreement, preferably written, whereby a property owner agrees to offer to sell property at a stipulated price within a defined period of time and which authorizes the listing real estate broker to solicit offers to purchase. The real estate broker who obtains the listing may be paid a fee or commission, either up front or at sale, as provided in the listing agreement. Other brokers participating in the transaction may also be compensated. There are many types of listings, as well as regional differences. The meaning of the names of types of listings also vary. Common categories of listings include:

• exclusive agency—same as exclusive right to sell, except the seller retains the right to sell the property directly to any other party not introduced through the listing agent without paying a commission or fee.

• exclusive right to sell—one broker is granted the exclusive right to sell the property. The listing may be entered into a multiple listing service, with a stated portion of compensation offered to other brokers, or retained by the listing broker, depending on the terms of the listing agreement. The listing broker is entitled to compensation under this agreement during the term of the agreement even if the seller or another party sells the property.

• exclusive right with exception -

same as exclusive right to sell, but with certain named parties excluded from the listing. For example, if a seller has negotiated with a neighbor to sell the property, but is uncertain as to whether the neighbor will actually purchase the property, the seller might exclude the neighbor from the listing. The effect would be that no commission or fee would be due to the listing broker in the event that the neighbor purchased the property.

- net listing—an older form, now disapproved in many jurisdictions, in which the seller agrees to sell a property for a particular stated price. Any amount received over that price represents the fee to the broker. Obvious problems with conflicts of interest and the potential for fraud make this uncommon today.

- open listing—an agreement by a seller with a broker that compensation will be paid to any broker who represents the actual buyer of the named property. In an open listing, the listing broker may not be compensated at all, or may be paid a fee in exchange for entering the listing into a multiple listing service. Open listings are more common with commercial, industrial, and special-purpose properties than with residential properties.

- probate listing—same as exclusive right to sell, except that price, terms, and broker compensation

are subject to the approval of a probate court judge. See also *agency, broker, multiple listing service,* and *Statute of Frauds.*

listing agent — a real estate agent who contracts with a property owner (on behalf of his or her broker) to solicit and procure offers to purchase the property according to the terms and conditions of the listing. The listing agent may be the procuring cause of the accepted offer to purchase, or the accepted offer may have been procured by another agent, one who is not a direct party to the listing agreement. See also *agent* and *broker* for the relationship between agents and brokers.

littoral — of or relating to the shores of lakes and oceans. See also *riparian.*

littoral land — land forming the shore of an ocean.

littoral rights — rights in real property comprised of a shore or shoreline.

livable — See *habitable.*

live load — a load on a floor of a building which is dynamic, variable, or subject to change or movement. Such loads are comprised of furniture, people, equipment, and other items not a part of the building structure.

living trust — a trust in effect during the life of the settlor, as opposed to a testamentary trust, which takes effect upon the death of the settlor. See also *settlor, testamentary trust, trust,* and *trustor.*

load – mass, product, or volume that is the object of transport or support.

load bearing – elements of a structural system that support other elements of the same system.

loan – the transfer of anything of value or utility on the condition of its return to the transferor or lender.

loan application – a form on which a prospective borrower/purchaser provides a history of personal, occupational, and financial information that the lender will rely on to determine whether the applicant satisfies the criteria established by the lender and the secondary mortgage market for making a loan in the amount requested for the desired property.

loan broker – See *mortgage broker*.

loan commitment – a written promise to fund a loan for an amount, interest rate, and term, on or before a specified date. In real estate, a loan commitment is obtained after completing a loan application, providing documentation of creditworthiness, and proving financial capacity to repay the loan. In addition to approving these items, the lender will also satisfy itself that the value of the property for which the loan is requested is within the loan-to-value ratio, and that the property is in good repair and is in an area that demonstrates that values will not be diminished by adverse conditions (e.g., proximity to existing or proposed highways, airports, industrial uses, natural hazard risk areas, etc.).

loan constant – the percentage rate computed by dividing the sum of the annual loan payments for a 12-month period, including principal and interest, by the unpaid balance of a mortgage. The loan constant will change annually as the loan is amortized. Over the life of a fixed rate loan, the loan constant will always rise. This may not be true for a variable interest rate loan if the loan permits negative amortization. See also *amortization, fixed interest rate loan, negative amortization,* and *variable interest rate loan.*

loan origination fee – a fee paid to a lender or mortgage broker for administrative and direct expenses associated with the processing of a loan application and funding the loan.

loan package – the entirety of a prospective borrower's loan application. Such a package may include the loan application, credit report, property appraisal, inspection reports, feasibility analysis, construction documents, governmental permits and entitlements, financial guarantees, corporate documents of the borrower, and the like.

loan points – fees paid to a lender or mortgage broker as compensation for arranging, processing, or funding a loan. These fees are calculated in terms of percentage points of the amount of the loan requested. A loan fee described as 1½ points, or 1.5%, of a loan of $200,000 means that a fee of $3,000 (0.015 x $200,000) will either be deducted from the loan, reducing the amount funded to $197,000 or the same fee will be paid as an additional closing cost. See also *Annual Percentage Rate* and *Truth in Lending Law (Regulation Z)*.

loan policy — (also called *lender's policy*) a policy of title insurance purchased by the borrower that insures the lender's interest in a property secured by a loan. Such a policy typically has a face value of the amount of the loan. See also *owner's policy* and *title insurance*.

loan ratio — See *loan-to-value ratio*.

loan-to-value ratio — a ratio expressed as a percentage reflecting the amount of the loan divided by the price of the property securing the loan. The proposed purchase of a $100,000 property using a mortgage of $80,000 indicates a loan-to-value ratio of 0.8 or 80%. Loan-to-value ratios are used to distinguish loan products. For example, lenders may offer a variety of 90%, 80%, 75%, and even 50% packages at different rates and terms. In general, lower loan-to-value ratios are associated with more favorable loan rates and terms.

lobby — the public area of a building used in conjunction with the entrance from the outside and the various points of access to the building's interior.

location — *situs*; place of being. See also *situs*.

lockbox — a device placed on or near a property listed for sale that may be accessed only by real estate agents or others, such as appraisers, authorized to open the device for purposes of obtaining keys necessary to gain entry to the property. The lockbox may be mechanical, requiring a special key or combination, or electronic, requiring an electronic device that will activate the release mechanism to present the key. Lockboxes are commonly used by real estate agents to facilitate the showing by other agents of a listed property. Access to lockboxes is restricted and defined by the MLS rules of the controlling local board (association) of Realtors®. See also *multiple listing service* and *board of Realtors®*.

lock-in — (1) the point in the loan application process where the interest rate and terms of the loan are guaranteed. In a rising interest-rate environment, there may be a fee charged to the borrower to obtain a "lock." (2) the time period within the loan term where no prepayment is allowed, or during which a prepayment penalty will apply.

loft — a small space above the main floor of a building, usually open to the area below. See also *mezzanine*.

long-term capital gain (loss) — an increase or decrease in the value of a capital asset realized after a period of ownership. Rules regarding long-term capital gains and losses are redefined from time to time in the Internal Revenue Code of the United States. Generally, a long-term gain or loss receives more favorable tax treatment than a short-term capital gain or loss. See also Capital gain, and Short-term capital gain.

long-term financing – a loan whose term is for an extended period of years. See also *interim financing*.

long-term lease – a lease having a term longer than one year.

longitude – the east–west lines of the spherical grid measured in relation to the north-south lines beginning at the Greenwich meridian.

loss of access – the deprivation of egress and ingress to private property.

loss payable clause – a term in an insurance policy specifying the order in which beneficiaries under the policy are paid. In a fire insurance policy on a property with a mortgage, the lender will be paid the balance of the loan on the property before the owner receives any funds.

lot, block, and tract (subdivision) – a type of legal description for land in developed areas where streets or other rights-of-way delineate large parcels of land referred to as blocks, which are then further subdivided into lots on which homes or other types of developments are built. An example would read "Lot 12 of Block 45 of Tract 3002 of the City of San Dunes, Desert County." Such a description would also reference an official plat filed with the clerk or recorder for that area which shows the location of the block and often the dimensions of the lots therein.

lot book – the official collection of plats, maps, and other documents that illustrate the situs and boundaries of parcels of land. Such books constitute the official recorded collection, which is indexed for public use and constructive notice.

lot line – a boundary line of a parcel or subdivision.

louver/louvre – an assembly or system of overlapping slats used as window coverings. Louvers may be movable or fixed.

love and affection – a recitation in documents of transfer indicating the absence of monetary consideration, but in its place a nonetheless valuable consideration whose sufficiency the parties acknowledge. Typically recited as consideration where a gift is intended.

low water line – an observable mark on the shore indicating the lowest water level either by tidal action or by simple depletion of water.

M

magistrate – a public employee with power as a civil or criminal officer. Examples are justices of the peace and judges of a police court.

MAI – Member, Appraisal Institute. a professional designation signifying a person who has achieved the required experience, passed rigorous examinations, and has prepared written appraisals that have led to the professional stature of Member of the Appraisal Institute, conferred by the American Institute of Real Estate Appraisers of the National Association of Realtors®.

main — a large pipe or conduit providing electricity, gas, or other utilities to or away from a branch line or circuit.

maintenance — acts related to keeping a property in good condition.

maintenance fee — in a homeowner's association, the periodic charge levied against individual homeowners for the purpose of maintaining the common areas. See also *common area* and *homeowners' association*.

majority — (1) the age at which a person, in the eyes of the law, is no longer considered a minor, that is, legal age; (2) in matters pertaining to tallying votes, a number greater than half.

maker — the person or entity (borrower) that executes a promissory note and thereby becomes the obligor liable to the payee (lender).

mall — (1) a public area for pedestrian flow between stores and other elements of a development. Many major commercial developments are interdependent uses of retail, office, lodging, and entertainment uses designed for ease of access connected or linked for a mall effect. (2) a shopping center consisting of a variety of contiguous stores.

management agreement — a contract between a property management company and its principal,

either an individual property owner or a group of owners such as a homeowners' association, to perform certain defined acts on behalf of the principal in consideration of a fee. Management companies acting under such contracts will perform such acts as collecting rents or dues, preparing budgets, supervising landscape maintenance, paying bills for services rendered, and providing overall management advisory services.

management company — a business entity charged with obligations defined in a management agreement. See also *management agreement*.

mandamus — Latin term meaning "We command." A writ of mandamus is issued by a superior court of competent jurisdiction ordering an inferior court, a governing body, a corporation, or an individual to perform some act of ministerial duty.

mansard roof — a roof that has two slopes on each side, the first or lower is the steepest.

mantel — (1) the lintel (top horizontal portion) of a fireplace; (2) a decorative shelf above a fireplace.

manufactured home — a residential structure created from materials that are suitable for quick production, easy assembly, are lightweight, and where desired, have easy portability, as in a mobile home.

manufactured housing — housing that is partially preassembled at a central location, then moved to the building site and completed.

marble – a harder, less porous version of limestone capable of being finished to a high polish and used for floors and countertops.

margin – in variable rate or adjustable rate loans, the percentage points that a lender adds to the index rate to arrive at the full interest rate. For example, a loan with an index rate of 7.5% and a margin of 2.5% would carry an interest rate of 10% (7.5% + 2.5%). During the life of a variable rate mortgage, the index rate will be the increment of the full interest rate that will change. The margin will remain constant. See also, *adjustable rate mortgage, index, interest cap, payment cap,* and *variable interest rate* .

marginal land – (1) land that is barely suitable, but not ideal, for a stated use; (2) income-producing land for which the income barely covers the carrying costs; (3) land that for any variety of reasons cannot be put to an economically productive use. Reasons include extreme terrain, geologic instability, soil chemistry, located in a frequent inundation area, and the like. See also, by contrast, *highest and best use.*

marginal tax rate – the tax rate that applies to the last dollar of earned income. For example, most of John Doe's income is taxed at 15%, but the last $300 is over the maximum amount for the 15% bracket, and is taxed at 28%. John's tax bracket is 15%; his marginal tax bracket is 28%.

marina – a small harbor with facilities for boats. See also *harbor.*

market approach – in valuation or appraisal terminology, the methodology of determining the market value of a property by comparing the subject property to similar properties that have recently been sold or are currently offered for sale. See also *appraisal* and *cost approach.*

market rent – the rent for a specific property as determined by current market conditions for similar property recently leased or currently offered for lease.

market value – the highest price in terms of money that a property will bring in a competitive and open market with no unusual or concealed circumstances where an informed and prudent buyer and seller bargain for a mutually acceptable purchase. This definition can change from one legal jurisdiction to another. If market value is subject to a judicial review, the definition for that jurisdiction must be adhered to. See also *arm's-length transaction.*

marketability – the probability of selling a particular property at a specified price and specified terms within a selected period of time.

marketability study – an analysis of a property to determine, at a given point in time and particular market conditions, the likely sale price and time on market. See also *comparative market analysis.*

marketable title – title to property that is free from exceptions or questions that pertain to validity of seller's ownership, and nature or number of encumbrances and would be readily insurable by a title insurance company and financeable by a mortgage lender. See also *title* and *title insurance.*

masonry — any work or material that involves the arrangement, manufacture, or design of a structure of brick, cement block, stone, or poured concrete.

master lease — the lease that is both senior in time and totality of property. An example of a master lease would be the lease of an office building in its entirety to a tenant who would in turn sublease individual office space to the tenants who would ultimately take physical possession and occupancy of the space. A master lease controls all subleases in the sense that the sublessees cannot take possession under terms more liberal or extensive than the master lease. See also *sublease.*

master plan — a comprehensive design and zoning document that defines and describes a proposed government subdivision, such as a city. See also *zoning.*

material fact — a fact, whose knowledge might cause a reasonable person to pursue or refrain from pursuing a course of action. Nondisclosure of a material fact by a principal or an agent may lead to a cause of action for recission or damages on the part of the party injured by the failure to disclose. See also *disclosure.*

materialman — a provider of material or supplies for an improvement project to real property for which a materialman's lien is provided as a remedy for nonpayment. See also *materialman's lien.*

materialman's lien — (also called "mechanic's lien")a statutory device designed to ensure that providers of materials and supplies used in the construction of repair of a structure receive priority in payment. Subject to rules that vary by jurisdiction, such a supplier may file a lien against the real property involved until payment is made.

maturity — the amount of time or termination stated on the face of an obligation by which the performance of the obligation is to be completed. For example, the maturity of a typical home mortgage is 30 years.

mean — the arithmetic average of a group of numbers. The arithmetic process involves adding the numbers given or observed and then dividing that sum by the number of items summed.

mean high water mark — an imaginary line on a shore subject to tides or other increases in water level, indicating the average level reached by the water during all relatively recent high water periods.

meander — to follow a winding or circuitous course. Usually applied to the line described by a river or stream. See also *meander line.*

meander line — a line used by a surveyor in a survey to indicate that a property is bounded by a watercourse, and that the watercourse it-self, not the line on the survey, forms the boundary. In other words, if the watercourse changes, the boundary line changes with it.

mechanic's lien — See *material-man's lien*.

median — a midpoint. In elementary statistics, the number that represents the center of an ordered array of numbers. The number in the position where half of the numbers are greater than, and half are less than, itself.

median strip — a portion of land that divides oncoming lanes of traffic on a roadway.

mediation — a consensual forum for disagreeing parties to a contract to attempt to resolve their differences in a nonbinding manner with the help of a third-party intermediary. See also *arbitration* and *mediator*.

mediator — a person who leads a mediation forum. An independent solution finder and facilitator.

meeting of the minds — a legal term describing the mutual agreement of the parties to be bound by a contract.

mensuration — the process or art of measuring.

mental capacity — See *capacity*.

merger of title — the combining by operation of law of a lesser and greater estate in one person. For example, if a lessee becomes the owner of the leased property, the leasehold is merged into the greater fee owner-

ship estate, and is thereby extinguished.

meridian — a set of agreed lines connecting the earth's poles which serve as north–south reference points in a grid used in a land measurement and description system known as the government survey method. See also *base line*.

mesne — something intermediate or intervening between other things. See also *mesne assignment*.

mesne assignment — an assignment of rights that passes from a grantor through one or more intermediaries to a grantee. For example, if Abel leases a building to Baker, who assigns his lease to Larry, who in turn assigns his lease to Mary, the assignments made by Baker and Larry would be called mesne assignments.

meter — (1) a unit of measurement equal to 39.37 inches; (2) a device for measuring consumption of gas, water, or electricity.

metes and bounds — a land locator and measurement system that uses a combination of surveyed marks and measurements together with landmarks and monuments. This system is often used in areas where there is no preexisting development plat that can be used to refer to specific parcels. It is most often found as a description of land of irregular shape or difficult terrain. See also *government rectangular survey method* and *lot, block, and tract (subdivision)*.

metropolitan area — a large city

and the zone surrounding it and influenced by it.

mezzanine — a partial floor area between two complete floors, as in the balcony of a theater. See also *loft*.

mile — a measurement of distance equal to 5,280 feet.

mill — one-tenth of 1 cent. Some property tax jurisdictions use this as a method of computing a tax assessment. If the property tax rate is 60 mills, a property with an assessed value of $200,000 would generate a tax of $12,000.

millwork — the wooden components of a building which are produced by machine off-site, such as doors, windows, trim and molding, etc.

mineral rights — the right to mine, pump, or extract minerals, petroleum, or other substances with or without the right to enter the surface of a particular property. Mineral rights are most often found as a reservation from the granting clause of a deed for the benefit of the grantor. Mineral rights may have been reserved many ownerships earlier, but an examination of title may be undertaken to discover whether there may be a right of the owner of the mineral rights to enter the subject property from its surface to mine or extract minerals, or whether such a mineral right has been judicially construed as an easement, which, if not used for a period of time, is deemed to have expired or been abandoned. Competent legal and title advice is critical to this exploration.

minimum lot — the smallest legal buildable lot, as determined by local zoning regulations. See also *zoning*.

mini-warehouse — a storage facility that is divisible into small compartments with individual access for the purpose of storage of personal property, business records and supplies, or other low-value articles for which ease of access is required. Mini-warehouses typically offer monthly rental storage spaces ranging in size from closets to two-car garages

minor — a person who has not reached the age of majority, that is, legal age; a juvenile.

minority interest — an ownership interest comprising less than half of a property or entity.

misdemeanor — an illegal act of a stature less severe than a felony for which the punishment may constitute a monetary fine, short-term incarceration, community service, or some combination thereof.

misrepresentation — a statement, representation, or concealment at variance with known or discoverable facts. Misrepresentation may be deliberate, negligent, or innocent, depending on the circumstances.

mistake — an unintentional error.

mistake of fact — a nonnegligent error in some factual matter that is material to a contract. For example, an erroneous assumption concerning the size of a parcel of land that was based on a professional survey might be considered a mistake of fact.

mistake of law – an erroneous conclusion regarding the effect of the law based on known facts. For example, an assumption that a parcel of land is zoned for commercial development when it is actually zoned as open space might be considered a mistake of law.

miter – to cut two pieces of material at a particular angle so they can be joined correctly. Sometimes a device called a miter box is used to control the cutting process.

mitigation of damages – a reduction of an award of damages (judgment) or contractually stipulated damages (liquidated damages the amount of which is derived from a mutually agreed formula) resulting from acts or circumstances over which the beneficiary of such monetized damages had some degree of control or influence.

mixed-use – a planned development that incorporates a variety of compatible uses. An example is a shopping mall that includes theaters, lodging, and multifamily residential structures.

MLS – See *multiple listing service.*

mobile home – a prefabricated living structure designed to be transported on streets and highways to a semi-permanent site. Most mobile homes are attached to foundations and connected to utilities within a special residential area zoned and designed to accommodate such structures. Many states regulate title and transfer issues as though the property were a motor vehicle. In some states, the sale of mobile homes does not require a real estate license. In many others, the initial sale of a mobile home from a factory does not require a license, but subsequent sales do. Mobile homes also present special title issues, because title to the structure may be separate from title to the land. See also *mobile home park.*

mobile home park – a special residential area zoned and designed to accommodate mobile homes. The land on which each mobile home is located may be leased or purchased by the owner of the mobile home, depending on the park.

model home – a structure in a residential subdivision that was constructed as an example or prototype of others to follow. A model home is sometimes used as a sales office for homes to be built in the future.

modular house – See *manufactured housing* and *prefabricated house.*

moisture barrier – a waterproof membrane applied to the floor or walls of a structure and designed to repel moisture.

molding – long strips of wood or other material designed to cover gaps between other materials or to act as decoration. See also *baseboard* and *trim.*

month-to-month tenancy – a periodic occupancy defined in a rental agreement which can be extended monthly by the payment of rent, or can be canceled by either party by giving 30 days' notice to the other party of its intent.

monument – (1) a permanent marker used by a surveyor; (2) a permanent sign marking the location of a tract of homes.

moratorium – in real estate, a suspension of the issuance of building permits for a period of time.

mortar – a mixture of sand, lime, or plaster, cement and water used as a glue between bricks, blocks, or stones.

mortgage – a written agreement that is used to create a lien on real property to secure a promissory note that is executed to provide the loan of funds for the purchase or refinance of the property. See also *trust deed*.

mortgage banker – a person or entity licensed in the jurisdiction of its business to solicit applications for the loan of funds, and to make such loans on its own account to borrowers for the purchase or refinance of real property. A mortgage banker may also be a mortgage broker for certain loans. See also *mortgage broker*.

mortgage broker – a person or entity licensed in the jurisdiction of its business to solicit applications for the loan of funds for the purpose of purchase or refinance of real property where such funds are provided by those other than the mortgage broker. A mortgage broker may also be a mortgage banker for certain loans. See *mortgage banker*.

mortgage company – a company that services mortgages. See also *mortgage servicing*.

mortgage constant – See also *loan constant*.

mortgage insurance – a form of decreasing term life insurance that is purchased specifically and solely to pay off the remaining balance of a mortgage at the death of the mortgagor. See also *private mortgage insurance*.

mortgage pool – a collection of individual mortgages that may be "securitized" and sold in shares as an investment.

mortgage servicing – the accounting and collection tasks associated with a mortgagee. These include collecting payments, monitoring taxes, foreclosing in the event of default, reconveying when the mortgage is paid in full, etc. These tasks may be performed by the mortgagee or by a firm hired for the purpose.

mortgagee – the person or entity who holds a mortgage as security for funds it has advanced; the lender. See also *mortgagor*.

mortgagee in possession – the post-foreclosure circumstance where the lender takes possession of the property and the rents or profits therefrom.

mortgagor – the party who gives a mortgage to a mortgagee. The borrower of funds secured by the mortgage. See also *mortgagee*.

mortise – a short dado cut for the purpose of receiving a tab for a joint. See also *dado*.

motel – (short for "motor hotel") a

lodging built near a major road or freeway and designed to accommodate people traveling by car.

mullion — a vertical structural element of a building which supports adjacent doors or windows.

multi-family structure — a residential structure built so as to accommodate living space for more than one dwelling unit attached to the others by common walls, floors, or attics.

multiple listing service (MLS) — an organization of real estate companies, agents, or associations who for their own convenience propound rules for the maintenance, publication, and sharing of data pertaining to the offering for sale of real property.

muntins — bars, traditionally of wood, that divide a window into individual panes.

mutual mistake — a shared misperception on the part of parties to a contract concerning a circumstance that is material to the contract. For example, Abel sells Baker a house, both erroneously believing it to have been designed by a famous architect. Mutual mistake may give rise to recission of a contract.

mutual water company — a public utility in which the customers are the owners.

N

naked title — (also called "bare legal title") The minimum title vested in the holder of a trust deed, without any of the privileges of possession and use. See also *equitable title* and *legal title*.

NAR — See *National Association of Realtors®*.

NAREB — See *National Association of Real Estate Brokers*.

narrative report — an appraisal report prepared in a style and format that extensively addresses economic, locational, physical, and market elements affecting the fair market value of the property appraised.

National Association of Real Estate Brokers (NAREB) — an organization founded in 1947 and composed primarily of African-American real estate brokers. Its members are known as Realtists®. It is one of the largest minority trade associations, with branches throughout the United States. Like the National Association of Realtors® (NAR), its members subscribe to a code of ethics.

National Association of Realtors® (NAR) — the largest and predominant trade association of the real estate industry. NAR membership branches include appraisers, residential and commercial real estate agents, property managers, and other organizations. NAR is responsible for prescribing a rigorous code of ethics for its members, monitoring and sponsoring legislation affecting property rights, as well as awarding certain professional designations connoting achievement in areas of specialization. Members of NAR must also belong to local and state associations of Realtors®. Although the word "Realtor®" has become nearly synonymous with "real estate agent," only members of NAR are entitled to call themselves Realtors®.

natural disaster — See *act of God.*

natural person — a human being as distinguished from "persons" created for legal convenience such as corporations or other entities whose existence is owed to legislative definition. See also *corporation.*

natural resources — the indigenous occurrence of materials lying in their natural state. Examples include forests, ore deposits, minerals, hydrocarbons, and mariculture. Often used to refer to all things in their natural state.

naturalization — the process whereby aliens earn the right to citizenship in a foreign country.

navigable — bodies of water (i.e., lakes, rivers, streams and oceans) that are suitable for use as passageways for the transportation of goods in commerce. In an international context, the term applies to bodies of water that are susceptible to the ebb and flow of tides. A common understanding of the term relates to waters on which watercraft may operate.

negative amortization — in variable interest rate or adjustable rate mortgages that contain a payment cap or limit, negative amortization occurs when the index rate rises to a level that, together with the addition of the margin, creates a monthly payment amount greater than that allowed by the payment cap. The difference between the interest amount that would have been payable in the uncapped payment over the capped payment is added to the outstanding loan balance thereby creating a growing loan balance, rather than an *amortizing* or decreasing loan balance. Negative amortization may occur in virtually any note or loan arrangement if the lender and borrower agree to it and the circumstances of its occurrence are clearly set forth. Naturally, the parties should be aware of the usury statutes in their jurisdiction. See also *adjustable rate mortgage, amortization, balloon payment, index, interest cap, margin, payment cap,* and *variable rate mortgage.*

negative cash flow — a situation that arises in income-producing property when the amount of income received is insufficient to cover the expenses of owning and operating the property. The difference, or shortfall, must be found in sources other than the income stream, most often the owner's funds. See also *cash flow* and *negative leverage.*

negative easement — an easement that prevents a property owner from using the property in a manner otherwise permitted by law. Examples include light and air easements and avigation easements. See also *easement*.

negative leverage – most commonly found in income property, a financial predicament that arises when the debt service for the property cannot be satisfied by the income from the property. This is a contributing factor to negative cash flow. See also *negative cash flow*.

negligence – failure to exercise reasonable care in the normal course of human activities given a set of circumstances.

negotiable instrument – any financial document that entitles the holder, bearer or payee to the amount shown in its face. Forms of negotiable instruments are currency, bearer bonds, checks made payable to cash, stock certificates, and notes. According to the Uniform Negotiable Instruments Act, an instrument is negotiable when (a) it is in writing; (b) it is signed; and (c) there is an unconditional promise or order to pay a certain amount of money on demand or at a definite future date, to the bearer, to the order, or to a named or certain drawee.

negotiation – the act of bargaining. The process whereby two or more parties communicate their respective demands, needs, and wants regarding an issue or subject, the successful completion of which is often memorialized, either as a matter of good judgment or law, in the form of a written contract or agreement.

neighborhood – an area of an urban *environment* distinguished from others by one or more characteristics that may be geographical, political, physical, cultural, ethnic, religious, school boundaries, or socioeconomic in nature.

neighborhood shopping center – a shopping center designed to accommodate the anticipated commerce from those living nearby. Such centers usually are comprised of a supermarket, drug/variety store, and in-line *shops* for such services and commodities as personal grooming, banking, medical offices, travel agencies, food service, and specialty shops.

net acre – that portion of an acre from which economic benefit can be derived directly. A net acre is usually a remaining area expressed in acres after the dedication of land for public use (streets, sidewalks, utilities, schools, fire stations, etc.), or the reservation of common areas such as a condominium complex's tennis courts, swimming pools, clubhouses, etc., are established, on which housing or commercial structures may be built. See also *acre*.

net after taxes – the income that may remain after deduction of allowable expenses and income tax is paid. See also *net before taxes* and *net income*.

net before taxes – net income remaining after payment of all operating and fixed expenses but before payment of income tax. See also *net after taxes* and *net income*.

net earnings – See *net income*.

net ground lease – a lease of land the terms of which require the lessee to pay some or all of the expenses of owning the land such as property taxes, insurance, and other expenses the lessor may have that are specific to the leased premises. The land subject to the lease may be improved or unimproved. See also *ground lease.*

net income – the amount remaining after deducting from gross income all cash expenses required to support the income-producing capacity of an asset. Net income is determined without regard for noncash accounting deductions such as depreciation, amortization of fees and commissions, and similar deductions. See also *gross income.*

net income multiplier – an informal valuation guideline used in multifamily property pricing. It is a market-derived factor calculated by dividing the net income of recently sold similar properties into their respective selling prices. That factor is then used as a multiplier to estimate the value of other properties. As a general example, if the average net income of similar triplexes in a given neighborhood is approximately $40,000 annually, and several triplexes have sold recently for $400,000, the indicated net income multiplier would be 10 ($400,000 ÷ $40,000). As a general guideline, triplexes similar to those recently sold in the same neighborhood would also be priced at 10 times the net income. See also *gross income multiplier.*

net lease – a lease that includes the provision that the Lessee pay some or

all of the expenses of operating the property such as property taxes, insurance, utilities, repairs, and maintenance. The various degrees of "netness" of a lease are not sufficiently standardized for universal classification. In some jurisdictions, for example, a "triple net" lease is one in which the tenant pays three of the major costs of ownership (insurance, taxes, and operating expenses) as part of the lease. It is best to review the lease contract carefully to determine who is responsible for any expenses. Generally, if the lease is silent on the payment of expenses, the burden of the expenses falls to the lessor. In an offer to lease that recites a "net-net" lease or "modified gross" lease, it is risky to assume the meanings of these terms. The precise meaning should be obtained in writing from the owner or broker.

net listing – a listing of real property that permits the listing agent to keep any consideration received over an amount guaranteed to the owner. This practice is fraught with ethical quandaries, so much so that such a listing arrangement is illegal in some states. See also *listing.*

net loss – (1) a loss that is realized after the deduction of all expenses, fees, and charges from the sale price of a property; (2) the net excess of expenses over income for an income-producing property over a stated period.

net operating income (NOI) – the amount remaining from gross income of an income property after the deduction of all fixed expenses, operating expenses, allowances for re-placement reserves, bad debts, and vacancy allowances. Debt service and income tax are not deducted.

net present value (NPV) — in financial analysis of income-producing assets, the sum of all cash flow over a number of periods plus the projected sale price discounted at a rate that reflects a financial goal or measure of certain criteria, less the original acquisition cost. If the resulting value is negative, the investment is generally unacceptable, but if positive, the investment may be considered. Consider a property that you know can be purchased today for $25,000. You are supremely confident that you can sell it for $40,000 four years from now. As a bonus, this property generates $4,000 per year of positive cash flow. If it is sold for the target amount at the end of the fourth year, the NPV arrived at by discounting the cash flows (including the net sale price) at 18%, your required risk rate, would then be $6,392. Stated another way, one could pay as much as $31,392 ($25,000 + $6,392) for the initial investment before its feasibility becomes marginal under the same assumptions. See also *internal rate of return*.

net proceeds — the amount available from a sale after all liens and expenses have been paid.

net profit — See *net proceeds*.

net rentable area — See *rentable area*.

net rental — the income from rent

that exceeds operating expenses. See also *net operating income*.

net sales area — the area of a retail premises where goods are displayed and sold. This area typically does not include storage/warehouse area, employee break or locker rooms, administrative offices, or corridors.

net spendable income — the amount available after each accounting or reporting period that is available for unrestricted distribution to an asset's owner.

net usable acre — See *net acre*.

net worth — the amount remaining after subtracting liabilities from assets; a measure of financial strength applied to individuals and business entities to help establish creditworthiness or to establish qualifications for some investment threshold. An example is a limited partnership offering that is restricted to individuals who have a net worth, exclusive of their primary residence and automobiles, in excess of $5,000,000.

newel — a vertical structural member of a stairway. In a circular stairway, it may be the center post. In other stairways it may be the post at the top or bottom.

no-bonus clause — in states where permitted, a lease clause whereby the lessee gives up its claim to any bonus value awarded in a condemnation of the leasehold estate. The lessee would be entitled to receive from the condemning agency only the value of the improvements made by the lessee to the premises and not the "bonus" value of the leasehold as measured by the difference between the positive difference between the market rent and the contract rent over the remaining life of the lease.

NOI – See *net operating income.*

nominal consideration – a consideration or amount not reflective of actual value, but sufficient to the parties to the contract or transaction to consummate the bargain. See also *love and affection* and *valuable consideration.*

nominal loan rate – the rate of interest stated on the face of the note. See *annual percentage rate* and *loan constant.*

nominee – a person or entity that may be substituted for a principal in a contract.

nonassumption clause – See *acceleration clause.*

nonbearing wall – a wall, usually within a structure, that has no significance to the structural integrity of the building. It holds nothing of a structural nature up or together; the building would stand without it. See also *bearing wall.*

noncompetition clause – a provision in a contract, lease or deed wherein a promise is made to refrain from engaging in or permitting some commercial enterprise or act on a particular premises, within a radius of a certain premises, or within a proscribed time period within a geographic boundary. For example, in a neighborhood shopping center, the supermarket operator may condition its occupancy on the shopping center owner not building another shopping center within a 10-mile radius of the subject that would include a competing supermarket.

nonconforming loan – a loan whose amount is in excess of that established by those entities, such as the Federal National Mortgage Association (FNMA or Fannie Mae) and others, that purchase such loans in the secondary mortgage market. This amount is subject to periodic review and change, and has been rising irregularly over the past several years. See also *conforming loan* and *jumbo loan.*

nonconforming use – in zoning matters, a use or structure occurring on a parcel that was in conformance with zoning regulations at some point in time, but would not now be allowed to be re-created either because building codes or environmental issues would preclude it, or because the zoning regulations for the subject area have been changed. Generally a nonconforming use is not an illegal use.

nondisturbance clause – a provision in a mortgage on a commercial building that provides in the event of a foreclosure on the mortgagor's/lessor's interest, those lessees' who are not in default shall have continued occupancy under their lease.

nonexclusive listing – a listing of real property wherein more than one agent is permitted to offer a property for sale under separate listing agreements. Compare *exclusive listing*. See also *listing*.

nonjudicial foreclosure – in states that recognize the securitization of a loan on real property by a trust deed rather than a mortgage, in the event of a fatal default (i.e., a default that calls for the forfeiture of the property), the property will be sold by the trustee named in the deed of trust for the benefit of the beneficiary (lender). All of this takes place without intervention of a court, but under the "power of sale" provision of the deed of trust executed by the trustor (borrower). This provides for an orderly process wherein the trustee follows a prescribed set of notice and procedural steps to regain possession of the property from the trustor without having to adjudicate the matter. In some states with antideficiency laws, a lender who chooses a nonjudicial foreclosure is limited to the recovery of the property and may not pursue the borrower for any shortfall in proceeds. See also *antideficiency laws, beneficiary, deed of trust, judicial foreclosure, nonrecourse loan, power of sale, trustee,* and *trustor*.

nonprofit corporation – a corporation, usually without shareholders, whose principal purpose is to perpetuate some religious, charitable, fraternal, or similar cause or association without regard for profits or earnings. An important privilege of such an organization is the tax-exempt status conferred on it by the Internal Revenue Service.

nonrecourse loan – a loan for which the sole source of satisfaction for default thereon is the property that was given as collateral. If the market value of such property does not offset the defaulted monetary debt, the debtor/trustor will have no personal liability for any shortfall. See also *antideficiency laws*.

nonrecurring closing costs – charges associated with closing an escrow which are singular in nature and will not form part of the regular monthly expense of owning the property. Loan fees, tax impounds, escrow charges, inspection fees, prepaid interest, and points are all examples of nonrecurring closing costs. Lenders sometimes require, and often allow, sellers or third parties to pay some or all of these costs on behalf of the borrower.

nonrecurring expense – an unusual expense that is unexpected or outside expenses normally incurred. An example is the expense associated with repairs resulting from a natural disaster.

normal wear and tear – the usual and expected consumption of a consumable asset in the course of its use. Examples are worn pathways on a carpet, tarnished metal fixtures on a heavily used door, burned-out light bulbs, etc. Normal wear and tear would not include a broken window, a missing door, pet-stained carpet, etc. Leases often use this phrase to indicate the dividing line between expenses attributable to the lessor and expenses chargeable to the lessee. Note that the length of the tenancy is a factor in determining what is normal. A long-term tenant might reasonably expect that property would be painted at the lessor's expense. Lessees may forfeit part or all of the damage deposit if excess wear and tear has occurred. See also *damage deposit.*

notary public – a minor officer of the state authorized to administer oaths and to validate identities and signatures on documents that require notarial scrutiny, especially for documents intended to be recorded or filed in the public records for purposes of giving *constructive notice.*

note – a document executed by the debtor that sets forth the amount, term, and interest rate of the debt, and also contains the operative words and phrases that constitute a promise to repay. When used in conjunction with real property, a note is often secured by a trust deed, which allows the lender to obtain lawful possession of the real property in the event of a default. See also *promissory note* and *trust deed.*

notice – (1) information passed from one person to the world at large given in a manner prescribed by law or contract to advise the public of an event or condition that the public should take note of and respond to as appropriate. Such a notice may be published in a newspaper of general circulation with the general intent of putting all on notice of such matters. Examples include a petition for a name change, the intent to sell assets of a business, the intent to sell alcoholic beverages, or a notice of trustee's sale under a deed of trust. (2)

information passed from one person to another as required by law or prudence. Examples include a lessor's notice to a lessee to pay rent within a specified time or vacate the premises, or a lessee's notice to lessor of its intent to exercise an option to extend its lease. See also *actual notice, constructive notice,* and *implied notice.*

notice of action – See *lis pendens.*

notice of cessation – a legal notice that work by a contractor on a building project has ceased. This notice is generally given by a contractor or a materialman to accelerate the process of filing mechanic's liens. See also *materialman's lien.*

notice of completion – a statement posted on the premises and filed for recordation to give notice, especially to those having the right to file mechanic's liens, that the work is considered complete. Depending on the jurisdiction, this starts a time period for filing claims for nonpayment and the like. See also *materialman's lien.*

notice of default – a warning that may be filed for recordation and/or sent to a person who may be in a material breach of a provision of a note, mortgage, or trust deed. If the default is not cured within a statutory or contractual period of time, the party providing the notice may move to foreclose. See also *foreclosure.*

notice of nonresponsibility – a written notice posted on the premises and filed for recordation stating that the owner of the subject premises is not responsible to third parties for payment or liability in matters undertaken by or on behalf of the work initiated by a lessee. Such a notice is filed when a lessee undertakes construction on leased premises for which the lessor may have granted consent but on which the lessor assumes no liability.

notice to quit — a written notice from lessor to *lessee* to vacate the leased premises prior to a certain date. A notice to quit may be given because of a breach of the lease or because the lease term has expired and the lessor wishes to regain possession of the property. See also *eviction*.

notorious possession — a required element of the *adverse possession* process which encompasses actual possession of the premises in an open manner that is opposed (hostile) to the owner of the real property. See also *adverse possession*.

novation — the substitution of a new contract, debt, or obligation for a previous or existing contract, debt or obligation between the same or different parties. There are three different types of novation in the context of real estate loans: (a) the debtor and creditor remain the same, but a new debt replaces the old; (b) the creditor and the debt remain the same, but a new debtor is substituted; (c) the debtor and the debt remain the same, but the creditor is replaced by another. The requirements for a novation are a valid original contract, an agreement by all parties to extinguish the previous obligation, the extinguishment of the

old contract, and the validity of the new contract.

NPV — See *net present value.*

nuisance — property or a condition on a property that is inconsistent with the surrounding uses or zoning, and which produces such annoyance, inconvenience, or harm to the public that the law will presume damages. An example is a vacant lot in a residential area used for open storage of gasoline. See also *attractive nuisance.*

null and void — having no further legally enforceable authority; having no effect.

nuncupative will — a will made orally, usually on a deathbed, before witnesses.

nut — colloquial term for overhead. See *overhead.*

O

oakum — a fibrous material made from hemp or rope impregnated with tar. It is used as a caulking material.

oath — (1) a solemn proclamation or attestation made under a moral or legal compulsion to subscribe publicly to a high standard of conduct for a specific purpose. An example is a public official's oath of office. See also *attest.* (2) an affirmation of the truth of a statement.

obligee — a promisee; the beneficiary or payee of a note or bond, or of a promise to do or not to do something. The party to whom another party owes a duty under a contract. See also *obligor* and *promisee*.

obligor – a promisor; a person who promises to pay a sum, or to do or refrain from doing some act; person who owes a duty to another under a contract. See also *obligee* and *promissor*.

obsolescence – the condition of having been made less useful by virtue of improved design, material, or construction permitting the creation of a thing of greater utility for the same or similar purpose. See also *external obsolescence* and *functional obsolescence*.

occupancy – the act or condition of habitation, control, or possession.

occupancy agreement – a contract between a seller and a prospective purchaser allowing the purchaser to occupy the premises prior to and in anticipation of the consummation of the purchase. An occupancy agreement (sometimes also called an early occupancy agreement) generally takes the form of a short-term lease, with cross references to the purchase contract. See also *early occupancy*.

occupancy permit – See *certificate of occupancy*.

occupant – (1) one who has taken possession; (2) a person with possessory rights to a property; (3) one who has actual or effective use and control of a property. See also *adverse possession*.

offer – (1) to present, with the intent of forming a valid agreement, the specifics of the circumstances, conditions, and reciprocal actions by the offeree under which the offeror will fully perform the agreement; (2) the specification of such circumstances, conditions, and reciprocal actions. An offer evidences the intent to be bound by a contract, assuming the party to whom the offer is made agrees to its terms. A listing in an MLS of a property does not generally constitute an offer, but rather is an invitation to an offer. In other words, the seller of the property is indicating that offers from buyers are welcome. See also *letter of intent, offer and acceptance, offeree,* and *offeror*.

offer and acceptance – concurrence or meeting of the minds resulting from an offer and the acceptance of the offer as made. Offer and acceptance are necessary elements of a valid contract. If the offeree changes the terms of the offer in any manner, the change is generally treated by law and custom as a counteroffer, soliciting an acceptance by the original offeror. A counteroffer is essentially an entirely new offer by the party making the counteroffer. Acceptance must be communicated effectively to the party making the offer or the counteroffer. Although laws and judicial construction vary by jurisdiction, acceptance generally must be communicated in the form in which the negotiations have been conducted. Thus, if negotiations have been conducted by means of a hand-delivered document, acceptance must also be hand-delivered. If negotiations have been conducted by fax, a faxed acceptance may be sufficient. Oral acceptances of written offers for real property may not be binding. Offers may be terminated by rejection, lapse of time, revocation prior to communication of acceptance, insanity, incapacity, or death of either party. See also *acceptance, counteroffer, offer, offeree, offeror, revocation,* and *Statute of Frauds.*

offer to sell — any solicitation of offers for real property.

offeree — the person or entity to whom or which the offer is extended. See also *offer* and *offeror.*

offeror — the person or entity extending an offer. See also *offer* and *offeree.*

office building — a structure divided into individual offices and used by a company or companies to conduct the planning, management, and marketing aspects of business. Office space is not generally used as an outlet for direct retail sales of products or for manufacturing. See also *commercial property, industrial property,* and *office space.*

office listing — a signed, valid listing of real property that is not placed in the MLS, but rather is made known only to agents of one real estate office or company at the specific request of the seller. Only agents from that company are promised a commission if they procure a buyer. Because of the potential for conflicts of interest in these arrangements, MLS rules often require that the agent tak-

ing such a listing have the seller sign a knowing waiver, indicating that the advantages of the wider exposure of the MLS have been explained to him or her. See also *agency, dual agency, exclusive listing,* and *multiple listing service.*

Office of Equal Opportunity — the federal agency under HUD that is primarily responsible for administering the Federal Fair Housing Act. See also *discrimination; Federal Fair Housing Act;* and *Housing and Urban Development, U. S. Department of.*

Office of Interstate Land Sales Registration — the federal agency under HUD that enforces and interprets federal regulation of interstate land sales. It was established in 1969 to protect the public against misleading practices in the sale of out-of-state recreational and investment properties. See also *Housing and Urban Development, U.S. Department of.*

Office of Management and Budget (OMB) — the Office that assists the President in the development and execution of policies and programs. OMB has a hand in the development and resolution of all the budget, policy, legislative, regulatory, procurement, and management issues on behalf of the President. OMB is composed of divisions organized either by agency and program area or by functional responsibilities. However, the work of OMB often requires a broad exposure to issues and programs outside of the direct area of assigned responsibility.

Office of Thrift Supervision (OTS)
— the federal agency under the Department of the Treasury that replaced the Federal Home Loan Bank Board (FHLBB) and assumed some functions of the Federal Savings and Loan Insurance Corporation (FSLIC) in 1989. See also *Federal Home Loan Bank Board* and *Federal Savings and Loan Insurance Corporation.*

office park — a development or zoning designation designed primarily for the construction and maintenance of office buildings. See also *industrial park* and *office space.*

office space — property that is designed for office use, whether currently configured as offices, or simply as open space without improvements within an office building. See also *commercial lease, office building,* and *tenant improvements.*

off-site — improvements or costs related to the development of a property that are not located on or directly attributable to the property. See also *off-site costs* and *off-site improvements.*

off-site costs — costs for improvements made for the benefit of a property but constructed on property other than the subject site. An example is the cost of extending utilities from the center of the street to the property line by a developer or owner. See also *off-site improvements* and *on-site improvements.*

off-site improvements — improvements to land that are not located on the land but that are related

to and were constructed to benefit the land. Streets, sewers, and utilities are all off-site improvements. See also *off-site costs* and *on-site costs.*

off-site management — property management functions performed by persons in a location other than the premises of the property being managed. Examples include leasing, billing, and accounting. See also *on-site management* and *property management.*

off-street parking — parking for a development, whether residential, commercial, or industrial, that is located in a designated area not on public streets. The most common examples are parking garages and parking lots.

oil and gas lease — a contract that permits the exploration and extraction of minerals and hydrocarbons (coal, oil and gas) from the surface or subsurface of the parcel described.

OMB — See *Office of Management and Budget.*

omnibus clause — a term in a will directing the disposition of property not specifically named in the will. See also *will.*

on center — a common method of measuring the distance between studs, joists, and other framing lumber. Rather than measuring from one board edge to another, the distance between boards is measured and marked at their center point. For example, residential building codes might call for "two by four (inch) framing spaced sixteen inches apart on center." For typical two by four construction, the midpoint is at three-fourths of an inch on the narrowest side. (Two by fours are actually 1½ inches by 3½ inches when finished.) This method makes it easier for carpenters to nail sheathing, such as plywood, consistently in the center of the framing member for the greatest strength. See also *framing*.

on title — having an interest in real property that is enumerated or described in a recorded document. See also *constructve notice* and *deed*.

on or before — a term in a contract referring to the date for the performance of some contractually referenced act, or for completion of the contract.

one-hour door — a door that is rated by an appropriate agency as being capable of resisting destruction by a typical fire for a period of at least 1 hour. Many building codes require these fire doors between garages and living areas in residential construction, and throughout a building in commercial construction.

one-hour wall — a wall that is rated by an appropriate agency as being capable of resisting destruction by a typical fire for a period of at least 1 hour. Many building codes require these fire walls between garages and living areas in residential construction.

one hundred percent commission — an arrangement between a real estate broker and a real estate salesperson in which the salesperson retains 100% of all commissions

generated by him or her. Such an arrangement is usually accompanied by a fee or rent schedule in which the salesperson compensates the broker for office space and/or services rendered.

on-site improvements — improvements to land that are located on and primarily benefit the land. Examples are houses, office buildings, and factories. See also *off-site costs*, *off-site improvements*, and *on-site costs*.

on-site management — an arrangement in which substantially all property management functions are performed by persons on the premises of the property being managed. Tenants often feel that an on-site manager is more responsive to problems with the property. See also *off-site management* and *property management*.

open and notorious — acts committed on the land of another of sufficiently prominent and conspicuous character that the legal owner of the land should be aware that another party may make a claim to the land. Examples include building a house on the land, or cultivating the land and reaping the harvest. It is an essential element of *adverse possession*. See also *adverse possession*.

open beam construction — a construction technique in which the structural beams of the roof are left exposed to the interior for visual interest. See also *half-timbered*.

open house — the practice of showing listed homes to the public during specific hours, often on weekends, as opposed to by individual appointment. Open houses are also sometimes held in homes that are not for sale for the purpose of displaying the historic or architectural significance of a home. See also *caravan*.

open listing — See *nonexclusive listing*.

open space — land held for the public benefit which by virtue of public policy or design is left in its natural state, or which is used only for conservation, light agricultural, or recreational purposes, such as wetlands, parkland, public squares, etc.

open-end mortgage — a mortgage that allows the mortgagor to obtain additional funds from the mortgagee after the initial commitment of funds up to a stated limit. See also *line of credit*.

operating budget — an itemized estimate of income, fixed and variable expenses, debt service, taxes and insurance, net operating income before taxes, and cash flow for a given project or business. Property managers may prepare an operating budget for each property they manage at the start of the fiscal year.

operating expense ratio — the ratio of operating expenses to gross income.

operating expenses — amounts expended to maintain an income-producing property. Such expenses might include property taxes, janitorial services, management salaries and expenses, utilities, insurance, cash re-serves for replacements, and supplies. Excluded are noncash expenses such as depreciation, expenses related to capital improvements, and all cash expenses attributable to debt service.

operating income — cash flow derived from a revenue-generating enterprise. Operating income from a real estate asset includes rents, fees, and commissions that are specific to the property.

operation of law — the manner in which the rights and obligations of parties to a transaction are affected and possibly altered by the application of the rules of applicable law to a transaction, independent of the wishes or intentions of the parties.

opinion of title — a judgment provided by a person competent to examine title, such as a title attorney or a title officer, as to the condition and validity of title to a particular parcel of land. An opinion is not a guarantee, but rather a statement that the person examining the title is qualified to do so and has exercised reasonable care and diligence. For this reason preliminary title reports coupled with title insurance have achieved increasing popularity. See also *abstract of title, preliminary title report, title,* and *title insurance.*

opportunity cost — the cost to pursue a course of action measured in terms of not taking alternative courses of action. The most common use of the concept is to compare investing a sum of money in a relatively risk-free investment, such as Treasury bonds or certificates of deposit, with the riskier contemplated investment, such as an apartment building. If the apartment building is estimated to return 10% per year while the risk-free investment returns 5%, and if the decision is made to invest in the apartment building, the *opportunity cost* is the 5% return the investor is foregoing by choosing the apartment option.

option – a right (but not a duty) to purchase or lease a property at an agreed price during an agreed time period. Most commonly in real estate, options are purchased for an agreed sum of money to secure a predetermined price on a parcel of property as long as the option is "exercised" on or before a certain expiration date. Options may not be of infinite duration and are subject to the Statute of Frauds. Exercising the option simply means completing the purchase. Buyers may seek an option because they want a guaranteed price on a future purchase. Sellers may wish to sell an option because if the buyer does not exercise the option, the seller typically keeps the option price (the option premium). Option may be granted as part of a lease or other contract or may be purchased outright. Lessees may also have a contractual option to extend the term of a lease or an option to expand the lease premises. See also *Statute of Frauds*.

option for additional space – a clause in a commercial lease that allows an existing tenant to rent additional space from a landlord at a predetermined price and terms.

option to renew – a clause in a lease that gives an existing tenant the right, upon written notice to extend the lease at a predetermined price and terms.

optionee – a person who holds the right to exercise the option. See also *option* and *optionor*

optionor – the person who granted the rights exercisable by the option. See also *option* and *optionee*.

or-more clause – a provision in a mortgage, trust deed, or land contract that permits the payment of additional principal to be applied without prepayment penalty after accounting for the regularly scheduled payment of principal and interest. Such a clause may be represented as follows: "...shall pay on the first day of each month the sum of $XXXX dollars, or more."

oral contract – an unwritten or only partially written agreement which in real estate is usually not enforceable. Same as *verbal contract*. See also *Statute of Frauds*.

order confirming sale – a court document signifying the court's approval of the price and terms of a judicially ordered sale of real property.

ordinances – laws originating from a county or municipality on matters of local governance. Ordinances usually regulate such matters as zoning, speed limits, parking charges, and fines. Ordinances do not have a priority over state or federal laws covering the same jurisdictional matter.

ordinary income – an income tax

term meaning a class of income that is taxed at the taxpayer's regular tax table rate. It is contrasted to income, such as capital gains and certain prizes, that receive unusual treatment, whether favorable or unfavorable. See also *capital gain, income,* and *income taxes.*

ordinary repairs — repairs to an improvement to real property that are necessary to maintain its functionality and prevent unusual wear and tear or decay. Examples include painting and plumbing repairs. See, by contrast, *capital improvement.*

oriel window — a bay or bow window located above the first floor supported by brackets (corbels) from underneath instead of by a foundation. See also *bay window, bow window,* and *corbel.*

orientation — the position and placing of a structure on a lot.

original cost — the purchase price of a property paid by the current owner.

origination fee — a fee charged to offset a direct expense of the loan process or to otherwise compensate a lender for a loan. Sometimes also called "points." Origination fees are generally quoted as a percentage of the loan amount. For example, a $200,000 loan at two points would carry an origination fee of $4,000. Such direct expenses might include a credit report, appraisal report, or other inspection for which a third party would be paid, although these charges are often also listed separately from the origination fee. See

also *point* and *Truth in Lending Law (Regulation Z).*

ostensible agency — agency duties and obligations created by means of ostensible authority. Sometimes also called "apparent agency." See also *agency* and *apparent authority.*

ostensible authority — See *apparent authority.*

OTS — See *Office of Thrift Supervision.*

outside of escrow — agreements, payments, or acts in connection with a real estate transaction that are performed separately from the escrow instructions and about which the escrow is not concerned. Although certain acts, such as the purchase of incidental personal property, are legitimately performed outside of escrow, the opportunity for fraud is always present. Many lenders require borrowers to sign a statement as a condition of the loan to the effect that there are no agreements outside of escrow. See also *escrow.*

outstanding balance — the unpaid balance of a loan at a particular point in time.

overage — an amount owed as additional rent over an agreed base amount. It is found as a contract term in certain commercial retail leases and is based on a percentage of income, less certain expenses, generated from the leased premises by the retail tenant. For example, assume that Abel leases a retail store location to Baker for "$3,000/month plus 5% of all gross sales over $5,000/month. In the first month of the lease, Baker grosses $10,000. Baker would owe Abel $3,250 ($3,000 plus 5% of $5,000). See also *lease*.

overbuilding – the construction of more housing, commercial space, or any other improvement to land than the market can absorb at a given price level. As overbuilding occurs, prices tend to fall.

overhang – (1) that portion of a roof which extends past an exterior wall; (2) that portion of a loan which is not secured by collateral.

overimprovement – an improvement to real property that costs more and is different from improvements that would lead to the highest and best use of the property. For example, a $100,000 addition to a $100,000 house in an area of $100,000 houses would probably be an overimprovement. See also *highest and best use*.

overpass – a method of joining or crossing perpendicular roads by means of elevating one of the roads above the other.

OWC – See *owner will carry*.

owner – (1) the person in whom is vested the legal or equitable title to real property; (2) any person with dominion over a property, whether real or personal, who has a right to enjoy and make use of it. See also *equitable title, legal title, ownership,* and *title*.

owner of record – the person who, according to public records, is the owner of a real or personal prop-

erty. He or she may or may not be the true legal owner.

owner/occupant – a person who owns and lives in a residential property.

owner's policy – a title insurance policy that protects the owner (buyer) of the property against defects in title. See also *lender's policy* and *title insurance*.

ownership – the bundle of rights to occupy, use, and enjoy property, to the exclusion of others. These rights include the rights to give, sell, or will the property to others.

owner will carry (OWC) – a term indicating the willingness of a seller of real property to extend financing to a qualified buyer. The financing may take the form of a first trust deed or secondary financing. It may be short or long term. See also *creative financing*.

P & I – principal and interest.

P & L – See *profit and loss statement*.

package a loan – the process by which a loan broker assembles a real estate loan application and supporting documents (tax returns, verifications of employment and income, credit reports, etc.) in preparation for submittal to a lending institution.

package mortgage – a mortgage

wherein a portion of the payment is allocated to amortizing the purchase price of personal property, especially appliances. The mortgage instrument generally deems the appliances to be fixtures.

package trust deed — See *package mortgage.*

pad — (1) any defined area of land on which a building may be built or on which another structure or device, such as a utility meter or air conditioner, may be placed; (2) the area in a mobile home park on which a mobile home may be placed; (3) the flat or legally buildable area of a larger parcel; (4) the collection of funds from one or more parties to an escrow in excess of known line item expenses so that sufficient funds are available for unforeseen costs.

PAM — pledged asset mortgage.

pane — an individual glass piece in a door or window.

panel — (1) a thin sheet of manufactured material, such as pressed board, gypsum, or rolled metal, that is used as a wall or ceiling surface; (2) a raised or recessed portion of a wall or ceiling, usually bordered by a frame; (3) the area inside an electrical supply box in which fuses or breakers are located.

panel heating — a radiant room heating system that is located in walls, floors, or ceilings, and that uses electricity, hot oil, hot air, or hot water as the heat source.

panel wall — (1) a wall using prefabricated flat structural elements composed of concrete, wood or metal for exterior surfacing; (2) a non-load-bearing interior wall, also called a "curtain wall."

panic peddling — the practice by a real estate licensee of soliciting listings through the illegal use of written or oral statements or through any other behavior that tends to create fear or alarm concerning the presence or imminent presence in the neighborhood of members of a minority status (race, gender, religious affiliation, handicap, familial status, or national origin). Sometimes also refers to creating alarm concerning geologic hazard or impending condition such as development of an airport, building a nearby highway/freeway, corrections facility, etc. See also *blockbusting.*

panic sale — See *distress sale.*

paper — (1) informal for documents, such as mortgages, deeds of trust, or land contracts, that are used instead of cash. especially if such financing is provided by the seller; (2) evidence of a loan.

par — the face or nominal value of a security or the current balance owing on a note without a discount. See also *discount.*

par value — the value that is printed on a stock certificate. Par value generally represents the legal or stated capital of the issuer on a per share basis.

parapet — a low or guarding wall

created by extending the exterior vertical surface of a structure above the roof plane.

parcel — (1) a portion of a larger land area; (2) a lot. See also *lot*.

parish — a political area established to administer the collection of taxes, enforce the law and operate a court system. A parish is the Louisiana equivalent of a county.

parity clause — a provision in a mortgage or deed of trust that allows the mortgage or deed of trust to secure more than one note, each with equal priority over the asset. See, by contrast, *subordination*.

park — a natural or improved section of land or water set aside for recreational or educational uses.

parking ratio — the number of off-street parking spaces divided by the number of units in the building or housing project served by that parking. Zoning laws often specify minimum parking ratios.

parkway — a multilane divided roadway with a landscaped median strip. It serves as an arterial road through a community.

parol evidence rule — a rule of evidence that prevents the parties to a written contract from attempting to alter the meaning of the contract in court through the introduction of contemporaneous oral declarations that are inconsistent with the written contract.

parquet flooring — a wooden tile flooring system that consists of short pieces of wood laid in a pattern of geometric shapes.

partial eviction — an act by a landlord that results in a tenant being unable to fully utilize the property as described in the occupancy agreement. For example, if a landlord refuses to repair a bathroom in an apartment, the tenant may argue that a partial eviction has occurred as a defense to an action by the landlord to compel rent payments. See also *constructive eviction*.

partial interest — any ownership interest that is less than a fee simple absolute. See also *fee simple absolute*.

partial reconveyance — a provision in a mortgage or deed of trust that allows a parcel of land, or a portion of a parcel of land, to be freed from serving as collateral for the mortgage or trust deed prior to the full satisfaction of the mortgage or trust deed. An example is a $1,000,000 construction loan secured by the land and improvements of a small development of four houses. Although the loan is secured by the entire property, a partial reconveyance clause would allow the builder to sell the houses one at a time, pay the lender a prorated share of the loan for each sale made (usually more than $250,000 each for the first few houses sold to protect the security interest of the lender), and deliver clear titles to the buyers.

partial release — See *partial reconveyance*.

partial taking — the involuntary transfer of title to only a portion of an owner's property under the laws of eminent domain. For example, if Abel owns 10 contiguous acres of land, and a condemnation proceeding takes 5 acres, Abel has suffered a partial taking. See also *before-and-after method, eminent domain, just compensation,* and *taking.*

partially amortized loan – a loan that includes some payments toward principal, but that does not fully retire the debt upon the completion of the loan term, requiring a balloon payment. See also *amortization* and *balloon payment.*

participating broker – (1) (also called a cooperating broker) most commonly, a real estate broker who represents the buyer in the sale of a property that is listed by another broker; (2) a broker who is among several brokers with a listing on a property, as in the case of a large condominium project in which several local real estate firms are contracted to sell the units.

participation –a lender's sharing in a portion of the profits, and sometimes the losses, of a project financed by the loan. See also *participation mortgage.*

participation certificate – a mortgage-backed security sold by the Federal Home Loan Mortgage Corporation (Freddie Mac) to finance the purchase of mortgages in the secondary market. Certificates are sold for a pool of mortgages or for a single large mortgage to institutions and individuals in denominations of $100,000 and more. The payment of

principal and interest is guarantied by the issuer.

participation mortgage – (1) a mortgage wherein the lender shares in the operating profits and/or capital gains realized by the property during the term of the mortgage; any mortgage in which the lender receives a return above the stated return on the note. Most commonly used in commercial mortgages. (2) a mortgage funded by more than one lender, usually because of the large size of the mortgage or because of a perceived high risk.

parties – the principals in a transaction or a court proceeding. Examples include buyer and seller, landlord and tenant, plaintiff and defendant. Real estate brokers are not typically parties to a real estate transaction.

partition – (1) an interior wall; (2) any vertical structure separating interior spaces (a bookcase in the middle of a room might be a partition);(3) a court order separating multiple ownership interests, usually to allow the individual owners to sell or otherwise convey their interests. For example, a married couple owning property as joint tenants may obtain a partition order as part of a divorce settlement.

partition action – a legal proceeding in which joint owners seek to recover their ownership interests. See *partition* and *severalty ownership.*

partner – a member of a limited or general partnership. See also *general partnership, limited partnership,* and *partnership.*

163

partnership — a voluntary or judicially determined (*de jure*) association of two or more legal persons for the purpose of carrying out a venture and sharing in the profits, losses, and liabilities incurred or created by their actions. See also *general partnership* and *limited partnership*.

party wall — a wall or partition constructed so as to create a physical boundary between properties. It is typically constructed on or very near the property boundary line. Both property owners benefiting from the presence of such a common wall may be required by contract or local laws to share the cost of construction and maintenance.

passive income — generally, income from rent, royalties, dividends, interest, and gain from the sale of securities. Passive income may be used to offset passive losses for federal income tax purposes. See also *passive investor* and *passive loss*.

passive investor — an investor who is not actively involved in the management and operation of a business or investment. One who contributes money or other assets, but not time or skills.

passive loss — a federal tax term meaning a loss from a passive investment. Passive investment losses are not treated in federal tax law as favorably as are losses generated by investments in which the investor plays an active role. See also *passive income* and *passive investor*.

passive solar heating — the practice of designing and orienting a building on its site in such a manner as to take maximum advantage of the heating capabilities of sunlight without the use of mechanical devices such as water-circulating pumps. Features such as south-facing windows, roof overhangs, and heat-storing walls exposed to the sun's rays can all be passive solar heating components.

pass-through — a tax term meaning that the taxable profits, deductible losses, and tax credits of a business enterprise or investment flow through the form of ownership (usually a partnership or trust that is not taxed) to the benefit and burden of the individual investors.

pass-through security — a mortgage-backed security issued by the Government National Mortgage Association (Ginnie Mae) in which cash flows from the underlying mortgages directly to the individual investors. These cash flows include any early payments of the mortgages. See also *Ginnie Mae*.

patent — a document issued by a governmental agency evidencing a transfer of title to real property from the government to an individual. See also *government patent*.

patent defect — (1) a flaw or defect in real or personal property subject to a sale that is plainly visible or easily discoverable by a reasonable person using ordinary care: a missing roof on a house, for example. See, by contrast, *latent defect*. (2) a defect in a legal description that cannot be corrected without recording a new description.

patio – a paved open area adjacent to or attached to a dwelling that is used mainly for social or recreational purposes.

patio home – a single-story dwelling that is attached on one side to another dwelling. On the side opposite the shared wall, the homes typically have a patio or small yard. See also *patio*.

pavilion – an inhabitable portion of a building that projects at ground level from the rest of the building; a wing; (2) a light, ornamental structure usually found in a park or garden, designed to provide a sense of enclosure; a gazebo.

payee – one to whom payment under a financial instrument such as a check, mortgage, or trust deed is made; the receiver or obligee. See also *payer*.

payor – one who renders payment under a financial instrument such as a check, mortgage or trust deed; the obligor. See also *payee*.

payment – (1) commonly the amount due monthly under a note or deed of trust; (2) any sum paid or payable to another party under the terms of a contract.

payment adjustment date – the date on which the payment under an adjustable rate mortgage or deed of trust may be subject to change (up or down) by virtue of an increase or decrease in the rate index. Payment adjustment dates can range from one month after the loan is funded to five years or more, depending on the loan. See also *adjustable rate mortgage, index, margin,* and *payment cap*.

payment cap – the maximum allowable periodic increase in a monthly payment or deed of trust under an adjustable rate instrument. For example, a mortgage with a $1,000/month payment and a 2% payment cap cannot increase to more than $1,020 at the next payment adjustment date. This does not mean that the interest rate increase must match the payment increase. If the allowable interest rate increase would have caused an increase in payment above the payment cap, the unpaid difference is added to the principal balance each month, resulting in negative amortization. See also *adjustable rate mortgage, index, margin, negative amortization, lifetime cap,* and *payment adjustment date*.

payoff – to satisfy or pay a debt in full.

payoff escrow – an escrow company or neutral third party employed to carry out mutual instructions to receive funds and issue documents evidencing the satisfaction of a debt.

pedestrian overpass – an elevated bridge for passage of nonmotorized vehicles and persons on foot over a busy roadway or railroad right-of-way.

pedestrian traffic count – the number of persons passing a particular point on foot over a particular period of time. Used in retail commercial environments to determine desirability and value of a retail location.

pedestrian underpass – a tunnel for passage of nonmotorized vehicles and persons on foot under a busy roadway or railroad right-of-way.

penalty – (1) a punishment, usually in monetary form, against a party to a contract for failing to perform an obligation or failing to refrain from an action prohibited by the contract; (2) a premium or bonus for the early payment of all or a predefined portion of the balance of a mortgage. See also *prepayment penalty.*

penny – originally, the price of different sizes of nails by the pound. An "8-penny nail" would cost 8 cents per pound. Now, a common unit of measurement for nails. For example, a "2-penny nail" (described as "2d") is 1 inch long.

penny nail – See *penny.*

penny stock – the stock of a small or minimally capitalized corporation that is publicly traded.

pension fund – an institutionally managed fund that may invest in mortgages, blue-chip stocks and bonds. The purpose of the fund is to provide retirement income for the employee group that contributes to it. Although pension fund managers do not typically originate mortgages, they are significant purchasers of mortgages and commercial paper. See also *secondary mortgage market.*

penthouse – (1) the uppermost apartment or floor in an apartment building or hotel Often a penthouse apartment steps back from the outside walls of the building to allow room for outside patios. (2) a small structure on the rooftop of a commercial building which houses mechanical equipment for elevators, HVAC, and the like.

per annum – Latin term meaning "by the year," yearly, annually.

per capita – Latin term meaning "by the head," or per person. Statistics such as average annual income, average annual consumption of sugar, and the like are often expressed using this term.

per diem – Latin term meaning "by the day." Costs such as rental charges in a holdover tenancy are calculated *per diem* for the actual number of days past the expiration of the lease the tenant remains in possession of the premises.

per se – Latin term meaning "in itself." Taken alone without reference to anything else.

per stirpes – Latin term meaning "by representation." In the law of descent of property, the term refers to taking title to property because of a deceased ancestor who was entitled to the property. For example, Abel dies, leaving property equally to Baker and Durwood. Durwood has two children who are his heirs. If Durwood dies before Abel, upon Abel's death Durwood's children would divide Durwood's share of Abel's property *per stirpes*, as representatives of Durwood.

percentage lease – a lease that includes a clause for the payment of rent based on a percentage of sales generated from tenant's operations on the leased premises. Most commonly found in leases for retailing uses. Often this type of rent will be computed as the greater of a stated percentage of sales volume or a monthly minimum market-rate rent.

percentage rent — See *percentage lease.*

perch — (also called *rod*) a unit of linear measurement equal to 16½ feet.

percolation — the absorption by the soil as a result of seepage of water or as the result of engineered drainage of a sanitary system.

percolation test — (also called a "perk test") a test to determine the rate, amount, and content of absorption and drainage of water, typically performed to determine the suitability of a site for construction generally or for a septic tank and leach field. See also *leach field* and *septic tank.*

perfect escrow — an escrow in which all required documents and funds are in the hands of the escrow agent. Nothing further is required from the parties to close the escrow. See also *closing* and *escrow.*

perfecting title — the process of eliminating any clouds or defects from the title to real property for purposes of obtaining a marketable title. See also *cloud on title, marketable title,* and *title.*

performance bond — a financial guarantee of contractual obligations. It is evidenced by a surety bond purchased in an amount representing

the estimated damage suffered through nonperformance of the act, and is payable to the party to whom the performance was to have been rendered. Commonly seen in larger construction contracts. See also *surety bond.*

pergola — a lightweight outdoor structure similar to an arbor or trellis, usually consisting of a row of parallel columns supporting an open roof of wood slats covered by vines; a covered walkway.

perimeter — (1) the outer boundary or edge of a parcel of land; (2) the length of the boundary of a parcel of land.

perimeter heating — (also called "baseboard heating") room heating from heat sources at the base of the walls.

periodic costs — certain fixed costs, such as property taxes and insurance, associated with ownership of real property, that recur at regular but infrequent intervals.

periodic tenancy — a leasehold estate defined by its term: week to week, month to month, year to year, etc. It may be established by contract or by judicial construction. The intervals between rent payments can establish the periodicity of the estate. Periodic tenancies can be terminated only at the end of the period by proper notice. See, by contrast, *tenancy at will.*

permanent loan — (also called takeout loan) a long -term mortgage made to pay off a short-term mortgage such as a construction or bridge loan.

permissive waste – the actionable failure of a tenant to maintain a property in reasonable repair, especially in an emergency in which the tenant's failure to act causes damage to the property. Failure by a tenant to notify a landlord of broken windows that allow rain to damage a property would be permissive waste.

perpetuity – (1) lasting until the end of time; (2) the illegal restraint on alienation of property for a length of time greater than the life of a person "in being" plus 21 years. See also *rule against perpetuities*.

person – a legal entity, usually defined by statute as one who (which) can enter into contracts, sue or be sued, or is otherwise afforded legal standing. Depending on the circumstances and the applicable law, a person may be a "natural person" (an individual), a partnership, a corporation, a municipality, or a foreign government.

personal liability – a type of legal responsibility for a debt or other obligation that places at risk the personal assets of the responsible party. It may be established by contract, by statute, or by judicial determination. Some real estate loans are "recourse" loans, which means that the borrower bears personal liability and that the assets of the borrower beyond the collateral of the real property may be at risk in the event of a default. See also *antideficiency laws* and *nonrecourse loan*.

personal loan – a loan made on the strength of the credit of the individual, absent collateral. Personal loans are unsecured and typically carry higher rates of interest than do secured loans such as mortgages.

personal property – (also called "personalty") all property other than real property; property that is tangible, movable, and not permanently attached to real property, or rights to intangible property, such as the right to benefit from a contract or bargain or to receive a royalty. See also *chattels* and *real estate*.

personal property broker – (1) a pawnbroker; (2) a lender who makes loans secured by personal property.

personal representative – the modern term for a person designated in a will as an executor or administrator. See also *executor/executrix*, and *administrator/administratrix*.

personalty – See *personal property*.

petition – a formal written request made of a government agency or official.

petition in bankruptcy – a paper filed by a debtor with a bankruptcy court that initiates the process of bankruptcy. See also *bankruptcy*.

petitioner – one who presents a petition to a court or other official body. See also *petition*.

petitioning creditor – a creditor who seeks, through a bankruptcy court filing, to have a debtor judged bankrupt. See also *bankruptcy*.

phase 1 audit – a professional environmental survey of a potential building site to determine the presence of environmental pollutants, hazards, and toxins. It includes a review of public records, but not a physical inspection of the site or chemical and biological testing. It is often required by commercial lenders because of the strict liability requirements of the Comprehensive Environmental Response, Compensation, and Liability Act of 1980 (CERCLA). Lenders generally wish to avoid making loans on properties that may require enormous cleanup costs. See also *Comprehensive Environmental Response Compensation and Liability Act of 1980.*

physical deterioration — the wearing-out of a structure (or personal property) either through the natural course of its use or through the lack of proper maintenance.

physical life — the actual length of time an improvement to real property may be usable, without regard for economic or functional obsolescence. For example, the potential physical longevity of a sports stadium may be much longer than its practical economic life. See also *obsolescence.*

picture window — a large fixed-glass window designed to admit light and/or frame a view.

pier — (1) a long, low structure that is connected to the shore and extends out over water, providing access to the water for purposes of strolling, fishing, or docking boats; (2) a pile or caisson driven into or

buried in the ground for purposes of supporting or strengthening a foundation system.

piggyback loan — (1) a loan made by two or more lenders on the same note and deed of trust, with each potentially taking an unequal interest and position of risk. For example, Abel purchases a $1,000,000 property with a 10% down payment. Bank A provides $800,000 in financing, and Bank B provides the remaining $100,000. (2) colloquially, any purchase money financing arrangement in which two or more loans are obtained at the same time through institutional lenders who are each aware of the other's participation in the financing. See, by contrast, *silent second.*

pilaster — a vertical column, either decorative or structural, that is attached to or protrudes from a wall.

pile — a column of steel, concrete, or wood that is mechanically driven into the ground to form a part of a subsurface structural system. See also *caissons* and *piledriver.*

piledriver — a large machine operated by steam or electricity, designed to power a heavy hammer that drives piles into the ground. See also *pile.*

pipeline — (1) a system consisting of pipes strung together in an extended array and designed to convey oil, gas, or water from one geographic area to another. pipelines may extend thousands of miles and may be above-ground, underground, or underwater. (2) colloquially, "in process," a series of steps in a predefined set of procedures. For example, a real estate loan in which the application is complete and is under review is said to be "in the pipeline."

pitch — (1) The angle of a roof expressed in the vertical distance (rise) divided by the horizontal distance (span). A typical sloped residential roof might be a "4 in 12," describing a 4-foot rise for every 12 feet horizontally. (2) a tarlike petroleum by-product used in roofing and some caulking applications.

PITI — principal, interest, taxes, insurance; the combined monthly dollar cost of principal, interest, property taxes, and insurance. These are the elements of a periodic loan payment (principal and interest) plus several other fixed costs of ownership. Depending on the loan, all these costs may be collected by the lender in the total monthly payment, or taxes and insurance may be the responsibility of the property owner. See also *impounds account* and *PITIA*.

PITIA — principal, interest, taxes, insurance, association dues; the combined monthly dollar cost of principal, interest, property taxes, insurance, and association dues. See also *PITI*.

place — (1) street name identifier, usually for a cul-de-sac, as in One Martin Place; (2) the act by a mortgage broker of choosing the lender who will fund a loan for a particular borrower. "The loan was placed with Bank A."

placement fee — a charge to a borrower by a mortgage lender for the service of negotiating a loan between a borrower and a lender.

plain language laws — a variety of federal and state laws designed to prevent confusion by laypersons over the meaning of a statute, contract, or other important document through the method of requiring that such documents be easily understandable to an average reader.

plaintiff — a person who brings or initiates a law suit; the complainant. See also *defendant*.

plank — a long piece of lumber measuring 2 to 4 inches thick and 8 inches or more wide.

planned unit development (PUD) — a planning and zoning term used to describe a subdivision in which the standard available zoning classifications do not apply. A master developer will, with the consent of the local governing authority, establish criteria for development of private and common area parcels specific to that subdivision. These may include special setback requirements, street lighting designs, street width standards, architectural styles, building height standards, land coverage ratios, common area park and amenity designs, and the like. Planned unit developments are often used to cluster homes closer together than would otherwise be allowed by local zoning laws. Unlike in a condominium, individual property owners own the land underneath their homes. See also *condominium*.

planning commission — an official body empowered to develop a master plan for the area and conduct hearings on planning and zoning matters brought before it. It may decide issues on appeal from subordinate staff rulings, applications for variances from the existing regulations, and recommend amendments to the zoning and planning laws.

plans – a set of detailed drawings illustrating the various systems of a structure, such as framing, foundation, electrical, plumbing, mechanical, roofing, etc.

plant – the place where a title company stores its records concerning the title history of real property in its jurisdiction. In the past, these records were maintained and searched on paper. Modern title plants are computerized and often are linked directly to the recorder's offices. See also *title insurance company*.

plaster – a powdered composition of lime, water, and sand that is mixed wet and applied to interior walls with a trowel as a finish material. It dries, becomes hard, and may be painted. See also *lath and plaster*.

plat map – a map of a town, subdivision, or section usually showing property boundaries, blocks, streets, and open-space areas. Subdividers begin the process of subdividing a new area by preparing a proposed plat map and submitting it to the local planning agency.

plate – a horizontal framing member that provides a base for the structure above it. For example, a sole plate is typically a long two by four piece of lumber attached to the

foundation and providing a base for the wall studs. A wall plate is a two by four parallel to the sole plate, laid along the top of the wall and forming a base for another story or the roof rafters. See also *sole plate*.

plaza – (1) a public square; (2) an open area in the center of a shopping complex; (3) the area in which toll booths are located on a toll road.

pledge – the transfer of title or the physical delivery of personal property to another party as security for a debt or other obligation. See pledged account loan for an example. See also *Uniform Commercial Code*.

pledged account loan – a type of flexible payment mortgage in which a certain sum is deposited by the borrower or a third party into a bank account pledged to the mortgage lender to be used as a source of funds to supplement the initial periodic mortgage payments. The account also provides additional collateral for the loan.

pledgee – the party to whom goods are pledged. See also *pledge*.

pledgor – the party who pledges personal property to another. See also *pledge*.

plot – (1) the act of calculating and drawing the configuration of a parcel of land from a description or surveyor's data; (2) a parcel of land on which an improvement is planned.

plot plan – a document showing the boundary dimensions, location of improvements, landscape layout, and other amenities and attributes specific to a particular parcel of land. See, by contrast, *plat map.*

plottage — (also called "assemblage") the act of assembling several smaller adjacent lots under one ownership for the purpose of creating value for the assembled parcel greater than the value for the lots or parcels individually.

plottage value — the increase in value resulting from adding an adjacent parcel or parcels to an existing parcel. For example, if three smaller parcels are purchased for $250,000 each, and the larger parcel formed by joining the three is worth $1,000,000 (because that land may now be put to a higher use), the plottage value is $250,000.

plumb — (1) true vertical. "Plumb and square" means that a structure or a part of a structure, such as a window or door opening, is perpendicular to the ground and that its corners form right angles. (2) a weight (plumb bob) attached to and suspended from a line or cord for determining a perpendicular line; (3) the act of installing piping and fixtures for plumbing.

plumbing — the piping and fixtures constituting a fresh- and waste-water system for a structure. Pipes, faucets, sinks, tubs, and toilets are all part of the plumbing.

ply — a layer of material in a multi-layer matrix or surface, as in plywood or belted tires.

plywood — sheets of wood comprised of three or more layers of ve-neer glued together. Plywood is commonly used as subfloor, roof decks, or exterior sheathing. Plywood is sold with both interior and exterior glue formulations. It comes in thicknesses ranging from 1/8 inch to 1 inch or more. The most common size is a 4-foot by 8-foot sheet, although other sizes are available. It may be engineered to resist stresses and used as a component of a shear wall. See also *shear wall* and *sheathing.*

PMI — See *private mortgage insurance.*

pocket card — an identification card issued by some states to indicate that the holder is a real estate licensee. It contains information such as the license number, expiration date, and type of license held.

pocket listing — an arrangement in which a seller has not signed a listing agreement but has made it known to one or more real estate brokers that a property might be available for purchase; knowledge of a potential seller who has not formalized a listing contract but is known to be a willing seller under acceptable terms and conditions. The broker cannot place the property in the MLS but has been verbally encouraged by the seller to seek buyers. Only written contracts for commissions are enforceable. In the event that the broker does procure a buyer, a written commission agreement should be signed before the presentation of an offer. See also *exclusive listing.*

point — in lending, a charge equal to 1% of the loan amount, paid to a lender or mortgage broker as an inducement to grant the loan. Points may be paid by either buyers or sellers (except in the case of VA or FHA loans, in which they are paid by the seller) and are construed by the IRS as deductible prepaid mortgage interest when they are paid in connection with a purchase money mortgage. They may be paid out of pocket or added to the loan balance, depending on the loan program. Points may also be used to buy down the loan interest rate for some period of time to make it easier to qualify for the loan. Points are a component of the APR of a loan. See also *annual percentage rate, buy-down,* and *loan origination fees.*

point letter — a letter from a lender to a borrower confirming the amount of points to be paid in connection with a loan. See also *point.*

point of beginning — a phrase used in surveying and legal descriptions that refers to an established point, monument, surveyor's tag, or other surveyor's reference of record which serves as the starting point and point of closure for a metes and bounds description. The description starts and ends at that point. See also *metes and bounds.*

police power — the constitutional authority of a state government, in turn delegated to local governments, to make rules to promote the public order, health, welfare, safety, morals, and prosperity. Established by the 10th Amendment of the U.S. Constitution, it forms the constitutional basis of much regulation concerning land use. Examples of police power

include zoning, eminent domain actions, building and safety codes, rent controls, and the like.

porch — a raised partially enclosed or unenclosed covered extension of a structure used for relaxing or as part of the entrance to a house.

porte cochere — a roof covering the area between a driveway and a building entrance, designed to shelter persons arriving or departing in vehicles from rain and snow.

portfolio loan — a loan originated and then retained by a lender. Not sold on the secondary market. Portfolio loans are not originated using the strict underwriting criteria of the secondary market. They provide lenders with more flexible lending guidelines, accompanied by presumably higher risk. On occasion, portfolio loans may be held for a year or two to verify a payment history, then sold on a secondary market as a "seasoned" loan. See also *seasoned loan* and *secondary mortgage market.*

portico — a formal walkway, entrance, or gathering area characterized by a colonnade-supported roof.

possession — (1) occupancy or control; dominion over an area; (2) in real estate contracts, the time at which control over the property and the right to inhabit it passes from seller to buyer or from landlord to tenant. Possession in this sense may occur at the close of escrow or later.

possessory interest — a right to exert control over a specific parcel of real property to the exclusion of others. Fee ownership and tenancy are examples of a possessory interest.

possessory rights – See *possessory interest.*

possibility of reverter – the future interest left a grantor or his heirs upon granting an estate that might "revert" to the grantor upon the occurrence of a default in a condition of title. For example, if Abel donates land to a school "as long as the property is used for the instruction of children age 5 to 10," there exists the possibility that title to the land will revert to Abel or his heirs if the school attempts to instruct older children using the property. See also *reversion.*

post – to display openly so as to give notice; literally, the attaching of a sign or a document on a conspicuous portion of the property. Posting of property commonly occurs to ward off trespassers, hunters, uninvited dumping, and the like. It may also be a requirement of an eviction proceeding in lieu of personal service of notice.

post and beam – (also called "post and lintel") a style of wood timber construction characterized by heavy vertical members (posts) supporting thick horizontal members (lintels or beams) such as headers and cross beams.

post and lintel – See *post and beam.*

postdate – to place a date on an instrument (such as a check) or other document that is later than the date the instrument is actually signed or

executed. A bank will not honor a postdated check until the date written on the check. In the case of a contract, opportunities for fraud make postdated contracts subject to careful judicial scrutiny in the event of a default or challenge.

poststressed concrete – a method of pouring concrete in which cables in sheaths are threaded throughout the site of the pour prior to application of the concrete. The cables are stretched and held in place, then the concrete is poured. After the concrete has cured, fittings are attached to the ends of the cables, and the tension in the cables is transmitted to the concrete. The technique has the effect of strengthening the concrete and limiting separation cracks.

potable – suitable for human consumption, usually with reference to water.

powder room – a rest room with sink, toilet, and sometimes other amenities such as seating areas, mirrors, and vanities. See also *bathroom.*

power of attorney – a written instrument whereby a principal grants certain powers to an agent (the attorney-in-fact) to act on the principal's behalf in certain situations for a specific period of time. The person so named need not be a licensed attorney, but does bear a fiduciary duty to the principal. An example is a person in the military who will be out of the country for an extended period and gives his or her spouse a power of attorney to purchase or sell a car or other property, open a bank account, settle a debt, etc. Powers of attorney may be general, giving the representative broad powers to act in a variety of circumstances for the principal, or special or limited, authorizing the representative to act in one particular capacity or transaction. Limited powers of attorney are commonly used in cases in which one owner of real property is authorized to act for the other in a sale. Powers of attorney may be recorded. See also *attorney-in-fact*.

power of sale — the contractual right of a lienholder to sell property serving as collateral for a loan or other obligation without judicial action in the event of a default. For example, if Abel purchases a condominium with the proceeds of a loan, the lender, the condominium association, and the tax assessor, as lienholders, may all have the power to sell Abel's property in the event of a default by Abel. State laws and lender practices vary considerably on this matter.

practicing law — performing services, such as drafting wills, giving advice concerning legal matters, and construing contracts, for which a license to practice law is required. Real estate brokers often perform activities that appear very close to the practice of law in the context of representing their clients. However, a broker's license may be revoked if it is determined that this inexact boundary has been crossed. As a result, many real estate contracts contain clauses urging both buyers and sellers to seek independent legal counsel.

preclosing — a preliminary meeting between representatives of the buyer, seller, closing agent, and possibly, lender, at which the documents necessary for closing escrow are prepared, discussed, and signed. Commonly used in complex escrows or escrows that are critically linked to other events such as other escrows.

preemption — the judicial doctrine that certain national laws and policies take precedence over state and local laws to the contrary. National clean air and water laws are one example.

preemption right — the right granted by the government to settlers on certain government land to purchase the land occupied by them at a fixed price in preference to other potential purchasers..

prefabricated house — a house partially or completely manufactured off-site and then assembled or installed at its final situs.

prelim — See *preliminary title report (prelim.)*.

preliminary costs — certain costs incurred in advance of and in preparation for a construction project. Such items as feasibility studies, market research, standby financing costs, and legal fees may all be preliminary costs.

preliminary title report (prelim) — a document issued by a title company in advance of the issuance of title insurance on a particular parcel of real property. It shows the condition of title as of the date of the creation of the report. Recorded liens such as mortgages and tax liens, recorded encumbrances such as easements and CC&Rs, and other items of record are noted and excluded from the proposed title policy as "exceptions to title." The report is not a guarantee that all items potentially affecting title are reflected. It forms the basis of the title company's willingness to issue title insurance but is not intended as a binding commitment to do so. See also *title* and *title insurance*.

premises – the entire property that is the subject of a document, lease, or contract. It may include the property site itself, the grounds, common areas, and other facilities that are intended to accompany the right to enjoy the property.

premium – (1) the periodic or one-time charge for obtaining insurance; (2) an additional charge for a special characteristic of an item, such as quality, scarcity, or other unusual and desirable attribute. Builders typically charge lot premiums for the most desirable lots in a development.

prenuptial agreement – a contract entered into prior to a marriage by prospective spouses in contemplation and consideration of the marriage. It seeks to establish an agreed division of property rights in the event of a divorce or the death of one or both spouses.

prepaid interest – interest paid before it has accrued and is due. The IRS disallows deductions for most

forms of prepaid interest with the important exception of points paid to obtain a purchase money mortgage, if they are reasonable and customary. These are deductible in the year they are paid. Points paid in connection with a refinance must be deducted over the life of the loan. See also *interest* and *points*.

prepaid items – costs associated with property ownership that may be due and payable at some later point in time but that are collected in a lump sum at the time of sale. Examples include taxes, insurance, and association dues. Some lenders, notably the VA and FHA, require that these funds be held in a reserve or impound account, and paid out as they are due. See also *impound account*, *reserves*, and *reserve account*.

prepayment – a payment, usually associated with a loan, made in advance of its due date. This may refer to the inclusion of extra interest in a monthly payment, or it may refer to the payment of the entire balance prior to the end of the financing term.

prepayment penalty – a contractually established fee paid by a borrower to a lender in the event of an early payoff of all or a significant fraction of a loan. A prepayment penalty clause is often associated with adjustable rate mortgage loans or loans with low up-front costs. In theory, it compensates the lender for the profit that the lender would have received had the loan been held for the full term. In many states, prepayment penalties are limited by law.

For example, the borrower might be allowed to pay off up to 20% of the principal each year without penalty, effectively limiting the time the penalty may be charged to five years. The penalty might be limited to six months' interest, but note that lenders may calculate the interest at the maximum rate the adjustable rate loan could have reached over the life of the loan, not at the actual rate at the time of the prepayment. The possibility of a prepayment penalty must be disclosed to borrowers in advance.

prepayment privilege — a contractual right granted under the terms of a loan to pay all or part of the unpaid balance without penalty at any time prior to maturity. In general, partial prepayments are applied to the payments due at the end of the loan, shortening the loan period but not providing a window in which no payments are due. See also *prepayment penalty.*

presale — an older practice in which builders offered condominiums or other properties for sale before they were built, in an effort to secure financing for the project. More recently, builders are required by law to wait until a final public report is issued and construction is under way. As a substitute, many builders ask potential buyers to sign an "interest list." Those doing so will be the first contacted when the properties become available for sale.

prescription — a method of acquiring the right to use a portion of the property of another through con-

tinuous usage of that portion of the property. See *prescriptive easement.*

prescriptive easement — a right to use the property of another in a manner not inconsistent with the owner's use. It is acquired by open and notorious usage adverse to the owner's interest over a statutory period of time (such as 20 years). For example, if Abel very publicly uses a path on Baker's property to reach the lakefront over the statutory period of time, he may acquire a prescriptive easement to continue the use which will run with the land and be valid against subsequent purchasers of Abel's land. See also *adverse possession.*

present value — a method of arriving at an appropriate price or value today for the right to receive either a level cash flow over time (present value of annuity), or a lump sum later in time (present value of 1). The essence of the concept is that money received today is generally preferred over money received later. The quantification of that preference is what determines the prevailing rate of interest at given time. See also *present value of annuity* and *present value of one dollar.*

present value of annuity — the value today of a level stream of income over a fixed number of periods, given a fixed rate of interest. See also *present value.*

present value of one dollar — the value today of one dollar received at a specific time in the future. See also *Inwood tables* and *present value.*

presumption – a judicial rule allowing the inference of a fact or circumstance from a known fact. For example, a homeowner who has lived for years in a house with a leaky roof may be judicially presumed to have known about the leak. Presumptions are generally subject to challenge or rebuttal.

prevailing party – the winning party in a lawsuit. Many real estate contracts provide that the losing party will pay the prevailing party's attorney fees.

prevailing rate – the average interest rate charged by lenders at a particular point in time for a particular type of loan. See also *prime rate*.

price – the consideration or value asked or paid to acquire goods or services. See also *asking price*.

price fixing – the illegal cooperative or collusive setting of price levels by competitors within an industry. In real estate, commissions are not set by law, but are subject to negotiation.

price takeoff method – See *quantity survey method*.

prima facie – Latin term meaning "at first sight"; obvious; presumed to be true unless rebutted.

primary mortgage market – business within the mortgage industry that originate mortgage loans. Examples include banks, savings and loans, credit unions, and mortgage bankers. Many of these loans are then packaged and sold to investors on the secondary mortgage market.

See also *secondary mortgage market*.

prime contractor – See *general contractor*.

prime lending rate – See *prime rate*.

prime rate – the rate of interest that the largest banks charge for short-term commercial loans to their most credit-worthy customers. This is usually the lowest rate of interest available for general commercial transactions other than real estate. Many large construction loans are tied to the prime rate in a formula such as "the monthly prime rate of Bank A plus three points." Some adjustable rate mortgage loans use it for the index portion of the interest rate computation as well.

prime tenant – the predominant or major tenant in a commercial or retail development. Typically, it is the tenant with the largest space, is the most visible, attracts large numbers of customers to the site, and is the economic key to the development in terms of rent paid and secondary traffic to smaller tenants.

primer – a type of paint intended to be applied before other paints. It is designed to adhere to both the base (the material being painted) and the topcoat (the final finish coat).

principal – (1) in contractual matters, the person who authorizes an agent to perform certain acts; (2) in lending, the amount of money borrowed or owing on a debt; (3) the main parties in a transaction. See, by contrast, *principle*.

principal balance – the amount owing on a debt at a particular point in time. In an escrow, the escrow officer will ask the seller's lender(s) for a determination of the principal balance on any outstanding loans on a property for the purpose of arranging payoffs. See also *demand*.

principal meridian – (also called "prime meridian") a geographical reference line running north and south and forming the regional basis for a government survey legal description of property. See also *base line* and *government rectangular survey method*.

principal residence – for income tax purposes, a dwelling occupied by an individual for at least two of the most recent five years. Federal income tax law treats gain on the sale of a principal residence more favorably than gain on the sale of other property. Current law allows individuals to sell their principal residence once every two years and earn up to $250,000 in capital gains tax-free. Married couples may earn up to $500,000.

principle – a fundamental truth; a settled concept. See, by contrast, *principal*.

prior appropriation – the right to continue to divert water from a public or shared source of water based on the history of past diversion.

priority – order of importance. In real estate transactions the general rule is that chronology controls priority, such as first deed to record, first encumbrance to be recorded,

and the like. Notes secured by trust deeds and mortgages will be honored or satisfied in foreclosures according to their priority of recordation. A third mortgagee might be paid in a foreclosure only in the event that there were sufficient funds from the sale of the property to pay the first and second mortgagees. Priority may be altered by agreement, by law, or by judicial order. See also *subrogation*.

priority clause – a clause in a junior lien or mortgage that specifically acknowledges or consents to the priority or superiority of another lien.

private land grant – a grant of land by the government to a private individual.

private mortgage insurance (PMI) – a form of insurance developed to protect lenders who offer high loan-to-value ratio mortgage loans. Loans exceeding an 80% loan-to-value ratio may require PMI. For example, if Bank A agrees to make Abel a $190,000 loan on a $200,000 property, it will contact a PMI company and arrange insurance for the first 20% of the purchase price or value ($40,000). The PMI company will charge Abel a monthly premium and possibly a setup fee for the insurance. In the event of a default by Abel, the PMI company will pay the lender up to $40,000 to cover any losses. In essence, PMI acts as a substitute for borrower equity, and the lender is able to offer a 95% loan on nearly the same basis as an 80% loan. This insurance may be terminated when the loan-to-value ratio exceeds 80%, either through appreciation in value or by principal reduction of the loan.

private offering – an offering of a real estate security that is exempt from government securities registration. See also *public offering*.

private property – real or personal property that is owned by persons or entities other than the government.

privity – a mutual or successive relationship based on a direct and uninterrupted interest in property rights. For example, in a real estate transaction, the buyer and the seller are in privity to one another. The real estate brokers involved are not.

pro forma – a Latin term meaning "for the sake of form."

pro forma **statement** – a financial statement based on assumed or anticipated facts, rather than actual results. Commonly seen as part of a prospectus offering a real estate security for sale, it relies on projections of income, expenses, sales, taxable income, and loss.

pro rata – a Latin term meaning "proportionally"; a share or portion of a charge or credit based on a predetermined formula or equitable division. For example, in the settlement of a class action lawsuit, the plaintiffs may receive an equal *pro rata* share of the settlement.

probate – the judicial process of proving the validity of a will and of overseeing the final distribution of the decedent's estate.

probate sale – a sale of property (usually real property) with the consent of or at the direction and supervision of a court of competent jurisdiction. Probate sales of real property listed by a real estate broker may require court confirmation and may be subject to overbid by other potential buyers at the confirmation hearing.

proceeds of sale – the net sums paid to a seller after deducting all settlement costs and satisfying any liens.

procuring cause – the claim made by a buyer's real estate agent that, but for his/her efforts, the foundation for negotiation and the consummation of a sale would not have occurred. Real estate listing contracts often call for the payment of a commission to the (buyer's) agent who is the procuring cause of the sale. In the case of buyers who have been shown the same property by more than one agent, this can be a contentious issue.

profit – (1) the net proceeds of a business transaction after all expenses are paid; (2) the gross proceeds from the sale of real property after all transaction costs (such as escrow, title, and commissions) and any outstanding debt obligations secured by the property are paid minus the original cost of the property to the seller and the cost of any capital improvements made by the seller; (3) any valuable gain.

profit *a prendre* – "right of common"; the right or estate in real property to take or enjoy some of the benefits of land belonging to another, such as soil, gravel, things mined, fruits and vegetables and the like. It differs from an easement in that materials are removed from the land. See also *easement*.

profit and loss statement (P & L) – a document or report in financial record keeping that summarizes all the income and expenses for an enterprise for a given period of time in order to show whether a profit or a loss occurred.

profitability – the degree to which an enterprise or project makes or is expected to make a profit. See also *profit*.

progress payments – portions of an approved construction loan that are distributed either to the borrower or to the contractors performing the work as the work is completed in preestablished stages. The lender typically disburses the funds as significant construction milestones are reached, such as foundation, rough framing, completed electrical and plumbing work, and the like. Such progress payments are designed to give the lender a measure of assurance that the project will be completed.

progression – an appraisal principle which holds that the value of a lesser property is enhanced when it is surrounded by more expensive properties. See also *regression*.

project – any planned construction development consisting of a commercial structure, multifamily units, or more than a few single-family homes.

promisee – the person to whom a promise is made.

promisor – the person who makes a promise.

promissory note – a financial document providing evidence of a debt and the terms under which it will be repaid.

promulgate – to publish or print, as in rules or administrative regulations.

property – anything that is or may be the subject of ownership; the unrestricted and exclusive right to a thing, including the rights to possess, enjoy, use, and dispose of it. Property may be a physical object, an idea, a work of art, a right to receive money, or an ephemeral right to something in the future.

property brief – a factual summary of the characteristics of a property for sale.

property line – See *boundaries*.

property management – the practice of leasing, managing, marketing, maintaining, and accounting for the real property of others. Property managers may or may not be real estate licensees, as dictated by state law. See also *Certified Property Manager*.

property report – a disclosure document required by the federal Interstate Land Sales Full Disclosure Act for subdivided lots sold using mechanisms of interstate commerce, such as mail, e-mail, fax, and telephone. It provides information con-

181

cerning the property and any planned improvements and gives the prospective purchaser from two to seven days to cancel the transaction. See also *Interstate Land Sales Full Disclosure Act*.

property tax — an tax assessed by state or local governments on real or personal property according to its value. Property taxes paid on real estate are generally distributed to state and local agencies to pay for schools, police and fire protection, and welfare. Some components of the property tax may be fixed, such as a school tax of $1,500.00 or a sewer bond of $25.00. The *ad valorem* portion of the tax is determined by the assessed value of the property times the tax rate. For example, a property assessed at $500,000 with a general tax rate of 2% will be taxed $10,000 for the year. Sometimes that tax rate is expressed in mils, or thousandths of a dollar, and sometimes it is simply expressed as "dollars of tax per one hundred dollars of value."

proprietary lease — a written lease used in the co-op form of ownership. In a co-op the buyer is both a stockholder in the co-op and a tenant. The buyer signs a lease in which he or she is authorized to occupy a particular unit. The rent is not fixed but is based on a proportional share of the ownership costs. See also *co-op*.

proprietor — the owner/operator of a business.

proration — the amount of or the act of determining a portion or share of a cost or benefit to be allocated

between two parties. Escrow officers must generally prorate taxes, association dues, interest, and insurance between the buyer and the seller at the close of escrow to ensure that each party pays the costs fairly attributable to it. For example, if the seller has paid property taxes in advance for a full year, and the escrow closes midyear, the escrow officer will prorate the taxes, giving that seller a credit from the buyer for the amount of tax the buyer would have otherwise been required to pay. See also *pro rata*.

prospect — (1) to mine or search for a valuable commodity. In real estate the term is used to identify the efforts used to find or cultivate potential buyers and sellers of real property. See also *farm*. (2) a person who has been identified as a potential client for a real estate broker or agent.

prospectus — a written disclosure of the financial implications of making a particular investment in a publicly offered security and required by law for most public offerings. See also *public offering*.

proxy — (1) a substitute; (2) a person empowered to cast the vote of another (e.g., the voting in a board of directors); (3) a document authorizing one person to act for another.

public domain land — land held or managed by the government for the use of the public.

public housing — housing built, provided by, or subsidized by the government for the benefit of the economically disadvantaged.

public land – land owned by governmental or quasi-governmental agencies when it is offered for sale.

public land system – a system of description of land for purposes of creating official records.

public offering – an offer to sell securities to the "public," as it is defined by various governmental agencies.

public records – documents filed and maintained by a governmental public repository for the purposes of safekeeping and for imparting constructive notice to the public as to the existence of documents, the date filed or recorded, and the parties to the document. These documents are admissible in a court of law and may be inspected by members of the public. Recorded wills, building permits, recorded trusts, and deeds are all examples of public records. See also *constructive notice.*

public report – a report prepared by a residential subdivider and required by law to be given to a prospective purchaser of a lot. It discloses matters pertaining to the condition of the development, the amenities planned, and the financial responsibility of the subdivider for the property to be sold.

public sale – an auction sale conducted after adequate notice at places and times accessible to the public to accomplish a conveyance required by law or contract. Sheriff's sales, trustee's sales, and tax sales are examples of public sales.

public utilities commission – a state agency empowered to regulate and set reasonable rates for public utilities. See also *public utility.*

public utility – a provider of essential public services or benefits, such as electricity, gas, water, cable television, and phone service. Companies providing these services are thought to have monopoly power and are generally regulated by a state public utilities commission.

PUD – See *planned unit development.*

puffer – a shill; a person employed to bid falsely or negotiate in order to inflate the price for his or her principal's benefit.

puffing – an exaggerated expression of opinion by a seller or a salesperson intended to induce a buyer to purchase. Not a misleading statement of fact. For example, the statement "This is the finest house you will ever find" might be puffing.

punch list – a list of defects or requested corrections compiled at the end of a construction process by a buyer, owner, architect, or other interested party. It details the final changes and fixes that are required before the project will be deemed acceptably complete. It is common practice for tract homebuilders to require escrow to close before all items on a punch list are complete. State builder liability laws and builder warranty policies are designed to ensure that the defects are corrected quickly following the close of escrow.

punitive damages – (also called "exemplary damages") money awarded to a plaintiff in a judicial proceeding that is intended to punish the defendant for particularly egregious behavior. Punitive damages are awarded separately from and in addition to compensatory or actual damages, which are damages for the actual loss of property or money.

pur autre vie – contemporaneous with the life of another. An estate *pur autre vie* is a property right in land held by one person as long as some other person is alive.

purchase agreement – a form, which when completed and signed by the appropriate parties, constitutes a binding contract.

purchase and leaseback – See *sale–leaseback.*

purchase money mortgage – (1) a mortgage entered into with a lender for the purpose of obtaining the cash used to purchase the property secured by the loan. See also *hard money loan* and *soft money loan.* (2) a mortgage loan given by a seller to a buyer to purchase the real property of the seller.

purchase money trust deed – See *purchase money mortgage.*

pylon – (1) a vertical structure to which high-power electric lines are attached; (2) a massive structure flanking an entry or the approach to a bridge.

pyramid roof – a roof in the shape of a pyramid, that is, a four-sided figure where the tops of the four roof sections meet at either a point or at a short ridge.

pyramid scheme – an illegal business enterprise in which investors are promised high returns, which are then paid from the funds received from new investors rather than from any actual profits the enterprise may make. Inevitably, the scheme collapses, as it becomes impossible to secure enough new investment.

pyramid zoning – the zoning practice of allowing less intensive land uses in more intensive zone designations. For example, a light industrial use would be permitted in a zone designated as heavy industrial. See also *zoning.*

pyramiding – the process of using the appreciation in real estate already owned to borrow more funds with which to acquire more real estate.

quad – (1) quadrant; (2) four of something; (3) an open space such as a plaza, usually bounded by buildings.

quadrangle – a square measurement of land area, 24 miles on each side, used in the government rectangular survey method. Each quadrangle contains 16 townships. See also *government rectangular survey method* and *township.*

quadrant – (1) one-fourth of a circle; (2) one corner of an intersection of two streets.

quadruplex – (also called a "fourplex") a multifamily residential structure containing four individual living units or apartments. A quadruplex is traditionally the largest multifamily structure qualifying for financing through government-insured and conventional financing sources. Sources of funding for five units and higher are more limited and tend to be more expensive.

qualified buyer – a buyer of real estate with the financial capability and creditworthiness (or the cash) to purchase a property at a particular price. In many states this qualification may be established through a prequalification letter from a lender or a verification of deposits by a bank or other financial institution. In some jurisdictions, the listing contract provides that the real estate broker is owed a commission immediately upon procuring a qualified buyer who agrees to the seller's price and terms. In many others, the commission becomes due only upon the consummation of the sale.

qualified fee – fee interest in real estate that may continue forever, but that also may end upon the occurrence of a specified event. An example is a grant of land to a school "as long as the land is used for educational purposes." If the school sells the land or changes its use, the land reverts to the grantor. Also called a *fee determinable*. See also *defeasible, fee, fee simple,* and *fee simple determinable.*

qualify – to meet the minimum criteria for approval of a particular loan. In many cases, both the borrower and the property must qualify. The borrower must meet the financial and credit criteria, and the property must appraise at a value sufficient to support the loan. See also *appraisal.*

quantity survey method – a cost estimating system that identifies all material and labor required to complete a job and then assigns costs to each element according to stage or module of assemblage or construction. It is most commonly used by construction cost estimators when bidding a job. Same as *unit-in-place method.*

quantum meruit – a Latin term meaning "as much as he deserves." It is an equity concept, applied by the courts to situations in which one party has received goods or services from another absent a specific or enforceable contract to pay for them. The law implies a promise to pay a reasonable amount to avoid unjust enrichment. See also *unjust enrichment.*

quarry tile – (1) natural stone tile, cut to shape rather than formed by hand or machine; (2): a variety of unglazed ceramic or clay tiles.

quarter – (1) See *quarter section;* (2) slang term for an area of a city.

quarter round – molding, usually made of wood, which in cross section has the shape of a quarter circle. See also *molding.*

quarter section – a square measurement of land area 2,640 feet on each side. It is equivalent to 160 acres and was traditionally the amount of land granted to homesteaders by the federal government in an effort to settle and develop frontier territory. See also *government rectangular survey method* and *section*.

quash – to annul, render void, or set aside. To quash a summons is to withdraw it.

quasi – as if it were; almost; analogous to; something that has the appearance of something else.

quasi-contract – the creation of rights and obligations inferred from the acts of one of the parties. Where no written or expressed contract exists, the acts of the parties create the inference of a contract.

quasi-judicial – actions or discretionary findings by someone who is not a judge but who is empowered to act in a judicial manner, and whose decisions have the force of law. Examples include actions or findings by representatives of regulatory agencies such as zoning commissions.

quay – a wharf used for the landing of ships or barges.

question of fact – an issue involving the resolution of a dispute over some event or state of affairs. Questions of fact are decided by the "trier of fact": either a jury, or in those cases in which there is no jury, a judge. See also *question of law*.

question of law – an issue involving interpretation of the law. At trial, questions of law are decided by a judge. See also *question of fact*.

quick assets – See *liquid assets*.

quid pro quo – a Latin term meaning "what for what"; something for something. In contract law, the term describes a mutual exchange of consideration. See also *consideration*.

quiet enjoyment – the right of a tenant or owner to use property without interference from others claiming the right to use the property. This term is often seen as a covenant in a deed or a lease.

quiet title action – a legal proceeding in which a property claimant forces another claimant or claimants into court to establish the true ownership of the property. The effect of the court's final ruling is to literally "quiet" the title to the property, eliminating clouds on title and making title marketable. See also *cloud on title, good title, marketable title*, and *title*.

quietus – final disposition of a debt or claim.

quitclaim deed – a deed given to convey whatever right, title, or interest the grantor may have, if any. The grantor does not warrant that he or she does in fact have some interest to the property. As a result, the quitclaim deed is often used to consolidate title in cases where there may be some doubt concerning possible parties to title. A common example is a requirement by title insurers that the spouse of a person who is conveying real estate held as "sole and separate property" execute a quitclaim deed on the property as a condition of title insurance. In essence the title insurer wants to be certain that any claim the spouse may have on the property is waived. See also *deed, grant deed, title,* and *warranty deed.*

quorum – the minimum number of people required to be present at the meeting of a deliberative body before actions of that body may be considered valid. Homeowners' association documents often specify such a quorum to guard against actions taken in secrecy.

R

rabbet – a method of obtaining a strong joint between two pieces of wood by cutting a deep groove in one piece into which the second piece is fitted and glued. See also *dado.*

racial steering – the illegal practice of directing potential buyers or renters belonging to a particular racial group to certain neighborhoods and away from others because of their race. See also *Federal Fair Housing Act.*

radiant heating – a method of heating the interior of structures, usually consisting of electrical coils or hot-water pipes placed in the floor, wall, or ceiling. This method heats the air in the room indirectly. See also *heating system.*

radiator – an exposed room heater that circulates steam or hot water within coils on the surface of the radiator. Heat is thereby transferred to the air in the room.

radon – an odorless radioactive gas naturally produced by rocks underground in certain areas of the country. Radon may build up to potentially unhealthful concentrations in basements or other tightly enclosed spaces. In areas of the country in which radon is known to present a problem, real estate contracts and state laws often provide for a radon inspection clause for buyers of real property.

radon testing – a real estate inspection designed to determine the presence and concentration of radon gas in a structure. See also *radon.*

rafters – horizontal or inclined structural beams of a building that support the roof. See also *joist.*

rail – (1) a horizontal element of a fence; (2) a finished board or other material designed as part of a stairway for a hand assist, required by most building codes for all but the shortest stairways; (3) a waist-high or taller barrier around a balcony, deck, or roof, designed to prevent persons from falling; (4) bands of steel on which trains and certain commuter vehicles move.

rake – a slope or incline from the perpendicular; the angle of incline, such as that measuring the rising floor of a theater. See also *rise.*

ranch-style house – originally, a

large, rambling, western-style, single-story house with a low pitched roof. The term now is used to describe virtually any single-level home.

range — (1) a strip of land 6 miles long, determined by a government survey, running in a north–south direction, lying east or west of a principal meridian. See also *government rectangular survey method, meridian,* and *township.* (2) a cooking stove with open burners or electric elements and an oven.

range lines — a series of government survey lines running north and south at 6-mile intervals, starting with the principal meridian and forming the east and west boundaries of townships. See also *government survey method, meridian,* and *township.*

rat wall — a low perimeter foundation wall that is both below and above grade, intended to prevent rodents and varmints from accessing the crawl space or sub-floor area.

ratable estate — property qualifying for taxation.

rate adjustment date — with respect to an adjustable rate mortgage, the date on which the borrower's interest rate may change. See also *adjustable rate mortgage, interest cap,* and *margin.*

rate index — any index established by, or designated in, an adjustable or variable interest rate loan as the reference or benchmark for changing the indexed rate component of the interest rate. Examples of a rate index are the LIBOR, 11th District cost

of funds, moving average of one-year T-bills, and the prime lending rate. See also *variable rate mortgage.*

rate of return — the financial return expressed as a percentage measuring the periodic earnings (either before or after expenses) against the initial investment, proposed purchase price, or appraised value. Such rates are usually and more meaningfully defined as rate of return on equity, after-tax rate of return, internal rate of return, financial management rate of return, net present value, and the like—each of which has its own particular relevancy in terms of the objective of the measurement. See also *internal rate of return* and *net present value.*

ratification — the adoption or approval of an act performed on behalf of a person without previous authorization, such as the approval by a principal of previously unauthorized acts of an agent after the acts have been performed. Ratification renders the prior act binding on the person who ratifies.

raw land — unimproved land; land in its natural state. See also *vacant land.*

raze — demolish, as in razing a building.

ready, willing, and able buyer — a buyer who is presently prepared to enter into a binding contract, wants to buy, and meets the financing and any other requirements of the purchase. The term is sometimes used in real estate listing contracts to indicate that only a broker who has procured such a buyer is entitled to a commission.

real estate – land and anything permanently affixed to the land. Examples include structures and items permanently attached to structures, such as wall-to-wall carpet, cabinets, built-in appliances, etc. Also called "real property." Those things that are not real estate are personal property. See also *fixtures* and *personal property*.

real estate agent – a licensed real estate salesperson. Real estate agents work under the supervision of a real estate broker and are licensed by the state to perform real estate services for a fee. See also *agent, licensee, real estate broker*, and *salesperson*.

real estate board – a trade organization whose members consist primarily of real estate brokers, salespersons, and professional persons in real estate–related industries. Most real estate boards sometimes also operate or own the local MLS service. They are usually members of the National Association of Realtors® (NAR) and the state association of Realtors®, and operate as nonprofit organizations governed by a board of directors elected from among the members. See also *association of Realtors®, multiple listing service* and *National Association of Realtors®*.

real estate broker – a real estate professional licensed by the state to sell real estate and oil and gas interests, to originate and sell mortgages, and to supervise other licensees, both salespersons and brokers. The principal broker of a real estate business is generally responsible for the acts of the licensees under him or her. The real estate broker's license is often more difficult to obtain than a salesperson's license, sometimes entailing a minimum work experience period and a more extensive test. See also *broker*.

real estate commission – (1) See *department of real estate*; (2) the type of fee paid to a real estate broker for professional services that is contingent on a particular result, such as the sale or rental of a property. Real estate professionals may charge other fees that are not commissions. See also *advance fees* and *commission*.

real estate contract – a document evidencing a sale or lease of real property.

Real Estate Investment Trust – See *REIT*.

real estate license – a state license granted to real estate salespersons, brokers, and in some states, real estate lenders, authorizing them to perform real estate services for other persons within that state. The license generally requires a course of study, a test or tests, a background check, and a commitment to continuing education. Broker's licenses may also require a period of experience as a salesperson. See also *license* and *real estate licensee*.

real estate licensee – the holder of a real estate license. In most states, a real estate licensee must disclose this fact to other parties in a transaction in which the licensee is a principal. See also *real estate license*.

real estate market — the balance between the supply of real property and the demand for it in a particular location at a particular time. See also *buyer's market* and *seller's market*.

real estate owned (REO) — real property that has been foreclosed by a lender and is now owned by the lender. See also *foreclosure*.

Real Estate Settlement Procedures Act (RESPA) — a 1974 federal law requiring the disclosure to borrowers on residential one- to four-unit properties of settlement (closing) procedures and loan costs by means of a pamphlet and forms prescribed by the U.S. Department of Housing and Urban Development (HUD). RESPA also regulates the relationship between real estate brokers, lenders, escrow companies, and title insurers, and generally prohibits kickbacks, referral fees, or steering agreements among them.

real estate syndicate — an organization of investors, usually in the form of a limited partnership, who have joined together for the purpose of pooling capital for the acquisition of real property interests.

real estate trust — a special arrangement under federal and state law whereby investors may pool funds for investments in real estate and mortgages and yet escape corporation taxes, profits being passed to individual investors who are taxed.

real property — same as *real estate*.

real property loan law (California) — See *mortgage loan broker law*.

real property sales contract — an agreement to convey title to real property upon satisfaction of specified conditions that does not require conveyance within one year of formation of the contract. See also *contract for deed* and *installment sale*.

real property securities registration — the general process of notifying the appropriate government agencies, including the Securities and Exchange Commission (SEC) and state securities commissions, of one's intention to offer securities backed by real estate to investors and thereafter complying with all required disclosures to investors. The intent of the registration is to prevent fraud and oppression. There are certain exemptions for the registration requirements for private offerings and securities not offered across state lines. See also *blue-sky laws* and *Securities and Exchange Commission (SEC)*.

realized gain — one measure of the profit made from the sale of a capital asset, usually calculated as the sale price less costs of sale, satisfaction of mortgages, and all other debts encumbering the property. See also *capital asset, capital gain,* and *recognized gain*.

Realtist® — a member of the largely African-American National Association of Real Estate Brokers (NAREB), an organization founded in 1947 and dedicated to promoting equal access to housing for all people. See also *National Association of Real Estate Brokers*.

Realtor® — a registered trademark signifying that the user is a member of the National Association of Realtors® (NAR). Not all licensees are members of the National Association of Realtors®. See also *licensee* and *National Association of Realtors®*.

Realtor®-associate — a real estate licensee who is a member of the National Association of Realtors® and who acts as a real estate salesperson under the supervision of a real estate broker. See also *real estate broker, real estate licensee,* and *National Association of Realtors®*.

Realtors® Land Institute (RLI) — a professional organization within the National Association of Realtors® that provides education and training to members concerning the marketing of land. It offers the professional designation ALC (Accredited Land Consultant).

Realtors® National Marketing Institute (RNMI) — a professional organization within the National Association of Realtors® that provides education concerning marketing, financial analysis, and investment analysis. It offers the professional designations CRB (Certified Residential Broker), CCLIM (Certified Commercial and Investment Member) , and CRS (Certified Residential Salesperson).

realty — of or pertaining to real property, real estate or land, whether improved or unimproved. See also *real estate.*

reasonable — fair, proper, suitable under the circumstances. Contract law often imposes a "reasonableness" standard on the parties for acts that are not specifically described in the contract. For example, if a real estate purchase contract allows a buyer to review and approve the preliminary title report, any disapproval of the report must generally be reasonable. An unreasonable disapproval may be a breach of contract.

reasonable time — any time for performance of some act required by a contract that is established by the parties themselves or by a third-party (judge, mediator, arbitrator) interpretation based on the whole of the circumstances of the transaction. For example, escrows sometimes close several days late. Courts have generally held that such a short delay does not constitute a breach unless the contract language specifies otherwise. See also *reasonable.*

reasonableness — reasonable behavior. See also *reasonable.*

reassessment — a change by an assessor in a value estimate of the thing (usually real estate) taxed, or in the amount of tax based on a formula or reappraisal. See also *appraisal, ad valorem tax, assessment, assessor,* and *property tax.*

rebar — metal rods incorporated in concrete used for structural applications. Rebar also limits cracking caused by thermal expansion of the concrete. See also *reinforced concrete.*

rebate — (1) generally, the return of a portion, or the entirety, of the purchase price or agreed value of a thing purchased or service rendered; (2) illegal kickbacks between real estate service providers. See also *Real Estate Settlement Procedures Act*. (3) a component of pricing in a mortgage loan. Mortgage brokers may use rebates from lending institutions to lower the rate or points charged to a borrower.

recapture — (1) recovery; the recognition of that portion of value previously treated as lost or consumed; (2) in tax law, the retroactive application of ordinary income tax rates to income (usually, the result of accelerated depreciation) that had previously been taxed at a more favorable rate. See also *depreciation* and *capital gains*.

recapture clause — a term found in some commercial leases allowing the landlord to retake possession of the leased premises if the tenant fails to meet financial projections that are part of a percentage lease. For example, if Abel leases a store to Baker on a percentage lease with a rent based on gross sales of $10,000/month or more, and Baker's store did only $3,000/ month in business, Abel would be able to terminate the lease under a recapture clause.

recapture rate — a financial term describing the portion of the capitalization rate required to return the investor's original investment over the life of a depreciating asset or expected holding period, such as an improvement to real property. See *capitalization (cap) rate* for an example.

recasting — a mutually-agreed

modification between a lender and a borrower of existing loan terms, usually as the result of financial distress on the part of a borrower. See also *novation*.

receipt — (1) a*ctual receipt*: the literal possession by a party to a transaction of some document or notice material to the transaction. If Abel hand-delivers his acceptance of Baker's offer to purchase Abel's farm directly to Baker, Baker is said to have actual receipt of the acceptance. (2) *constructive receipt*: an income tax rule that a person is deemed to have received income for tax purposes when he or she is entitled to the money, whether or not he or she actually receives it. (3) *deposit receipt*: in some jurisdictions, a real estate purchase contract is also called a deposit receipt and serves as evidence of the buyer's good faith deposit.

receiver — an entity appointed by a court as a representative of the court to guard against the dissipation of assets that are the subject of litigation or that may be used to satisfy a judgment. See also *bankruptcy* and *trustee*.

reciprocal easements — easements typically found in multioccupant commercial or residential planned developments in which common areas are set aside for the use and benefit of all the occupants. Such easements provide for the mutual and nonexclusive use of parking, sidewalks, elevators, escalators, recreational amenities, and the like. See also *easement*.

reciprocity — (1) mutuality; (2) between states, the mutual recognition of licensed professionals to practice in each other's jurisdiction.

recital — the statement of a fact or premise in a document that forms the basis or justification for the substance of the agreement.

recital of consideration — a formal written statement of the consideration passing between the parties to a contract. It is often found in deeds, and is intended to prevent any challenge to a transfer of real property based on inadequate or nonexistent consideration. See also *consideration.*

reclamation — the act of changing the nature or character of land with marginal value in order to create a higher or better use opportunity for that land and, therefore, greater value. Certain types of reclamation activities commonly practiced in the past, such as draining and filling swamps, damming rivers, and building levees to hold back floodwaters are now environmentally controversial.

recognition — a tax term denoting the point in time at which a taxable event occurs. It may be at the time income is received, or at an earlier or later time, depending on the specific application of the tax laws. For example, the tax on the capital gain attributable to income property may be deferred through the use of a Section 1031 exchange, while tax may be due immediately on interest deemed earned by a taxpayer (as in the case of a no-interest loan to a relative) whether or not it was actually received. See also *imputed interest* and *Section 1031 exchange.*

recognized gain — the gain that qualifies for taxation at the sale or other disposition of an asset. See also *realized gain.*

reconciliation — in real estate appraisal, the process by which estimates of value derived through different techniques (such as direct sales approach, income approach, and cost approach) are analyzed to arrive at a final estimate of value. Reconciliation is not a simple averaging process, and involves considerable judgment on the part of the appraiser. See also *appraisal.*

recondition — to restore a property to marketable condition without a major remodel. See also *rehabilitate* and *remodel.*

reconveyance — (1) the transfer of the title to real property secured by a deed of trust from the trustee to the trustor upon satisfaction of the debt represented by the note secured by the deed of trust. In practice, a reconveyance occurs when an owner pays off a loan and then keeps the property, or when a transfer of the property occurs in which the old loan is paid off through the proceeds of a new loan or by cash. See also *title, trust deed, trustee,* and *trustor.* (2) the document evidencing such a transfer of title.

record owner — the owner of property as described in a recorded document from which ownership is generally inferred. See also *equitable title* and *legal title*.

recordation — See *recording*.

recorded map — a plan or map of a parcel of real property recorded in a county recorder's office illustrating or describing existing or planned improvements and property boundaries for purposes of establishing official and lawful recognition and notice.

recorded plat — (also called a *plat map*) a subdivision map that is recorded with a court recorder. See also *subdivision* and *Subdivision Map Act*.

Recorder — the county public official responsible for maintaining orderly official public records concerning title to real estate within the county.

Recorder's Office — the place where documents relating to real estate title are placed or filed for public notice and reference are maintained.

recording — the process of placing a document on file in a designated public office for the purpose of giving public notice of the subject and parties to the document. Deeds, mortgages, trust deeds, contracts for sale, land contracts, leases, options, liens, easements, and assignments are examples of documents that may be recorded.

recording acts — a general category of legislation enabling and authorizing the filing of certain documents and maps for public notice.

recording fee — fees established at a county level to cover the administrative costs of recording of documents and maps.

recourse — the right of a holder of a negotiable instrument to recover against a party who is secondarily liable. For example, if a real estate broker accepts a deposit check from a buyer, then endorses it "without recourse" to be deposited into escrow, neither the escrow company nor the seller can pursue the broker if the check is dishonored.

recourse loan — a loan in which the borrower is personally liable for the debt in the event that the collateral pledged to secure the loan is inadequate to repay a defaulted loan. For example, assume that Abel borrows $300,000 from BakerBank in order to purchase a $350,000 house. Three years later Abel defaults. The home has declined in value to $250,000, due to adverse market conditions. After BakerBank forecloses and sells the home, Abel would still owe BakerBank $50,000 from any other assets that he may have. See also *antideficiency laws* and *nonrecourse loan*.

recovery fund — a trust fund available in certain states to compensate clients of real estate licensees who have been injured by some dereliction of duty or fraud by the licensee in the course of a real estate transaction. Aggrieved clients may make application to the fund in cases where the licensee is unable or unwilling to provide a recovery. Recovery limits tend to be low.

rectangular survey method – See *government rectangular survey method.*

red flag – a fact which, when it becomes known to a party to a transaction, should alert that party that there may be other, as yet unknown facts or circumstances detrimental to the advisability of the transaction. For example, if a deposit check to escrow written by a buyer of real property bounces, the seller should be alert that there may be financial problems that might make the escrow difficult to close.

red tag – a term used by building officials to describe the posting of notices on a property deemed dangerous or unfit for human habitation. See also *condemnation.*

reddendum – a reservation clause in a deed or lease withholding a portion of the estate from the grantee or lessee.

redeem – to buy back; repurchase; recover.

redemption – buying back one's property after a judicial or lien sale.

redemption, equitable right of – the right of a former property owner to reclaim his or her property after a judicial foreclosure. There is generally no right of redemption in a non-judicial foreclosure. See also *judicial foreclosure, non-judicial foreclosure, redemption, redemption period,* and *trustee's sale.*

redemption period – the statutory period of time in which a property owner who has lost the property to a judicial foreclosure or unpaid tax sale may repurchase the property for the amount of the debt or tax lien plus foreclosure costs.

redevelopment – generally refers to a wholesale reconfiguration and/or rehabilitation of a blighted or distressed area. The new uses may be the same or different from the previous uses. Redevelopment is often accompanied and encouraged by tax incentives.

redevelopment agency – a local government agency charged with planning and overseeing redevelopment projects within its jurisdiction. See also *redevelopment.*

redlining – an illegal lending practice, denying real estate loans in a particular geographic area (usually those containing large minority populations) because of alleged higher lending risks without consideration of the credit-worthiness of the individual applicant. See *Federal Fair Housing Act.*

reentry – the process of lawfully regaining possession of a property occupied by another. A right of reentry clause is sometimes included in a lease document.

referee – a person appointed by a court to act on its behalf in certain routine or administrative matters within its jurisdiction. A common example is a bankruptcy referee.

referral – the recommending to a client of a professional of another specialty, discipline, or geographic area. Real estate agents may refer relocating clients to an agent in their new area.

referral fee — a fee paid to a person who arranges a direct relationship with a professional of another specialty or discipline or geographic area. Referral fees are subject to considerable state and federal regulation and must generally be disclosed to the parties involved in a transaction.

refinance — to pay off a debt with funds from a new, extended, increased, or renegotiated borrowing. Refinances are common when interest rates decline. It may make financial sense to pay the costs associated with a new loan if the new interest rate is attractively below the existing loan rate. Note that in some states, the refinance of a purchase money loan removes the antideficiency protection associated with the loan. The new loan may become a recourse debt on which the borrower is personally liable. See also *antideficiency laws, nonrecourse loan, purchase money loan,* and *recourse loan.*

reformation — an action to correct a technical mistake in a deed or other document.

reformation deed — See *correction deed.*

regional shopping center — a shopping center serving a major population center with at least one major full-line department store and related smaller shops and related complementary uses. Such a center will typically be a minimum of 300,000 square feet, and will be located at or along the intersections of

major arterial roads or highways. Many such centers have become destination centers featuring, in addition to retail elements, lodging, entertainment, transportation, and housing.

register — a gridlike device attached to a ducting system to aid in directing air circulation. See also *duct.*

registrar of deeds — See *recorder's office.*

regression — (1) an appraisal principle holding that the value of a superior property in an area of lower-quality properties is diminished by the presence of the inferior properties; the converse of *progression;* (2) a mathematical and statistical tool of financial analysis that allows estimates of the relative influences a number of variables have on a target variable. For example, a developer might want to perform a regression analysis to determine the relative value to home buyers of location, square footage, amenities, proximity to schools, etc.

Regulation Z — See *Truth in Lending Law.*

rehab — informal for (1) to rehabilitate; (2) a rehabilitated structure..

rehabilitate — the act of repairing, reconstructing, or improving after damage, destruction, or disrepair from neglect to a state or condition closely resembling the original plan and character. See, by contrast, *recondition* and *remodel.*

reinforced concrete — concrete incorporating a grid of steel or iron wire and/or *rebar*. Reinforced concrete can carry greater loads and resists cracking better than unreinforced concrete. It is often engineered as a structural material in place of wood or steel beams. See also *rebar*.

reinforcing – strengthening; a combining of elements in construction to create greater structural integrity.

reinstatement – the curing of a default; a payment or performance that restores a defaulting party to its original position. A borrower in default on a real estate loan typically may cure the default up to the point of foreclosure by paying all sums then due, plus any collection costs. See also *acceleration clause, foreclosure,* and *redemption*.

reinsurance – a form of insurance purchased by insurance companies to spread the risk of the policies it issues among several insurers.

reissue rate – (also called a "short-term rate") a discounted premium for the issuance of a policy of title insurance within a short period of time after the initial policy is issued. The period is usually five years or less from the date of the original policy purchase.

REIT (Real Estate Investment Trust) – an investment conduit designed to provide investors with a tradable interest in a pool of real estate–related assets. REITs are required to pass through 95% of their net taxable income to investors. Ownership in a REIT is evidenced by

shares that are freely tradable. As a part owner of real property, the investor receives capital gain tax treatment on any capital gains.

related parties – parties to a financial transaction who might be expected to have something closer than an arms-length relationship. This concept has primary importance in the Internal Revenue Code. Examples include close family members, subsidiary companies, shared ownership interests, and those parties with fiduciary relationships, such as a trustee and a beneficiary. Transactions between related parties are carefully scrutinized by the IRS for evidence of a transaction that has been illegally manipulated to obtain a tax-advantaged result.

relation back doctrine – in real estate practice, the principle that the death or incapacity of a transferor of real property in escrow at the time of the death or incapacity does not invalidate the transfer. Delivery of the deed to the grantee is said to relate back to the time the grantor deposited it.

release – (1) abandonment of a right, claim, or privilege, whether for consideration, or gratuitous; (2) a document given in satisfaction of performance under a note or other security instrument. In mortgage vernacular it may also be referred to as a reconveyance or discharge. See also *discharge* and *reconveyance*.

release clause – (also called "partial release clause") a contractual agreement providing that a lien as to a specifically described lot or area shall be removed from the blanket lien on the entire area upon the payment of a specific sum of money to the holder of the trust deed or mortgage. See also *blanket mortgage* and *partial release.*

release deed – an instrument executed by the trustee reconveying to the trustor the real estate that secured the loan after the debt has been paid in full. See also *deed of reconveyance* and *reconveyance.*

release of lien – the process by which a recorded lien on real property is removed. For example, if Abel owns a $300,000 house with a $100,000 mortgage, and pays the mortgage in full, Abel will ask the lender to record a lien release, indicating that the debt has been satisfied. See also *lien* and *reconveyance.*

reliction – increase of land area by the gradual withdrawal of a river, lake, pond, creek, sea, ocean, or other body of water. See also *accretion* and *alluvium/alluvion.*

relief – (1) the remedy or redress sought by a plaintiff in a lawsuit. See also *remedy.* (2) the elevations or changes in height of a parcel of land, as seen from above. See also *relief map* and *topography.*

relief map – a map drawn or manufactured in such a way as to illustrate multi-dimensionally the topography or terrain of an area. See also *topography.*

relinquished property – (also called "downleg") the real property

traded or sold in a Section 1031 tax-deferred exchange. The property newly acquired in an exchange is called the replacement property. See also *replacement property* and *Section 1031 exchange.*

relocation – the transfer of a person or family from one city to another when occasioned by a new job or a job transfer.

relocation clause – a lease provision giving the landlord the right to move the tenants to other premises in the event of a remodel, or to accommodate a larger tenant that wants the specific space.

relocation company – a company retained by businesses to facilitate employee moves. Relocation companies assist in the sale and purchase of homes for the employee. They may purchase the employee's home outright (with funds provided by the employer) in order to make funds available for the employee's move and purchase of a new home. Relocation companies typically work on a referral fee basis with local real estate companies in order to sell the acquired homes.

remainder – (1) the remnant of an estate in land linked to and dependent on a prior estate created by the same instrument and at the same time. For example, Jones conveys a farm to Swenson for the life of Swenson, with a remainder interest in Barbanell. When Swenson dies the remainder estate passes to Barbanell. See, by contrast, *reversion.* (2) in a will, the balance of the estate after all specific bequests have been satisfied. See also *remainderman*.

remainderman – the person entitled to the remainder. See also *remainder*.

remediation – the process of cleaning up land that has been contaminated with hazardous substances. It may be required under terms of the Comprehensive Environmental Response Compensation and Liability Act (CERCLA) after an environmental audit. See also *Comprehensive Environmental Response Compensation and Liability Act (CERCLA)*, *environmental audit*, and *Superfund*.

remedy – the means employed to enforce a right or redress an injury. For example, in a breach of contract lawsuit, the remedy might be an award of money damages, or an order compelling specific performance of some act on the part of the defendant. See also *damages* and *specific performance*.

remise – to remit or give up something. Often used in a quitclaim deed.

remnant – a parcel remaining to a property owner after a taking in eminent domain that is of a size, shape, or location that renders such a parcel essentially without utility or value. See also *eminent domain*.

remodel – to change or upgrade the utility of a structure. Implies making structural alterations, not merely cosmetic changes. See, by contrast, *recondition*, *rehabilitate*, and *renovate*.

rendering – See *artist's rendering*.

renegotiable rate mortgage – an older type of short-term loan secured by a long-term mortgage that provides for renegotiation, at predetermined intervals, of the interest rate. See also *adjustable rate mortgage*.

renegotiation – the process of changing or adjusting the terms of a contract. Such a process may involve as its subject the term, premises, rate of interest, amount due, fair market rent, and the like.

renewal – the improved character and enhanced values associated with a geographic area that has been redeveloped. See also *redevelopment*.

renewal option – in a lease, the option (usually held by the lessee) to extend the term of the lease under certain stated circumstances and restrictions. It is designed to give the lessee confidence that the property will be available for an extendable period of time.

renovate – to return a property to its original character and condition. A renovation might include elements of reconditioning and remodeling. Portions of the premises may be cleaned, repaired, and restored, while inappropriate additions might be removed. See also *recondition* and *remodel*.

rent – (1) any consideration named in a lease (or the formula for determining the consideration) owed by the tenant to the landlord for the use and occupancy of the premises; (2) the fixed amount (paid periodically according to a rental agreement) owed by a tenant to a landlord as payment for the tenant's occupancy of real property. See also *landlord, lease,* and *tenant;* (3) the act of offering real property for purposes of tenancy.

rent controls — restrictions on rents, rental terms, and/or rent increases prescribed by local government in an attempt (a) to diminish the effects of rampant rent inflation, or (b) to protect or establish an affordable rental housing stock, however that might be defined.

rent escalator — a clause in a lease that allows the landlord to raise the rent based on a formula tied to some other index of costs. For example, a lease might have yearly rent increases tied to the Consumer Price Index.

rent roll — an independently prepared or certified list of the tenants occupying a building along with the terms of their occupancies. Lenders may require certified rent rolls as a condition of a loan. See also *estoppel certificate.*

rent subsidy — a local, state, or federal economic aid program intended to assist those who qualify as low- or moderate-income wage earners by providing a portion of their rent obligation. The subsidy is usually determined by a formula based on the person's income and the amount of the rent.

rent up — the process of initially renting a new building to tenants.

rentable area — the interior space, measured in square feet, for which rent is charged. Such space is usually exclusive of common areas or areas that are of functional benefit only to the landlord, or which are shared among tenants, such as a common kitchen area, common rest rooms, or an elevator shaft. See also *usable area.*

rental agent — a person who acts as a compensated intermediary between landlords and tenants. In many states a rental agent is required to have a real estate license.

rental agreement — See *lease.*

rental concession — reductions in rent, free rent, free tenant improvements, or other inducements offered by a landlord to a commercial tenant to induce the signing of a long-term lease. Rental concessions are features of slow rental markets and tend to disappear as the market tightens.

rental pool — an agreement between owners of (usually contiguous) rental property to make their units available for rental through a rental agent and share in the proceeds of the rentals, regardless of which units are actually rented. This arrangement is most common in seasonal and resort areas.

rental value — the value of a premises for purposes of determining rent; the amount of rent determined by applying principles of appraisal analysis.

REO — See *real estate owned.*

repairs — a category of work or expense that is intended to restore a property to its initial working condition. A repair is not a capital investment. For example, patching a hole in the roof is a repair; replacing the entire roof is a capital improvement. See also *capital expenditure, capital improvement,* and *maintenance.*

replacement cost – the cost to replace a structure with one having utility equivalent to that being appraised, but constructed with modern materials and according to current standards and design. It is one measure of the value of the building for appraisal or insurance purposes.

replacement property – (also called "up-leg") the real property traded for or purchased in a Section 1031 tax-deferred exchange. The property sold in such an exchange is called the relinquished property. See also *Section 1031 exchange.*

replacement reserves – (also called "reserve for replacements") an accounting term meaning monies set aside in the operating budget for an income-producing property or homeowners' association for the replacement of certain consumable items, such as roofs, pool heaters, and carpeting. See also *replacements.*

replacements – (1) substitutions; (2) consumable or depreciating elements of an improvement to real property that have been or will need to be replaced prior to the full depreciation of the structure. Examples include roofs, carpets, furnaces, water heaters, etc. See also *replacement reserves.*

replevin – a legal action to recover personal property when the payment of money damages is insufficient. Such an action might be brought to recover an heirloom of great sentimental value that was confiscated to secure an unpaid hotel bill.

representation – (1) a statement of fact made to induce another to enter into a contract. If untrue, material, and relied on by the other party, it may form the basis for a lawsuit for rescission or damages. See also *damages, misrepresentation,* and *mutual mistake recission.* (2) any writing, conduct, or utterance that may be taken or was intended to be taken by a reasonable person as a statement of fact; (3) actions taken on behalf of another under the terms of agency. See also *agency.*

reproduction cost – the cost of replacing an improvement to real property with one that is the exact replica, having the same quality of workmanship, materials, design, and layout; the cost to duplicate an asset. Reproduction cost may be higher or lower than replacement cost. See also *replacement cost.*

request for notice of default – a recorded document in which an interested party, such as a lender (especially second trust deed holders) or a beneficiary under a trust, asks to receive written notification should the property become subject to foreclosure by some other party, such as the first trust deed holder, a homeowners' association, or a taxing agency. It is designed to protect the party recording the document by giving timely notice of the risk to their interest. See also *notice of default.*

request for reconveyance – a demand made by a trustor under the terms of a deed of trust for an instrument (usually, a deed in recordable form) from the trustee, indicating the satisfaction of the note securing the deed of trust. The effect of a deed of reconveyance is to acknowledge the satisfaction and to remove the lien of the note and deed of trust from the public record. Such requests are commonly made by escrow companies in a sale of property in which the existing loans will be paid off. See also *reconveyance.*

re-recording – (also called "correction deed") the recording in the public records of an instrument that corrects errors in a previously recorded instrument. See also *reformation.*

rescind – to void or cancel. See also *rescission.*

rescission – the cancellation of a contract and restoration of the parties to the same position they held before the contract was formed. Some, but not all, breaches of contract may give rise to a right of rescission on behalf of the nonbreaching party. See also *cancel.*

reservation – a clause in a granting instrument such as a deed in which the grantor creates and reserves to himself or herself some specific right or interest. For example, Abel sells his farm to Baker but retains a life estate for himself. The life estate is a reservation. Other examples include easements running with the land in favor of the grantor. See also *remainder.*

reserves – (1) in a common interest subdivision, an accumulation of funds collected from owners for future replacement and major maintenance of the common area and facilities or for emergency use; (2) with regard to mortgage loans, the cash a borrower is required to have on hand after paying all loan and property acquisition costs. Reserves of several months' living expenses are sometimes required by lenders as added security in a high loan-to-value ratio loan program.

reservoir – a lake, pool, or tank designed to retain a reserve supply of water for an individual home or an entire community.

residence – a person's home or place of abode. A person may have many residences, but only one domicile. Residence can refer to an actual structure or to the state or country (etc.) in which the individual lives. See also *domicile.*

residence, sale of principal – the residence that is also a person's domicile. Under law, a principal residence is a dwelling in which a person has lived for at least two of the most recent past five years. Federal income tax law now allows individuals to earn up to $250,000 free of capital gains tax on the sale of a principal personal residence. The process may be repeated every two years. For married couples the limit is $500,000. There is no minimum age as there was under previous law. The effect of this change has been to make it easier for persons of all ages to buy more or less expensive homes over the course of their lives as their lifestyles require, with less regard for adverse tax consequences. See also *domicile*.

resident manager – a property manager who lives on the premises of the managed property.

residential building rate – the quantity of residential property construction within a given geographical area, measured in units (housing starts) per 1,000 people over a specified period, usually a month or a financial quarter.

residential property – (1) property intended for or used as human dwellings; (2) houses, condominiums, planned unit developments (PUDs), co-ops, and apartment buildings; (3) unimproved property designated on a zoning map as residential.

residual – that which remains after something else is consumed. The value of an improvement after its economic life has been completed. See also *salvage value*.

residual appraisal process – an appraisal method in which the value of land or improvements is calculated by capitalizing the income attributable to it. The goal is to separate the land from the improvement in a financial model and to determine how much income each is capable of generating independently. See also *capitalization*.

residuary estate – any property of a decedent that remains after the execution of a will, following the

payment of debts, administrative expenses, and all other liabilities.

Resolution Trust Corporation (RTC) – a federal agency created in 1990 as part of FIRREA for receiving and disposing of the assets of a large number of financial institutions that had become insolvent in the wake of the financial deregulation of the early 1980s. The RTC packaged and sold pools of nonperforming loans and foreclosed properties to investors. By the late 1997, with most of the troubled assets liquidated, the functions of the RTC were transferred to the FDIC and the agency was eliminated. See also *Federal Deposit Insurance Corporation (FDIC)* and *Financial Institutions Reform, Recovery, and Enforcement Act (FIRREA)*.

resort property – (1) a property constructed for recreation uses that includes lodging facilities; (2) residential property at or near recreational sites such as mountains, lakes, seashore, tennis or golf resorts, etc.

RESPA – See *Real Estate Settlement Procedures Act*.

respondeat superior – a legal theory holding that an employer is liable for the acts of its employees when a wrongful act is committed while the employee was acting within the scope of his or her duties. The doctrine is often applied to hold real estate brokers liable for the acts of the agents they supervise.

restraint of trade – contracts, combinations, or agreements that tend to or are designed to stifle or eliminate competition, fix prices, or otherwise interfere with the ordinary course of commerce, business, and trade to the detriment of consumers. Restraint of trade is illegal under federal and most state laws. It arises in the real estate industry when brokers attempt to fix commissions, refuse to deal with competitors, or without disclosure steer consumers to settlement service companies (lenders, escrow, title) owned or controlled by the broker. See also *antitrust laws*.

restraint on alienation — a restriction in a grant on the sale of certain property or assets. Because the right to transfer property freely is an important part of the "bundle of rights" enjoyed by property owners, unreasonable restraints on alienation will not be upheld by the courts. A contract that includes a prohibition against the sale of land to "anyone named Smith" will be void as to that restriction. Similarly, covenants based on race, ethnicity, religion, gender, familial status, and handicap are void under a number of antidiscrimination laws. The void element does not generally void the transfer or grant. By contrast, a restriction on a corporation against selling additional stock the effect of which would be financially damaging in a discernible way to the original founding investors might be permitted. See also *alienation* and *rule against perpetuities*.

restriction — a limitation on the use of real property. The two general types of property restrictions are (a) public restrictions imposed by a gov-

ernmental authority having the appropriate jurisdiction in the form of zoning (e.g., Wright purchases land from Hunt that has a zoning restriction limiting the height of any structure to 28 feet); and (b) private restrictions between private parties in the form of covenants, conditions, and restrictions contained or referenced in instruments of conveyance or contained in specific planned community rules. Restrictions may also appear in a deed: "Garza conveys to Harris as long as Harris uses the property for a fishing camp." See also *covenants* and *zoning*.

restrictive covenant — a private limitation on the permitted uses of real property created by deed or other instrument. Sometimes called private zoning. Restrictive covenants run with the land and are binding on subsequent purchasers. An example is a covenant permitting no more than one house per acre on a parcel of land. Restrictive covenants on individual properties are not favored by courts because of the permanent limitations they place on changing uses to which land may be put. Hence, these covenants are construed narrowly by the courts. Contrast with a public restriction arising from zoning restrictions or negotiations with an entitlement-granting entity with the statutory authority to establish and regulate land uses. See also *restriction* and *zoning*.

resubdivision — the process of replatting (remapping) an existing subdivision for the purposes of changing lot sizes or configuration, or street patterns. Occasionally, a resubdivision or replatting is required by a governmental agency when it wants to renegotiate the entitlements associated with the development plan. See also *subdivision map act.*

resulting trust — a trust arising from a court's conclusion that although no fraud has occurred, by virtue of the relationship of the parties and the factual circumstances, title to property has been passed to party A but was intended for the benefit of party B. A is said to hold the title in trust for B. See also *equitable title, legal title,* and *trust.*

retainage — that portion of payment due a contractor for construction work that is held back by the property owner until the work is complete, and either lien releases have been obtained, or the statutory time for filing mechanic's liens has passed. A typical retainage is 10% of the job cost. It is established by contract between the property owner and contractor.

retaining wall — a wall of sufficient structural strength to prevent the lateral movement of earth.

retaliatory eviction — an eviction of a tenant motivated by the landlord's displeasure at some complaint made by the tenant. The Uniform Residential Landlord and Tenant Act, and state and federal laws may protect a tenant against eviction based on a good faith complaint of substandard conditions or the need for repairs. See also *eviction.*

retire a debt — to pay off a loan.

retrospective value — the value of the property as of a previous date. This may be used in matters of probate or descendant estate taxation where the value on the date of death may be required.

return — any of a variety of measures of income received or earned from an investment. See also *yield.*

revaluation — See *reassessment.*

revaluation clause — a lease clause that establishes the timing and methodology of rent adjustment based on the market value of the property. Usually found in long-term leases where the exact rent payable is not predetermined for a future period, it establishes the procedures for selecting a mutually agreed appraiser and appraising the property to arrive at a value to use in a formula for determining market rent. For example, a commercial lease might be based on 1% of the market value per month. If the property is worth $500,000 at the beginning of the lease, the rent will be $5,000/month. If at a later adjustment period, the value of the building is $700,000, the rent will be set at $7,000/month.

revenue stamps — (also called tax stamps) a tax collected at the time of transfer of real property, the amount of and payment for which are evidenced by stamps affixed to the deed or other document of transfer.

reverse annuity mortgage — a form of mortgage in which elderly homeowners receive monthly annuity payments from a lender based on the value of a mortgage placed on the home. The mortgage may come due on a specific date, or upon the occurrence of a particular event, such as the death of the mortgagor. The income may allow homeowners to stay in their homes rather than selling and moving because of financial circumstances.

reverse leverage – the opposite of leverage. A circumstance where the income plus appreciation of the asset against which money has been borrowed is less than the cost of the borrowed funds. See also *leverage*.

reversion – the residue of an estate left by operation of law to a grantor or his or her heirs in a circumstance in which the grantor has transferred less than the whole of his or her estate. Any right to future possession or enjoyment of a property by a grantor or the grantor's heirs. See, by contrast, *remainder*.

reversionary interest – the future interest that a grantor or his or her heirs has in lands or other property upon the termination of the preceding estate. For example, if Abel places a property in trust for Baker for the life of Baker, Abel or his heirs will receive the property by means of reversion when Baker dies. A reversionary interest is identical in principle to a remainder interest except that a remainder interest passes to a third party rather than reverting to the grantor. See also *remainder* and *remainderman*.

reversioner – a person who is entitled to an estate in reversion; a person who will succeed to an estate in

the future as a result of an operation of law. See also *remainder, remainderman,* and *reversionary interest*.

reverter – the possibility that a reversion will occur. For example, if Abel grants land to a church as long as the property is used for religious purposes, there exists the possibility that the land will revert to Abel or his heirs if the church uses the property for some other purpose. See also *reversion*.

review appraisal – a second appraisal of real property for purposes of obtaining a loan. A review appraisal may be discretionary, ordered by the lender to verify the value of a property, or it may be a condition of the particular loan program. For example, many jumbo loan programs require review appraisals. A review appraisal may be a separate and complete appraisal (a field appraisal) or simply a review by a second qualified appraiser of the facts relied on by the first appraiser (a desk appraisal). See also *appraisal, appraiser,* and *jumbo loan*.

revocable – capable of being revoked. See also *revoke*.

revocation – the act of terminating, canceling, or annulling. Most common in the sense of having one's license (driver's, broker's, liquor, etc.) nullified for cause by the authority granting the license. Can also apply to contracts such as real estate listings in which the principal reserves the right to revoke the agency contract.

revoke – to make void by taking

back or recalling; cancel, rescind, annul, reverse.

rider — (1) See *addendum*; (2) a small sign attached to a large one. Commonly seen on real estate signs in which the larger sign contains the name and phone number of the real estate broker or agent, and the smaller sign contains a remark specific to the property, such as "Pool," "Ocean View," or "Sold." (3) additional clause or coverage added to an insurance policy.

ridge — the high point formed by at least one sloping side.

ridgeboard — in roof construction, the board located at the peak of the roof where rafters meet and to which they attach.

right of contribution — the right at law of one who has satisfied some joint obligation on behalf of himself and another party to receive compensation from that party for an appropriate pro rate share. For example, if one tenant in common pays the property taxes on a jointly owned property, he or she will be entitled to compensation from the other tenant in common for that tenant's share. The principle also applies to defendants held jointly liable in a lawsuit. See also *joint and several liability* and *tenancy in common*.

right of first refusal — the right granted by a property owner to any other person to have the first opportunity to purchase or lease a specific property at such time as the owner has a bona fide offer to lease or purchase from a third party. A right of first refusal may not

first refusal may not necessarily contain a preestablished price, term, or other conditions required to complete the transaction. It does not give the holder of the right an immediate or determinable right to purchase the property. It can be construed as an invitation to negotiate which is superior as to third persons. See, by contrast, *option*.

right of reentry — the right of a grantor to resume possession of property upon the occurrence of some breach or failure of the condition of the grant. See also *reentry*.

right of survivorship — a unique characteristic of a *joint tenancy* that gives the surviving tenant (owner) the interest previously held by the deceased joint tenant, without need for, or requirement of probate proceedings. In other words, title passes automatically upon the death of one joint tenant to the other(s). See also *joint tenancy* and *Uniform Simultaneous Death Act*.

right-of-way — (1) the right to pass on or over or to cross another's property (private) or a public transportation structure such as a street, bridge, or tunnel (public). Right-of-way includes but is not limited to the right to drive on a public street, to place and maintain utility service equipment on private property (e.g., the natural gas pipeline from the street to the gas meter) and the like. In this context the right-of-way is an easement. See also *easement*. (2) a strip of land on which train track is constructed. Used in this sense, the right-of-way is the land itself.

right, title, and interest – phrase commonly contained in instruments of conveyance that is understood and accepted to mean that the conveyance purports to pass no interest superior than that held by the grantor. It does not define grantor's right, title, and interest to the subject property. See also *quitclaim deed.*

right-to-use – the legal right to occupy or otherwise utilize a property. The phrase most commonly applies to interests created under a time-share arrangement or a club membership.

rill erosion – erosion or loss of soil caused by heavy rains creating ruts and channels in recently plowed or tilled soil.

riparian – having to do with the bank of a river or stream. See also *littoral.*

riparian owner – an owner of property that includes the bank of a river or stream.

riparian rights – those rights of a landowner whose property borders on a stream or other body of moving water to use and enjoy a portion of the water and other benefits of the watercourse, such as land deposited accretion. See also *accretion.*

riparian water – water that flows below the highest line of normal flow of a river or stream. Not floodwater.

rise – the vertical measurement of a slope in terms of the length of its horizontal plane. Often used to describe the angle of a roof. For example, a typical shingle roof might be

described as a "4/12" or a "4 in 12", meaning that the roof rises 4 feet vertically for every 12 feet horizontally.

riser – (1) the vertical element of a stair step; (2) a pipe or duct rising vertically in a building.

risk of loss – the allocation of responsibility for damage to improvements to real property during the course of a transaction involving that property. Under the Uniform Vendor and Purchaser Act, adopted in whole or in part by many states, the purchaser can void a real estate purchase contract if the property is substantially taken (by eminent domain), destroyed, or damaged without fault on the part of the purchaser prior to the close of escrow or the delivery of possession to the purchaser. Allocation of this risk is primarily by contract, and many real estate purchase contracts specify which party is responsible for loss or damage prior to the close of escrow.

RLI – See *Realtors® Land Institute.*

RNMI – Realtors® *National Marketing Institute.*

road – (1) a rural street without sidewalks or curbs; (2) any street.

rock wool – a fibrous insulation material made from molten mineral rock through which air is blown. When cool, it is applied to wall and ceiling cavities for heat or sound insulation.

rod – (also called *perch*)unit of length equal to 16½ feet.

roll roofing — an asphalt-treated felt material that is rolled in sheets after manufacture. It is unrolled and attached to the roof in the course of installation. It may be left uncovered for an inexpensive, but not durable roof covering, or covered by shingles for greater permanence.

rollover — income tax provisions allowing deferral of tax upon the transfer of some asset until a later time.

rollover paper — short-term debt (often with no payments) that may be extended ("rolled over") to a longer-term form of debt with periodic payments.

Roman bath — a bath characterized by a large tile or marble tub recessed below the level of the floor.

Roman brick — brick of nominal dimensions of 2 by 4 by 12 inches. It is narrower and longer than standard building brick.

roof — the uppermost surface of a structure; the structural element designed to shed water; the top of a building.

roof cover — the outer layer of the roof. It may be rolled roofing, shingles, metal such as copper or steel, or virtually any other material.

roof sheathing — (1) boards or sheet plywood applied to the exterior of the roof rafters and to which the exterior roofing materials are attached; (2) flat material covering the roof and designed to make the roof waterproof. This is often a layer of felt impregnated with asphalt or tar (roofing felt). It is often covered by shingles of wood, clay, cement, fiberglass, ceramic, or some other material (the roof covering). See also *roof covering, roof shingles,* and *roofing felt.*

roof shingles — small pieces of wood, composite material, or fiberglass that are applied to a roof in overlapping rows and designed to protect the roof from wind and rain. Shingles in and of themselves may not prevent water infiltration unless the pitch of the roof is very steep.

roof tile — thick formed tiles composed of clay, cement, ceramic, or other materials and applied to a roof.

roofing felt — thick felt or paper impregnated with a waterproof tar-based substance.

room — an enclosed interior portion of a structure, accessible through a door or doors, and designed for a special purpose such as sleeping or dining or social gatherings.

room count — the number of rooms in a structure. The methodology of room counting varies regionally. Generally the total room count of a dwelling unit will exclude hallways, utility rooms, porches, breezeways, garages, and other rooms which are not primary areas of habitation such as a kitchen, living room, or bedroom. Bathrooms are often counted separately.

roominghouse — a house in which individual bedrooms are rented to paying guests.

rotunda — a circular building or room with a domed roof.

row house – (also called townhouse) a residential dwelling, characteristically two or three stories, with common walls on two sides and attached by those common walls to similarly configured dwellings. See also *townhouse*.

royalty – money paid to the owner of a mineral right to allow removal of the minerals. Examples include oil, gas, stone, sand, etc. royalties are typically calculated on the value or volume of the material removed. See also *depletion*.

RRM – See *renegotiable rate mortgage*.

RTC – See *Resolution Trust Corporation*.

Rule 10-B5 – an antifraud provision of the Securities Act of 1934. It is administered by the Securities and Exchange Commission and prohibits deceptive practices in connection with the sale of any security. Even if the issuer of securities is exempt from the more formal registration requirements of the Act, deceptive practices are still prohibited and subject to penalty. See also *security*.

Rule 147 – an intrastate exemption to the registration requirements of the Securities Act of 1934. In general, the company offering the securities must (a) be incorporated in the state where it is offering the securities; (b) carry out a significant amount of its business in that state; and (c) make offers and sales only to residents of that state.

rule against perpetuities – in common law, the legal principle that no interest in property is good unless it must by its terms vest within 21 years nine months (to provide for posthumous birth) after some life or lives in being at the time of creation of the interest. In other words, the law disapproves the transfer of indefinite estates that may or may not spring into being in the far future. Some states have developed a statutory period different from the common law rule. See also *common law*, *estate*, and *vested interest*.

Rule of 72 – a rule of thumb allowing estimates of the time a given sum of money will take to double at a specified rate of return. The formula is [$72 \div r$ (*the rate of return*)]. For example, at an interest rate of 8%, it will take approximately nine years for the investment to double.

Rule of 78s – a method that many lenders use to calculate the interest due on prepayment in an installment loan where there is "add-on" interest. The effect of the rule is that an early prepayment of the loan will not save as much in interest charges as the borrower is likely to expect based on the assumption that equal amounts of interest are payable each month. For example, in a 12-month loan of $100,000 with 10% add-on interest, the lender is entitled to 12/78 of the total interest charge in the first month ($1,538.46), 11/78 the second month ($1,410.26), and so on. If the loan is prepaid at six months, the lender will be entitled to 57/78 of the total finance charge ($7,307.69), while the borrower would save only 21/78 ($2,692.31).

Rules 506 and 507 — (also called "private placement") exemptions to the registration requirements of the Securities Act of 1934. They are among various regulations designed to define exempt private placements (security offerings that are not made to the public at large). In general, the targeted investors must be either accredited by the SEC (banks, pension funds, insurance companies, and certain wealthy individuals) or otherwise sophisticated with regard to the investment offered. The rules are complex, and a sale to even one investor who does not qualify may make the entire offering subject to penalty.

running with the land — a right or liability passing as part of the transfer of land; a covenant or easement that passes from one owner successively to the next.

rural — having an agrarian quality; concerning the country as opposed to the city or the suburbs of the city.

R-value — a method of comparing the efficiency of various types of insulation, or the thermal efficiency of windows, doors, and roofing materials. The product is assigned a number based on its resistance to the transmission of heat and its manufactured thickness. The higher the number, the greater the insulating ability of the product. R-values of 15 to 30 are common for insulation in residential buildings.

S

S corporation — (also called *Subchapter S corporation*) a type of corporation in which the shareholders are taxed as they would be in a partnership. Although the corporation can retain earnings, the shareholders must pay tax on it in the year it is earned. The corporation itself does not pay corporate income tax. The S corporation also offers investors limitations on personal liability for the debts and liabilities of the corporation. Currently, S corporations are limited to 75 investors. See also *corporation*.

safe harbor rule — any of a variety of formal or informal rules acknowledged by a government agency that, if complied with, offer an individual or business the presumption of legality for activities which might otherwise be subject to case-by-case scrutiny. Examples include tax rules covering Section 1031 exchanges and the enumerated broker practices that lead the IRS to treat real estate salespersons as independent contractors rather than employees.

safety clause — a provision in a listing contract that protects the listing broker's claim to a commission if a sale is made after expiration of the listing contract (and within a specified period of time) by the seller to a buyer who was introduced to the property by the listing broker during the listing period. See also *procuring cause*.

SAIF – See *Savings Association Insurance Fund.*

sale – (1) the actual transfer of title to real or personal property accompanied by consideration received from the party acquiring title. See also *title* and *consideration.* (2) colloquially, an agreement to transfer title accompanied by consideration.

sale-leaseback – conveyance of interest in a property by a seller who simultaneously leases (back) the property in order to maintain uninterrupted occupancy while recognizing a capital gain on the sale of the asset. Most commonly used in commercial property where a single user such as a manufacturing company owns a manufacturing site that it wants to retain, but from which it also wants to generate capital for plant modernization, expansion, or some other corporate purpose.

sales associate – See *salesperson.*

sales comparison approach – See *market approach.*

sales contract – a written or oral agreement that sets forth the terms of a transaction agreed between buyer and seller. A sales contract involving the sale of real property must generally be in writing to be enforceable. See also *Statute of Frauds.*

sales kit – a package of information and supplies assembled to aid the listing presentation and closing or to promote a particular property to a buyer. Such a kit or package would contain the appropriate forms, promotional materials about the listing broker and agent, pens, rulers, measuring devices, camera, and branded leave-behind materials.

salesperson – (also called *sales associate*) a person with a real estate sales (agent's) license who, for compensation or other valuable consideration, performs the acts authorized by the license while under the supervision of a real estate broker. A salesperson (a) sells or offers to sell, buys or offers to buy, solicits prospective sellers or purchasers of, solicits or obtains listings of, or negotiates the purchase, sale, or exchange of real property or a business opportunity; (b) leases or rents or offers to lease or rent, or places for rent, or solicits listings of places for rent, or solicits for prospective tenants, or negotiates the sale, purchase, or exchanges of leases on real property, or on a business opportunity, or collects rents from real property, or improvements thereon, or from business opportunities; (c) assists or offers to assist in filing an application for the purchase or lease of, or in locating or entering on, lands owned by the state or federal government; (d) solicits borrowers or lenders for loans, or negotiates loans, or collects payments or performs services for borrowers or lenders or note owners in connection with loans secured directly or collaterally by liens on real property or on a business opportunity; (e) sells or offers to sell, buys or offers to buy, or exchanges or offers to exchange a real property sales contract, or a promissory note secured directly or collaterally by a lien on real property or on a business opportunity, and performs services for the holders thereof. The acts a salesperson is authorized to perform are more limited than those allowed to brokers. See also *broker*.

salvage value – in taxation, the value below which an asset may not be depreciated, a value determined as if the asset has reached the point of its economic and functional obsolescence; a value that would reasonably be assigned to an asset as scrap. See also *depreciation*.

SAM – See *shared appreciation mortgage*.

sandwich beam – (also called a "flitch beam") a beam comprised of at least two timbers with a steel plate placed between. The timbers and the plate are then bolted together to make one strong beam. See also *glue-laminated beam*.

sandwich lease – a leasehold estate in which the lessor has acquired a leasehold interest from an owner or another lessee, and has in turn subleased the premises to a subtenant. All leases that lie between the original lessor and the ultimate subtenant are sandwich leases. See also *sublease*.

sanitary sewer – a system of plumbing that carries wastewater and waterborne effluent from its source to a treatment facility. This system is usually not intended for stormwater or other drainage requiring treatment different from sanitary sewer or no treatment at all.

SARA – See *Superfund*.

sash – a movable wood or metal frame into which window glass is fitted.

satellite tenant – a tenant in a shopping center who occupies a smaller space than the major or anchor tenants and depends on the anchor tenants to attract business. See also *anchor tenant*.

satisfaction – the discharge or payment in full of a debt or judgment.

satisfaction of mortgage – a certificate issued by the holder of a mortgage when the mortgage is paid in full. It may be recorded to place the world at large on notice that the mortgage has been paid.

saturation zone – the strata of ground below the upper layer where water collects and subsequently feeds springs, wells, and other hydrologic geostructures. It is below the level of surface groundwater and subsurface water that is available to plant roots.

savings and loan association – a federal- or state-chartered depository institution whose primary business is the origination, servicing, and sometimes holding of mortgages on residential property. The distinguishing characteristics between S&Ls and commercial banks are diminishing. Although commercial banks make residential loans, they are more apt to deal in commercial lines of credit, small business loans, auto loans, merchant credit card account transactions, and other types of nonresidential lending. Generally, savings and loan associations are regulated by the Office of Thrift Supervision. Funds on deposit with S&Ls are insured up to $100,000 per depositor by the Savings Association Insurance Fund (SAIF), a division of the Federal Deposit Insurance Corporation (FDIC). See also *bank, Federal Deposit Insurance Corporation,* and *Savings Association Insurance Fund.*

Savings Association Insurance Fund (SAIF) — federally required deposit insurance maintained by savings and loan associations for the protection of their depositors. The fund replaced the *Federal Savings and Loan Insurance Corporation (FSLIC)* and is administered by the *Federal Deposit Insurance Corporation (FDIC).* In general, deposits are insured to $100,000 per account or depositor for loss due to the failure of the savings and loan institution.

sawtooth roof — a roof consisting of a series of single pitched roofs with skylights and resembling the profile of a saw blade. Used in earlier factory design to allow increased light and ventilation.

SBA — See *Small Business Administration.*

scale — (1) in engineering and architecture, a dimensional relationship between an object on a drawing, a map, or a model and the object in the real world that it represents. In architectural drafting it is used to describe the proportion of the size of the drawing to the size of the intended finished product. For example, a map may be drawn on a scale of 1 inch to 1,000 feet. (2) an in-

strument with graduated markings used to measure illustrations and figures in blueprints to establish the size and dimension of the figure represented by the illustration or blueprint.

scantling lumber — boards used in construction that have been cut to nonstandard dimensions.

scarcity — in economics, the lack of supply of some desired commodity compared to its effective demand. See also *demand, effective demand,* and *supply.*

scenic easement — an easement created for the benefit of a particular property or for benefit of the public for the express purpose of maintaining and preserving an existing view or an existing view past another property. A public example is a restriction on development on roads surrounding a park. A private scenic easement might be purchased by a homeowner with a view from a neighbor whose property, if developed past a certain height, would interfere with that view. Similar easements may be granted or reserved in densely built urban areas for the preservation of air and light so that an existing property will not lose its exposure to the warmth and light of the sun or the benefit of a pleasant natural breeze. See also *easement* and *light and air easement.*

schematic design — a preliminary step in the architectural design process between conceptual design and final working drawings where sufficient detail is represented to establish the building's vocabulary (visible elements, facial material, glazing, roofing systems, HVAC, etc.), height, area, volume, relationship of building location to property boundaries, parking, shape, etc. This level of detail is used for preliminary cost estimating, governmental approvals where needed, preparation of marketing plans and materials, and mortgage applications.

scope of authority – in agency law, the range of actions an agent is permitted to undertake on behalf of a principal. It is not necessary that the principal actually approve all the actions, only that the type of action taken is reasonably implied by the agency relationship. The concept is important because, generally, a principal may be bound by the actions taken by an agent within the scope of his or her authority. Moreover, a principal may be liable for the negligent acts of an agent operating within the scope of his or her authority. See also *agency* and *respondeat superior*.

scratch coat – the first layer of stucco or plaster on which another layer or layers will be applied. The second coat is called a brown coat, while the final surface is called a *finish coat*. See also *brown coat, finish coat, plaster*, and *stucco*.

seal – (1) the official mark of a government official or notary public impressed on a document for signifying authenticity; (2) a coating applied to protect from the elements.

seasoned loan – a loan of suffi-

cient age to establish that the borrower has made regular payments according to the terms of the note. This is a subjective criteria used by investors to determine the marketability of the loan or the prospective creditworthiness of the borrower. Certain loans may need to be seasoned before they can be sold on the secondary market. See also *portfolio loan* and *secondary mortgage market*.

second – (1) 1/60 of a degree. In surveying, this is a component of a measurement in a metes and bounds description that uses degrees, minutes, and seconds of a hypothetical circle overlaid on the area to be described. An excerpt from a property description using this method might read as follows: 97° 14″ 25′ (i.e., 97 degrees, 14 minutes, 25 seconds). See also *metes and bounds*. (2) a second mortgage or trust deed.

second mortgage – a mortgage that is junior, or subordinate, to the mortgage that was recorded first in time, or that for some other reason (such as subordination) has been assigned a lower-priority claim against the asset mortgaged. "Second mortgage" is a general term that refers to all junior financing, whether second, third, fourth, or greater in position of priority. It is usually the case that the first mortgage, aside from having been recorded ahead of all other mortgages, contains the longest term, lowest interest rate, and the largest amount financed. A second mortgage, to reflect the presumed higher risk of the transaction, characteristically carries a higher rate of interest, shorter term, and smaller amount financed. In the event of a default and foreclosure, the holder of the first mortgage will be paid first, while the holders of secondary financing instruments will be paid according to their priority until the funds available from the sale are exhausted. A second mortgage may be part of the purchase financing, or it may have been taken out later in time. The source of funds for a second mortgage may be banks, savings and loans, private parties, and even the seller of the property. See also *foreclosure, mortgage, priority, second trust deed, trust deed,* and *subordination.*

second trust deed — analogous to a second mortgage. See *trust deed* and *mortgage* for the differences between the instruments. See also *second mortgage.*

secondary financing — junior financing placed on a property at the time of purchase and as part of the purchase price. Some government-guaranteed loan programs do not permit secondary financing, while others place restrictions on it. See also *junior mortgage.*

secondary location — a location that is not the best location. In a commercial sense, it is the location farthest from the anchor or prime tenants, parking, or general flow of vehicular or pedestrian traffic.

secondary mortgage market — a marketplace for financial instruments where loans originated by institutional lenders and mortgage bankers are in turn sold at a discount in order to replace the funds originally advanced so that additional mortgages may be originated. Large investment banking firms, governmental, and quasi-governmental agencies purchase portfolios or pools of these mortgages, often totaling millions of dollars. The primary lending criteria used in the origination of these loans at the consumer level are established by these secondary market purchasers. These criteria include loan-to-value ratios, buyer income-to-debt and housing cost ratios, credit-worthiness thresholds and maximum loan amounts for conventional-type loans. Typically, after the originating lender sells a loan, it continues to service the loan. That is, it collects the monthly payments and passes the payments to the loan purchaser (less a small servicing fee), oversees the performance of the borrower, institutes foreclosure proceedings when necessary, and the like. These purchasers of pools of mortgages in the secondary market, Federal National Mortgage Association (FNMA or "Fannie Mae"), Federal Home Loan Bank Board (FHLMC or "Freddie Mac"), Government National Mortgage Association (GNMA or "Ginnie Mae"), sell bonds or other publicly traded securities that provide the funding for their purchases of mortgage pools. A primary factor influencing consumer mortgage interest rates is the interest rate that must be paid to the purchasers of these bonds and securities. See also *Fannie Mae, Freddie Mac, Ginnie Mae,* and *servicing.*

secret profit — any sum of money

or other item of value paid to a real estate licensee that is not disclosed to the licensee's principal, the other party in a real estate transaction, and the employing broker. In general, all compensation paid to an agent must be disclosed to all the parties in the transaction. See also *agency, dual agency,* and *Real Estate Settlement Procedures Act.*

section – in government land survey, an area of land 1 mile square comprised of 640 acres. See also *government rectangular survey method* and *township.*

Section 1031 exchange – a provision of the Internal Revenue Code that allows sellers of property held for investment purposes to purchase another, more valuable property, and by complying with certain requirements, defer tax on the gain of the sale until a later time. In general, the property purchased should cost at least as much as the property sold, the new loan should be for at least as much as the old loan, and the seller must either transfer both properties simultaneously, or use an accommodator to hold the proceeds of the sale until the new purchase is consummated. A failure of any of a number of conditions will render the transaction immediately taxable. See also *accomodator, boot, delayed exchange, Internal Revenue Code, like-kind exchange, relinquished property, replacement property,* and *Starker exchange.*

Section 203 (b) – a mortgage insurance program offered by the Federal Housing Administration (FHA). It helps make possible the sale of mortgages in the secondary market, and generally increases the funds available for mortgage loans. See also *secondary mortgage market, Federal Housing Administration (FHA),* and *mortgage insurance.*

Section Eight Program – a federal program offering rent subsidies for low- and moderate-income tenants. The subsidy is paid to the landlord by the Department of Housing and Urban Development (HUD). See also *Housing and Urban Development, U.S. Department of,* and *rent subsidy.*

secured party – a person having a security interest created by a debt instrument such as mortgage, installment contract, or Uniform Commercial Code filing. See also *unsecured loan.*

Securities and Exchange Commission (SEC) – an independent, nonpartisan, quasi-judicial regulatory agency with responsibility for administering the federal securities laws. The purpose of these laws is to protect investors in securities markets and to ensure that investors have access to disclosure of all material information concerning publicly traded securities. The Commission also regulates firms engaged in the purchase or sale of securities, people who provide investment advice, and investment companies.

security – (1) the property pledged as collateral against a debt; (2) written evidence of an ownership interest in an asset or business. Common stock in a publicly traded company is one example of a security. Real estate investments are also sometimes offered in the form of a security. Securities are closely regulated by state and federal laws. See also *blue-sky laws* and *real property securities registration*.

security agreement – a document that creates a lien on personal property in order to secure performance of an obligation. The Uniform Commercial Code (UCC) provides for a streamlined notice known as a "short-form filing" or a "UCC-1" as evidence of a security agreement. It may be recorded against real property on which the personal property is located. It is most commonly seen in circumstances in which a business that owns real property has purchased equipment using the proceeds of a loan. See also *Uniform Commercial Code*.

security deposit – a sum of money in addition to rent, typically paid by the tenant to the landlord at the beginning of the rental term. Some or all of it may be refundable at the end of the tenancy. It is held by the landlord to offset unusual expenses occasioned by a breach by the tenant of the lease or excessive wear and tear on the rented property. The precise uses of such funds and their refundability are governed both by the lease itself and the laws of the jurisdiction in which the property is located.

security interest – the rights of a creditor in the property pledged as collateral. See also *collateral*.

seisin – the actual possession of real property under claim of a freehold estate. See, by contrast, *trespass*.

seizure – the act of taking possession of a property by an officer of court.

self-help – any of a number of extralegal methods employed by landlords to cure a lease default or remove a tenant. Examples include changing the locks, cutting off utilities, removing the tenant's furniture, etc. For the most part, these techniques are illegal. Landlords must generally follow applicable state laws to resolve disputes with tenants. See also *eviction*.

seller – a vendor; one who has sold or offered to sell anything of value. See also *buyer*.

seller financing – a financing method in which the seller extends credit to a buyer for all or part of the purchase price. The seller takes back a note in the amount of credit extended. It is secured by a mortgage or deed of trust, the security instrument. The seller may have a mortgage which is recorded before any other mortgage instrument, thereby creating a first mortgage, or the seller may extend credit in a subordinate position to the first mortgage (a second mortgage). The seller then occupies the position of any lender. He or she receives payments until the debt is paid in full. He or she also will have the right to foreclose if the obligation is in default. See also *creative financing*.

seller's market – an active real estate market characterized by an abundance of buyers compared to the number of homes on the market.

Prices tend to escalate rapidly. Offers are made and accepted at or above the listed price. Multiple offers are common, and seller concessions are rare. See also *buyer's market.*

selling broker – the real estate broker representing the buyer in a transaction. Where dual agency is permitted, the selling broker may also be the listing broker. See also *agency, buyer-broker agreement, dual agency,* and *listing agent.*

SEM – *See shared equity mortgage.*

semiannual – occurring twice in a year. See, by contrast, *biannual.*

sensitivity analysis – in commercial investment property transactions, an analysis of financial performance based on the interrelationship of changing variables. An example is the impact on the return on equity when operating expenses escalate faster than originally projected, or the impact of the bankruptcy of an anchor tenant in a shopping center, or the effect of refinancing on internal rate of return.

separate property – (also called "sole and separate property") property that is not community property in states that have community property statutes. Property owned prior to marriage, or acquired by inheritance and that is not commingled with the community property. If Alice, a married woman in a community property state, inherits $5,000, that money is her sole and separate property. If Alice deposits that $5,000 check into the community joint checking account or uses it to pay off

the mortgage on the community property home, it may lose its separate property classification. State laws vary considerably. See also *community property.*

septic tank – a subsurface container located in areas where there is no municipal sanitation system and into which domestic effluence is discharged for bacterial treatment and subsequent drainage. See also *leach field.*

sequestration order – a judicial writ authorizing the preemptive taking of land or personal property to secure a defendant's performance under a pending or actual court order. For example, the receipts of a business may be sequestered in order to pay court-awarded damages. See also *writ.*

service life – (also called *economic life*) the period of time over which an improvement to real property may produce income above the income the land itself would produce. For example, an apartment building in an urban area might eventually deteriorate to the point at which the value of the land as a parking lot would exceed the value of the land with the apartment building.

service line – a pipe or electrical wire or conduit running from the main line to individual properties or spaces and designed for providing some form of utility service to the property or space.

service of process – an official court-ordered notice given or sent to someone informing them that an action has been brought, that their presence is required to give testimony, or to otherwise inform them of a judicial matter concerning them. The rules concerning "effective" service are complex and vary by the type of action and by jurisdiction. In some cases, publication in a newspaper of general circulation may be the only service possible.

service road – See *frontage road.*

servicing –collecting payments on secured loans such as mortgages and trust deeds, and passing those payments along to the holder of the loan. These duties include administration, accounting, collection, verification of insurance and tax service, and foreclosure where necessary. Servicing may be performed in-house by the lender that originated the loan, or contracted out to another lender or a separate mortgage servicing company.

servient tenement (estate) – land on which an easement has been created for the benefit of another property. For example, if Baker has a right-of-way easement across Abel's property for the purpose of reaching a public road, Abel's land is the servient tenement. See also *dominant tenement* and *easement.*

servitude – an estate in land that carries the burden of an easement. Servitudes may be personal, generally ending with the life of the person benefited. For example, Abel grants land to Baker with the provision that Abel should be allowed to hunt and fish on the land for as long as he lives. Servitudes may also be real, and generally run with the land. For example, Abel grants land to Baker with the provision that Baker allow Abel, his heirs and assigns, to pass over Baker's property to reach a public road. See also *easement* and *running with the land.*

setback – in land planning, the distance from a lot line, easement, or existing structure that cannot be encroached on by a new improvement.

set-off – (1) a claim a defendant makes against a plaintiff, arising out of circumstances extrinsic to the plaintiff's claim against the defendant. For example, if Abel sues Baker for damages for trespass, and then Baker countersues Abel on an unrelated contract matter, the suit by Baker would be a set-off. (2) any adjustment intended to mitigate the effect of a claim, award, judgment, or penalty.

settlement – (1) (also called *closing*) the process of concluding a real estate transaction by paying all necessary expenses, making all prorations and adjustments, delivering deeds, paying lender demands, etc.; (2) the compromise of a claim or a lawsuit short of a trial or a final administrative proceeding.

settlement statement – (also called *closing statement*) a written accounting given to each party in a transaction showing the flow of funds and other items of value in satisfaction of a contract. Such an accounting may be given by the escrow holder, broker, attorney, or other party with a fiduciary duty to the buyer or seller.

settling — a change in the compaction or density of the earth. When settling occurs in land on which a structure is built, the structure may experience damage, evidenced by out-of-square doors and windows, interior and exterior cracks, and uneven floors. Licensed geologists and geotechnical engineers are qualified to determine the existence, extent, and cause of settling.

settlor — (also called *trustor*) one who creates a trust.

severalty ownership — See *tenancy in severalty.*

severance — the act of partitioning or separating something from something else. Common real estate applications are (1) the act that changes the nature of a joint tenancy into a tenancy of common. See also *joint tenancy* and *tenancy in common.* (2) harvesting of growing crops or the removal of fixtures from real estate. In both cases, the objects are "severed" from the land and become personal property. (3) the division of a single lawsuit into two or more.

severance damages — damage or lessened value in property remaining after the purpose of a condemnation action is fulfilled. The damage may be disproportional to the size of land taken versus the size of land remaining. For example, if an owner of a 5-acre industrial tract of land in an area in which zoning requires a 4-acre or larger parcel lost 2 acres in a condemnation proceeding, the remainder of his or her land may be essentially valueless. See also *condemnation* and *just compensation.*

sewer — See *sanitary sewer.*

shake — a hard, thick wood shingle. See also *shingle.*

shared appreciation mortgage (SAM) — a loan wherein the lender participates after a specific number of months in the appreciation in the value of the property. This type of loan is usually written at below-market interest rates and requires repayment or refinancing at the time the lender takes its share of the appreciation. See also *equity sharing.*

shared equity mortgage (SEM) — a loan that gives the lender a predetermined percentage share of the equity in a home at the time of resale. A lender will typically contribute equity funds toward the purchase in order to receive a share of equity on resale.

shareholder — one who owns stock in a corporation.

shear wall — a structural wall engineered to provide enhanced lateral stability. A shear wall may be covered by plywood in a designated thickness and nailed according to a specified pattern.

sheathing — the covering of bare studs or rafters with another material, such as plywood, particleboard, gypsum board, or insulated wrap.

shell lease — a commercial lease in which the tenant leases the unfinished shell of a building once it is weathertight. The tenant then provides all interior improvements, such as walls, plumbing, heating, and air conditioning.

shelter belt — a line of trees planted to protected a structure or road or other area from wind or blizzards.

sheriff's deed — the name of a deed given in post-foreclosure sales of property in some jurisdictions (i.e., a sheriff's sale). See also *sheriff's sale*.

sheriff's sale — a sale, usually by auction, conducted by the county sheriff or other court-appointed official, of property ordered sold by a court. Reasons for the sale might include tax lien forfeits, attachments, and mortgage defaults. Not all jurisdictions employ sheriff's sales. See also *judicial foreclosure* and *nonjudicial foreclosure*.

shingle — a construction material consisting of thin, small pieces of almost any substance (most commonly wood) that is used to cover an exterior surface, such as a roof or a wall, in an overlapping manner. See also *shake*.

shoe — a decorative molding that covers the joining of a floor and wall.

shopping a loan — the process by which a mortgage broker packages and presents an individual borrower's loan application to several lenders, in an effort to obtain the best loan possible for the applicant.

shopping center — a planned development zoned and designed for the construction and operation of buildings and parking to accommo-

date various retail enterprises. The four general classes of shopping centers are (a) strip mall: a modern mix of a few small local business, such as convenience markets, haircut and nail shops, and dry cleaners, often located on corners near residential districts; (b) neighborhood shopping center: usually consists of a supermarket, gas station, variety store, and several smaller shops; (c) community shopping center: may contain a large supermarket, department stores, retail shops, and restaurants; larger than neighborhood centers; (d) regional shopping center: a very large master-planned complex, including several major department stores, dozens of smaller retail shops, restaurants, movie theaters, day care, and possibly skating rinks, amusement parks, or other attractions that create a destination orientation. It may be enclosed and will usually have parking for thousands of cars.

shoreline — the lands along navigable water between the high and low water marks. Each state has its own rules concerning ownership of shorelines. Many coastal states now prohibit private ownership of land below the mean high-tide line, in an effort to promote public access to beaches, waterways, and mariculture.

shoring — (1) the reinforcement of the walls of an excavation to prevent collapse; (2) temporary reinforcement of a structural member during construction.

short form — a summary document that recites the essential facts of a contract for real estate, such as an option, lease, or purchase contract (i.e., parties, term of lease, property, and operative language). The purpose of this document is to allow recordation of the document without divulging the detailed terms of the agreement.

short rate – a higher *pro rata* premium charged by an insurance company for early cancellation of a policy. For example, if a homeowner purchases a one-year homeowner's insurance policy for a $600 annual premium, and then cancels after one month, the insurance company might charge more than 1/12 of the premium paid to offset the costs of administration.

short sale – a sale of real property for an amount less than the unpaid balance of its first mortgage. The sale proceeds, after costs such as real estate commissions, escrow, and title, are passed along to the lender, who agrees to accept the proceeds as payment in full, despite the shortfall. Such a sale requires the consent of the lender and may create taxable gain for the seller to the extent of the debt forgiven by the lender. Short sales may also affect the credit of the seller. Despite the difficulties, short sales have become a popular alternative to foreclosure in states in which purchase money real estate loans are nonrecourse. See also *foreclosure, nonrecourse loan,* and *recourse loan.*

short-term capital gain – an income tax term meaning gain from the sale or exchange of an asset that was held for less than the period to qualify for long-term capital gain. See

also *long-term capital gain.*

short-term lease – a general phrase indicating a lease with a term of a few months to a few years, depending on the type of lease. The phrase implies a period of time that is not suitable for undertaking financing, new construction, or the addition of expensive fixtures.

sick building syndrome – a term applied to the recently recognized phenomenon that indoor air pollutants, such as gases given off from construction adhesives, plastics, or concentrations of pollutants due to reduced fresh-air replacement in newer thermally efficient buildings, may make some individuals ill.

side – the position a real estate licensee represents in a transaction. If an agent represents both landlord and lessee or buyer and seller, the agent is said to have handled both sides of the transaction.

siding – the finish applied to an exterior building surface, except for glass and concrete. Examples of siding materials include wood boards, aluminum sheets, shingles, composite materials, and stucco.

sign – (1) the act of affixing a signature to a document; (2) any written display designed to attract public attention, such as a "For Sale" sign in the front yard of a house.

signature – the affixing of one's name to a document, usually by means of handwriting. Commonly done for purposes of attesting to the validity of the signature, executing a contract, or otherwise giving the document effect. Valid signatures need not be in handwriting. Depending on the circumstances and the jurisdiction, they may be in the form of a mark, a stamp, printing, or a facsimile.

silent partner – an investor who takes no active part in the management of an enterprise.

silent second – an unrecorded second trust deed or second mortgage secured by real property. Silent seconds may be left unrecorded to mislead the first trust deed or mortgage holder. In other words, the buyer is pretending that the money received through the silent second is actually a portion of the buyer's own down payment. When used as part of the purchase money in a real estate sale, silent seconds may be construed as lender fraud by a court.

sill – (1) a horizontal beam or board that forms the bottom of the frame for an opening such as a door sill or windowsill; (2) (also called "mud sill") the horizontal wood member resting directly on the foundation, forming a base for the wall studs and supporting the walls of a structure.

simple interest – the interest paid on a deposit account or debt that is not compounded or amortizing. Usually simple interest is short term. Interest may be payable periodically with the total due in a lump sum at the end of the term (a straight note), or the interest and principal may be due together at the end of the term. For example, a $100,000 loan at

simple interest for one year at 8% would require a total payment of $100,800. See also *interest-only loan* and *straight note.*

simultaneous issue – the issuance of owner's and lender's policies of title insurance at the same time. Such issuance often carries a discount to the premium payer. See also *title insurance.*

single – a person who has never been married.

single agency – agency relationship characterized by the fact that the agent represents only one party in the transaction, usually either the buyer or the seller. See also *agency* and *dual agency.*

single-family home – a structure constructed to accommodate living space for one family per vertical unit. In other words, no other living units will be above or below. It may be detached, having no common walls, or attached, such as a row house or townhouse having one or more common structural elements with a separate entrance to the outside. See, by contrast, *multifamily structure.*

single-loaded street – a street on which homes have been built along one side only. The other side is usually a slope, either up or down. Single-loaded streets are considered attractive to homebuyers because they reduce the appearance of density.

single-purpose property – a property whose design, construction, and use preclude uses other than that for which it was built. Examples include an oil refinery, power plant, dam, and hazardous waste dump.

sinking fund — a savings account established to accumulate funds calculated to achieve a target sum at a future date. A sinking fund might be established to replace a roof in 20 years. The cost of the roof is estimated and deposits are credited to an interest-bearing account that will reach the estimate for the new roof at the time it is needed. Sinking funds are common methods of savings for replacements in a homeowners association.

site — the location, orientation, or position of a plot of land considered for development.

site analysis — the study of the location of a parcel of land for determining its suitability for a particular use or its highest and best economic use.

site development — the preparation of the land for the construction of the ultimate structures. This may include the demolition of existing structures, grading and compaction of the soil, placement of utility lines, creation of interior on-site roads and parking, and the like.

site plan — an illustration showing the placement of buildings and amenities on a parcel of land. Such a plan will often show access points to a public right-of-way, proximity to neighboring structures, and dimensional data and calculations.

situs — the location where something exists in the eyes of the law for purposes of jurisdiction, taxation, regulation, or for some other public purpose.

skeleton — the structural frame of a building.

skin — an informal expression referring the exterior covering of the frame of a building.

skylight — an opening in a roof that is covered by glass or plastic and designed to admit light into a building.

slab — a flat horizontal area of poured concrete.

slander of title — an oral or written statement that is untrue and made with the malicious intent of calling into question a person's title to real or personal property. The statement must be conveyed to a third party and must result in damage to the holder of title.

slant drilling — the subsurface mining of a property from adjacent land. Generally, used in the removal of oil and gas where surface rights or access cannot be obtained.

sledgehammer — a large, heavy hammer wielded with both hands and used in construction.

sleeper — a piece of lumber, steel, or concrete resting directly on the ground and designed to support a structure. A ground-level wood deck may rest on pressure-treated, rot-resistant wood sleepers.

sleeper note — a promissory note in which the principal and interest are payable on a future date.

slip – a space in or around a dock where a boat may be tethered. See also *dock*.

Small Business Administration (SBA) – a federal agency whose purpose is to promote the growth and health of small business through education, consulting, and the lending of money. The SBA makes direct low-interest-rate loans and participates or guarantees loans made by private lenders.

Small Business Administration (SBA) Loan – one of a variety of loans made to small business with some form of Small Business Administration (SBA) participation. These include the 7(a) loan program, the Certified Development Company (503/504) loan program, and the Small Business Investment Company (SBIC) program. In addition, the SBA now administers a Microloan Program and has established a revolving line of credit called CAP-Line.

small claims court – a special court whose jurisdiction is limited to disputes involving relatively low dollar amounts. The limit varies by jurisdiction, but is usually between $1,000 and $10,000. Parties represent themselves without benefit of counsel in the courtroom. Filing fees are low, the wait for a court date is usually short, and the proceedings are informal.

SMSA – See *Standard Metropolitan Statistical Area.*

Society of Real Estate Appraisers (SREA) – an international group that merged with the American Institute of Real Estate Appraisers to form the Appraisal Institute.

soffit – the finished underside of an exposed architectural element such as a roof overhang, the underside of a stairway, or a duct run.

soft costs – costs associated with the construction of an improvement to real property that are not direct ("sticks and bricks") costs of the construction. Examples include architectural fees, commissions, attorney fees, engineering costs, etc. See, by contrast, *hard costs.*

soft money loan – a purchase money real estate loan, a loan whose proceeds go directly to purchase the property that serves as collateral for the loan. See, by contrast, *hard money loan* and *purchase money loan.*

soil – the top layer of dirt used in agriculture.

soil bank – a program administered by the Department of Agriculture in which farmers are paid to remove land from production for soil conservation purposes.

soil pipe – a sanitary sewer pipe, running from a building to the main sewer.

solar easement – an easement designed to preserve or establish a property owner's access to direct sunlight. Solar easements are generally established by private agreement. One property owner purchases the easement from another. In crowded urban environments, the right to receive direct sunlight not blocked by neighboring buildings can be very valuable. See also *easement* and *light and air easement.*

solar heating – heating systems driven entirely or assisted by the energy of the sun. One example of active solar heating is a rooftop solar collector through which water flows. The water is heated by the sun, and is in turn circulated to heat the interior of the structure. Passive solar heating depends on the design, materials, and siting of the structure to take maximum advantage of the heat energy of the sun.

sold-out second – a second trust deed holder who has been left with no security, no proceeds, and a defaulted loan due to a foreclosure by a trust deed holder with a higher-priority claim. In some jurisdictions, even some jurisdictions with antideficiency laws, a sold-out second may pursue the borrower personally for the shortfall. See also *antideficiency laws* and *foreclosure.*

sole plate – the board or beam on which vertical studs rest and are attached.

sole proprietorship – a form of business ownership in which an individual, not a partnership or corporation, owns all the assets of a business and reports all the income on his or her personal tax return. See also *corporation, limited liability company,* and *partnership.*

sole tenancy – See *tenancy in severalty.*

solvent – (1) able to meet one's immediate financial obligations; (2) any liquid used to dissolve another substance. Water is a solvent, as is paint thinner.

space heater – a small heating device intended to heat a room rather than an entire building.

space plan – a preliminary drawing or series of drawings prepared by an architect to illustrate the interior functionality of how interior building space will be laid out. Such drawings include dimensional layouts of offices, rest rooms, entrances, reception areas, conference rooms, warehouse space, showroom facilities and the like.

span – the distance between two load-bearing members that will support a beam or arch. Building codes specify the strength and size of materials used to connect spans of different sizes and purposes.

spandrel – (1) the space between the bottom framing of a window and the top framing the window below it; (2) triangular space formed beneath the stringer of a stairway; (3) roughly triangular space formed between the outside curve of one-half of an arch and any right-angle structure framing it.

spec builder – a "speculative" builder; one who builds with the expectation of immediate resale for a profit.

spec home – an individual house built with the intention to resell immediately for a profit.

special agent – a person acting

under a limited authority as to scope of the agency and time of performance; an agent who has been engaged by a principal for a particular transaction rather than for more general purposes. See also *agency, agent, limited power of attorney,* and *power of attorney.*

special assessment – (1) a charge levied by a homeowners' association on members of the association for payment of unusual or unanticipated financial obligations. A homeowners' association might assess an additional monthly fee to undertake litigation for a construction defect problem in a condominium complex, or charge a one-time fee for the replacement of a community pool. (2) a levy imposed by a taxing authority on specific properties that will be benefited by the improvements paid for with the assessment, as opposed to a general property tax. Such a charge by a taxing authority might include the costs of street lighting for a particular neighborhood or the relocation of overhead utility lines to below the ground in a limited area.

special benefit – the value added to a property by a government-created improvement. The concept is used primarily to arrive at the just compensation owed to a property owner whose land was partially taken in a condemnation proceeding. For example, assume that Abel owns 100 acres worth $2,000,000 prior to the condemnation of 50 acres. After the condemnation, Abel's remaining 50 acres might be appraised at $1,500,000 instead of $1,000,000

because the improvement the government has made to the condemned land (a road, school, airport, etc.) has actually increased the value of Abel's remaining land. The special benefit would be the $500,000 increment, which would be deducted from any compensation paid to Abel for the taking of his land. See also *before-and-after method, just compensation,* and *severance damages.*

special conditions – conditions (also called *contingencies*) in a real estate contract that must be satisfied before the contract is binding on the party in whose favor the condition runs. Examples include appraisal contingencies, termite clearances, submittal of prequalification letters, etc. A failure of a special condition (e.g., if the property does not appraise at the purchase price) may allow the party who is benefited by the condition to rescind the contract. See also *contingency.*

special partner – See *limited partnership.*

special power of attorney – See *limited power of attorney.*

special-purpose property – a property that is constructed for a single and limited type of use, and which is not economically convertible to an alternative use such as a church, meatpacking plant, power plant, etc.

special use permit – a zoning variance that allows a specific type of building or use that is inconsistent with the current zoning, based on an application that sets forth extraordinary circumstances and justification. See also *variance*.

specific lien – a lien, such as a mortgage or trust deed, against a particular property. See, by contrast, *general lien*.

specific performance – in contract law, a remedy sought in litigation that would compel the opposing party to perform specific acts or refrain from performing acts required in the contract. It is applied by courts when money damages alone will not make the injured party whole. An example is an action brought to compel the return of a family heirloom from a landlord who is holding it as security for a lease.

specifications – written supplements to blueprints that detail the materials, colors, brands of appliances, and other features of a structure. They are provided to the contractor to form a complete guide to building the property.

speculative building – the act of building a structure for resale, such as a house, commercial building, or industrial building, without first having located a purchaser.

speculator – (1) a real estate investor who expects a substantial portion of the profit to come from market appreciation, as opposed to existing income, of a property; (2) a builder who builds individual properties anticipating that a buyer will be found when the property is complete.

spendable income – in real estate investment, the income from an investment remaining after payment of all expenses and income taxes.

spendthrift trust – a trust created to provide income for the beneficiary while protecting the assets of the trust from encumbrance by the beneficiary.

spite fence – a fence constructed as an affront to a neighbor. Such a fence is usually of extreme proportion and little aesthetic merit. Many jurisdictions have building codes that regulate fence construction.

split financing – a financing method sometimes used by builders in which the land and the proposed improvements to land are financed separately.

split rate – methods of investment analysis in which return attributable to land and building, or to income and debt, or to income and tax shelter, or to equity and income, are calculated separately.

split-level – a multilevel home in which at least one level occurs "between stories"; that is, at least one living area is separated from the others by less than a full flight of stairs. Split-level homes are often built on gently sloping lots.

splitting fees – the practice of sharing compensation either as a result of being a cooperating broker, subagent, or someone to whom a referral fee is due. Fees are usually not paid to those not possessing a real estate license. See also *cooperating broker, finder's fee,* and *referral fee*.

spot loan – a loan made by a lender

for an individual unit in a condominium project in which the lender has no experience or lending history. Some lenders require that the entire project be approved by the lender before any loans will be made.

spot zoning — a land use of limited area granted by the zoning authority that is within but different from an existing zoning classification. It may be granted to permit a special use that makes sense to the surrounding community: for example, a grocery store in a residential area not otherwise close to supermarkets.

spreading agreement — an agreement between borrower and lender that collateral in the form of real property other than that being purchased or refinanced will be provided to secure a loan. The mortgage collateralization is spread to property in addition to the one for which a mortgage is sought. See also *anaconda mortgage* and *dragnet clause*.

sprinkler system — a systematic method of providing water to specific areas either for irrigation or the suppression of fire.

spur — a short segment of railroad track that leads off a main line and services a specific business, such as a manufacturing plant.

square — (1) in the government rectangular survey method, an area of land 24 miles on a side; (2) a method of measure for roofing material, equal to an area 10 feet by 10 feet; (3) a device the measures right angles for cutting or joining building materials.

square-foot method — an appraisal method of determining the value (or cost of construction) of a property by estimating the square-foot cost of replicating the building.

squatter — one who illegally occupies the property of another without a claim of right to possession. See also *adverse possession*.

SREA — See *Society of Real Estate Appraisers.*

staging — (1) a temporary scaffold used during construction; (2) the practice of preparing a property for showing to prospective buyers. It might include cleaning, opening curtains, placement of flowers, adjusting lighting to the best effect, etc.

stain — a thin water- or petroleum-based liquid designed to protect and give color to wood without completely hiding the grain.

staking — the act of inserting small vertical markers into the ground to mark lot boundary points or corner points of a proposed structure or improvement to assure accurate placement of improvements.

Standard Metropolitan Statistical Area (SMSA) — a designation given by the federal Office of Management and Budget (OMB) to a county that contains at least one city with a population over 50,000. Such a designation is part of the qualifying standard in applying for certain federal aid and grants. It is also an important source of census data used for making business location decisions.

standard parallels — in the government rectangular survey method, a series of imaginary lines running east-west, parallel to the base lines, and spaced 24 miles apart. They form the north-south boundaries of squares or quadrangles. See also *base line, government rectangular survey meridian, method, quadrangle,* and *square.*

standards of practice — an elaboration of some of the elements of the Code of Ethics of the National Association of Realtors® (NAR), published by the Professional Standards Committee of the NAR. These interpretations may be used by Realtors® to defend against a charge that a violation of the code occurred. See also *Code of Ethics* and *National Association of Realtors®.*

standby commitment — an agreement between a borrower and a lender where, in exchange for a standby fee, the lender agrees to keep a specific sum of money available as a loan to the borrower until a certain date. The borrower in essence has an option on a loan, lending credibility to the development package, but is not obligated to take the loan. A standby commitment is typically used by real estate developers in the course of obtaining land and government approvals for a development package. Ideally, when all preliminaries are completed, the loan will be ready to go. As a practical matter, standby loan rates are high, so the developer has every incentive to obtain alternative financing when funds are actually needed. See also *standby fee.*

standby fee — a fee paid to a lender for a standby commitment. In the event that the borrower does not close the loan during the agreed standby period, the fee may be retained by the lender.

standby loan — See *standby commitment.*

standing loan — (1) an agreement by a lender to extend interim or construction financing for a specified period of time, usually to allow a developer additional time to obtain takeout financing. See also *construction loan, gap financing,* and *takeout loan.* (2) See *interest-only loan.*

standing timber — uncut timber; trees.

standing water — water that has collected in a place that does not drain naturally.

Starker exchange — See *delayed exchange.*

starter — (1) a previous policy of title insurance that is used as the basis for the new policy. A starter allows the title company to limit title search costs. (2) a (usually inexpensive) first home or a property that is being represented as ideally suited for that purpose.

starts — the number of units of new construction in a given period. It is a measure of the size of a part of the construction economy at a particular point in time. See also *housing starts.*

startup costs — the initial funds necessary to begin a new project, enterprise, or business. It is not intended to constitute the entire capitalization.

statement of identity information — a form completed by the buyer and the seller that is used for title insurance purposes to assure that there is no confusion of identity with those of the same or similar names and to assure that there are no unknown judgments against the person seeking title insurance. See also *title insurance.*

statement of record — a document filed with the Department of Housing and Urban Development (HUD) by a subdivider of real estate who intends to sell the properties by means of interstate commerce (mail, telephone, television, fax, phone, etc.) See also *Interstate Land Sales Full Disclosure Act.*

statute — a law created by the legislative process. See also *case law* and *common law.*

Statute of Frauds — a law from seventeenth-century England governing contracts. Versions of this law have been adopted by most jurisdictions in the United States as well as by the Uniform Commercial Code. The primary effect is to require that certain contracts, such as those pertaining to real estate and having a duration of a year or more, be in writing. It was adopted to prevent fraud and perjury. Under the Statute of Frauds, courts will not enforce oral contracts that fall within the covered categories.

statute of limitations — laws that specify the length of time a plaintiff

(or a prosecutor) has to bring a cause of action. Such time periods begin at the occurrence of the event or circumstance giving rise to the cause of action or, alternatively, at the discovery by the plaintiff of the event or circumstance giving rise to a cause of action. In real estate, the issue is often litigated because of undisclosed hidden defects in real property. By the time the purchaser of the property discovers the defect, the statutory period in which to sue may have passed. Some statutes of limitation therefore contain terms such as "five years from the sale or three years from the discovery of the defect, whichever is earlier."

statutory foreclosure — (also called a *nonjudicial foreclosure*) foreclosure action brought under the terms of a deed of trust or mortgage without judicial action or intervention. Foreclosure authorized by statute. See, by contrast, *judicial foreclosure.*

statutory law — the body of law created by the acts of legislatures, as opposed to administrative regulations, executive orders, and case law.

statutory lien — an involuntary lien created as a matter of law such as a court-ordered lien, attachment, or a tax lien. Not a mortgage or trust deed.

statutory notice — notice required to be given as stated in specific legislation pertaining to an action.

statutory right of redemption — a right granted under state laws (different in each state) giving a person the right to redeem (buy back) a property lost in a judicial foreclosure or tax sale for a specific period of time after the foreclosure. The redeeming party must generally pay all foreclosure costs, back interest, and the full encumbrance. Statutory redemption periods range up to a year after the sale. There is generally no right of redemption in a nonjudicial foreclosure such as a trustee's sale. See also *judicial foreclosure* and *nonjudicial foreclosure*. See, by contrast, *redemption, equitable right*.

steering — the illegal practice of showing or presenting properties to buyers who are members of a protected class (race, ethnicity, handicap, marital status, etc.) in a manner designed to keep that protected class isolated to a particular area, or to introduce those of a protected class to an area with the intent of generating unstable market conditions. Steering can be blatant (a refusal to show African-Americans homes in white neighborhoods), or more subtle (showing young single buyers condominiums instead of detached houses). See also *blockbusting* and *Federal Fair Housing Act*.

stepped-up basis — in the area of federal estate taxation, the new basis in property for federal taxation purposes acquired from the decedent as of the date of death. In general, the basis is the fair market value of the property at the time of death, or six months after the death, regardless of the decedent's original cost or depreciated basis. See also *basis* and *fair market value*.

stigma — a negative association at-

tributed to a particular property, reducing its marketability and value. Examples might be a murder occurring in the house, proximity to a waste dump or landfill, a history of geological problems, or a past lawsuit over construction defects.

Straight-line depreciation — a method of accounting for the diminution of value of an asset over time by dividing the cost of the asset less its salvage value by the number of years of its expected (or statutory) useful life. The equal yearly percentage of value thus derived may be a deduction from adjusted income for income tax purposes. Tax law in this area changes frequently. See also *basis* and *depreciation*.

straight note — a promissory note serving as evidence of a nonamortizing loan that calls for the payment of the entire original principal on a specific date. Interest may be paid periodically or accrue until the principal is due. Straight notes are often short-term (three- to five-year) secondary financing used in conjunction with a first trust deed or mortgage for a real estate purchase.

straw man — a person or entity who, in order to the conceal the identity of the ultimate purchaser, purchases a property on their behalf. Historically, trusts, attorneys, foreign corporations, and shell or dummy corporations performed these duties. Such activity is not recommend for real estate licensees in view of strict codes of ethics, disclosure requirements, and other laws pertaining to secret profit, unjust enrichment, breach of fiduciary duty, etc.

street – a surfaced road serving local traffic.

street improvement bonds – bonds issued by local government for the construction or repair of local streets. The property owners are assessed their *pro rata* share of the principal and interest of the bond payment which is generally paid with the property tax statement. See also *bond*.

strict foreclosure – a rarely employed method of foreclosure in which, by contract or by judicial decree, the debtor relinquishes the property to the lender immediately in the event of a default, without a formal sale. See also *foreclosure, judicial foreclosure*, and *nonjudicial foreclosure*.

strict liability – liability that does not require a finding of fault or negligence or intent. In other words, if a person performs some act, he or she is held liable for the results. Strict liability has been imposed by the federal Comprehensive Environmental Response, Compensation, and Liability Act of 1980 (CERCLA) and the Superfund Amendment and Reauthorization Act of 1986 (SARA) for the presence of certain toxic substances on some commercial and industrial real property. See also *Environmental Protection Agency* and *Superfund*.

string – See *stringer*.

stringer – the slanted sides of a staircase.

stringpiece – a long, heavy horizontal timber that functions as a structural support for cross members that rest on it.

strip center – a retail center comprised of several small stores arranged in a lineal design. Usually does not have a large anchor tenant.

structural alteration – any change made to the existing layout of space in a structure that requires moving walls or adding new space. A room addition is a structural alteration. Remodeling a kitchen by refacing cabinets and changing appliances is not.

structural defect – a design or construction error that causes the structural integrity of a building or other structure to be unreliable or dangerous.

structure – a built improvement to real estate.

stucco – a cement or plaster compound applied wet to exterior wall surfaces as the final structural and aesthetic treatment. It hardens quickly and adds strength to the structure.

stud – a light vertical support, usually made of wood or metal used in the construction of walls. For residential construction, studs are usually 2-inch by 4-inch by 96-inch wooden timbers. Steel studs are becoming popular in residential construction, and are common in commercial buildings.

studio apartment – a living unit consisting of a multipurpose room with living, sleeping, and cooking functions combined in one room, usually with an attached small bath. also called an efficiency apartment.

subagency – an agency relationship characterized by a delegation of agency duties from one agent to another. See also *subagent*.

subagent – an agent for one party (usually the buyer) who has previously committed to be the agent for the other party (usually the seller). Historically, the listing of a property in the multiple listing service included an offer of subagency to brokers who showed the listed property. In effect, the broker who showed the property to the buyer acted as a delegate of the listing agent, and was expected to represent the interests of the seller. Buyers objected that they were not being represented effectively and modern MLS practice generally allows seller's agents to offer fee sharing without requiring subagency. See also *agency, dual agency, single agency,* and *subagency*.

subchapter S corporation – See *S corporation*.

subcontractor – (1) a contractor who works for a general contractor. Usually it is a specialty contractor, such as one responsible for concrete, glazing, steel, drywall, or painting, working under an agreement with the general contractor. The general contractor manages all of the subcontracting work and usually is responsible for paying the subcontractors. See also *general contractor*. (2) a contractor with a license other than a general contractor's license.

subdivider – an owner or an owner's agent who obtains the entitlements from the granting authorities to create smaller legal parcels or lots from larger parcels. See also *subdivision* and *subdivision map act*.

subdivision – a grouping of lots or parcels that were formerly a part of a larger parcel.

subdivision map – a map or plat showing the lots and streets of an area to be developed under a common plan. When approved and adopted by appropriate agencies, it becomes the basis for the legal descriptions of the properties it contains.

subdivision map act – state laws, often contained in the government code, that define the responsibilities and limitations of power for municipalities with regard to the subdivision of land.

subfloor – the subsurface deck or slab, either laid on joists or directly on the ground, on which the finished floor material, such as carpet, wood, or tile, will be installed.

subjacent support – the structural support that the surface of a parcel receives from the subsurface soil and rock or strata. See also *lateral and subjacent support*.

subject property – (1) the property or parcel that is the object of the transaction; the thing that is bargained for; (2) an appraisal term referring to the property being appraised.

subject to — the practice of a buyer purchasing a property from a seller, while leaving at least one existing loan in place. The buyer makes the payments under the loan but does not formally assume the loan. There are risks to this strategy for both the buyer and the seller, especially in jurisdictions with enforceable due-on-sale clauses in the loan.

sublease — a lease of property already leased from the owner or another lessee. The sublease will often be for a shorter term, for only a portion of the master lease area, or some combination. It may well be for a greater amount of rent. A sublease can not create a leasehold estate larger than that creating the master lease. If the lessee transfers his or her entire interest to a sublessee, an assignment of lease is created. See also *assignment of lease* and *sandwich lease*.

sublessee — (also called *subtenant*) one who subleases from another. See also *sublease*.

sublessor — one who subleases to another. See also *sublease*.

submittal notice — written notice by a broker to a seller setting forth the names of persons to whom the broker has shown the property. It is designed to forestall arguments about procuring cause. See also *procuring cause*.

subordinated ground lease — a ground lease, or lease of bare land, wherein the landlord allows the tenant's lender to foreclose on the landlord's interest in the event that the tenant defaults on the loan. The landlord subordinates his estate (subjects it to a lower priority) to the lease.

subordination — the act of permitting one's estate or security interest in real property to be reduced to a lesser priority. This is done in situations where it is considered to be a temporary condition; there is adequate compensation for the risk; and an analysis of the probability of a default is made and determined to be remote.

subpoena — a command by an official body to appear at a certain place and time and to give testimony on a specified matter.

subpoena duces tecum — a Latin term meaning an order by an official body to appear and produce a specified document or documents.

subprime — refers to the quality of loan as an investment or to the borrower whose creditworthiness is below average.

subrogation — a situation where one party is substituted for another and allowed to pursue some lawful claim or right. In the business of insurance, subrogation allows the insurance company to sue in the place of the policyholder and keep all damages awarded in order to recoup the amounts paid to the insured.

subscribe — to sign at the end of a document.

subsequent bona fide purchaser — one who has purchased property of value without any notice of defects concerning its title, and without knowingly being a part of an illegal transaction. Thus, If Abel purchases a farm from Baker, not knowing that Baker has mortgaged the farm to Charlie, Abel may prevail against a claim for the property by Charlie, especially if Charlie failed to record his interest properly. See also *actual notice, constructive notice,* and *recording.*

subsidence — a geologic failure of the subsurface strata, causing land to sink vertically.

subsidized housing — residential rentals or buildings in which the rents themselves are supported in part by government funds or guarantees.

subsidized rent — residential rents that are paid in whole or part through government-funded programs for low- or moderate-income individuals and families.

substitution — an appraisal principle which holds that a prudent buyer would pay no more for real property than the cost of buying or building an equally desirable property, assuming no unreasonable delay was required.

substitution of collateral — a provision in a mortgage that permits the borrower to request that the lender grant a release of one property from the mortgage and substitute other property acceptable to the lender.

substitution of trustee — the act or document used to replace a trustee under a deed of trust. Because deeds of trust are often bought and sold on

the secondary mortgage market, this substitution is a common practice.

subsurface easement — the right to install water, sewer, power lines, and the like under the property of another. See also *easement, dominant tenement,* and *servient tenement (estate).*

subsurface rights — the rights to the benefits of the property beneath the surface. Usually refers to the right to mine minerals or pump gas, oil, or water. It may or may not be accompanied by the right of surface entry.

subtenant — See *sublessee.*

suburb — a community near a larger city and linked to it economically. For example, residents of a suburb might work and shop in the city.

successors and assigns — words of limitation used in deeds in which property is transferred to a corporation rather than an individual. A corporation does not have heirs, but rather has "assigns"—those who are entitled to the benefits of a corporation's assets.

sufferance — at the will of another. A tenancy at sufferance is a tenancy that may be terminated at any time by the owner of the property. See also *tenancy at sufferance.*

summary possession — an uncommon expedited legal process in which a landlord is granted the immediate right to remove a possessor who was a former tenant but who is remaining on the property without consent. See *eviction* and *tenancy at sufferance.*

summons – a legal notice that a lawsuit has been filed against a defendant. It serves both as a notice and as a means of acquiring jurisdiction over a party. It generally contains information about the action, and where and when to appear to answer the complaint. If a duly served defendant fails to appear, a *default judgment* may be entered against him or her. See also *default judgment.*

sump – a pit or tank used to hold fluids temporarily until they can be disposed of permanently, usually by means of a pump. Basements often have a sump for purposes of allowing small amounts of water to collect without flooding the entire basement.

superadequacy – an overimprovement to real property. An overimprovement is one whose cost exceeds the value it adds to the property. An example is a private sauna in a one-bedroom apartment.

Superfund – Superfund Amendment and Reauthorization Act of 1986 (SARA); an amendment to the federal Comprehensive Environmental Response, Compensation, and Liability Act of 1980 (CERCLA) that actively mandates, funds, and supports urgent cleanup of hazardous and toxic material on public and private property. It imposes strict liability on landowners, landlords, and lenders. See also *Comprehensive Environmental Response, Compensation, and Liability Act of 1980.*

supervise – to oversee the work of another. See also *supervisory broker.*

supervisory broker – (also called designated broker) the broker in a real estate office who is designated to oversee and review the work of the agents and brokers in that office. Department of real estate regulations and liability laws make the supervising broker generally liable for the negligence of his or her agents.

supply – (1) the amount of any product or material that is available for purchase; (2) a means of supplying a utility to a structure, or within a structure, to fixtures. For example, a water pipe running from the wall under a sink to the faucet is a supply line.

supply and demand – the motivating principles of a market economy. When the supply increases compared to its effective demand (desire to buy coupled with the funds to do so) the price will tend to decline. When the effective demand increases relative to existing supply, prices tend to rise.

support deed – a deed used to convey property in exchange for a promise by the recipient of the deed to financially support the maker of the deed for the life of the maker. This type of deed has been accompanied by so much fraud that courts tend to view them narrowly. If the recipient at any time fails in his or her obligation to reasonably support the maker of the deed, a court may invalidate the transfer surety–one who agrees to be a guarantor for another. The arrangement is often secured through the purchase by the parties of a surety bond. The person who requires the assurances of the surety is the obligee. The person or company whose performance is to be guaranteed is the principal, while the guarantor bond company is the surety. A surety bond in the form of a completion and performance bond is often required of general contractors on large projects to help assure that the work contracted for will be completed properly and on schedule. See also *surety bond.*

surety bond — a form of insurance that is purchased to cover the risk of loss in the event that the principal fails to perform as contracted. After performance has been tendered properly, the bond is void. If performance is not tendered properly, the surety company pays the obligee up to the amount of the bond, and will have recourse against the principal for losses suffered. See *support deed* for a discussion. See also *completion bond.*

surface water — groundwater from a storm that has not been artificially channeled or concentrated. In most states, landowners are not liable to adjacent landowners for damage caused by surface water running across their property.

surrender — the early release, by contract between the parties, of a possessory right to land (ownership, lease, etc.) to one who has an estate in remainder, reversion, or who is the lessor. The effect is to merge the lesser estate into the greater. Surrender differs from abandonment in that it is bilateral, requiring a formal agreement. See also *abandonment.*

survey — (1) the act of determining the location, orientation, size, boundaries, and configuration of land through field measurement; (2) the written summary of a survey.

survivorship — See *right of survivorship.*

suspension — as applied to a real estate licensee, the temporary revocation of the privileges of the license by a state department of real estate or a real estate commissioner, due to a violation or violations of the state's licensing laws. During the suspension period, the licensee may not engage in real estate activities requiring a license.

sweat equity — the value added to a property (usually a "fixer") through the labor of the owner in such activities as remodeling and rehabilitation. See also *fixer.*

swing loan — (also called a *bridge loan*) a temporary loan designed to allow the purchase of one property before the sale of another whose equity is essential to the purchase. The loan is usually very short term (a few months to a year, and often carries a high rate of interest and high costs. Sometimes the loan is secured by both properties ("cross-collateralization"). See also *bridge loan* and *cross-collateralization.*

syndication — the combination of investors for the purpose of pooling their funds into a centrally managed investment vehicle. A generic term that may allude to a real estate investment trust (REIT), a limited partnership, a limited liability company, a corporation, or any other legal entity.

T

T-bill — See *Treasury bill.*

tacking — (1) combining successive periods of possession by different parties in order to satisfy the time requirement for adverse possession. Each adverse possessor's possession period must have been continuous and the possessors must be related in interest, such as ancestor and heir. See also *adverse possession.* (2) in federal income tax law, the carryover of holding periods from one property to another; (3) in the area of finance, the term is applied to the questionable practice of a third (or later) lien holder acquiring the first mortgage, thereby attempting to thwart any claim of the second or any other intermediate lien holder. This practice is rarely successful where priorities of time of recordation are recognized. See also *priority.*

take-down — (1) a draw or demand against a preapproved limit in a construction loan for a progress payment to contractors. See also *progress payments.* (2) a draw or demand to acquire one or more parcels of land in an assemblage program where the lender has committed funds for that purpose.

take-off — the practice of using blueprints, plans, and specifications to estimate the amount and cost of materials needed for construction.

take-out commitment — a contract between a lender and borrower wherein the lender agrees to loan funds to pay all or substantially all of the accrued balance of a construction loan at a defined rate and term. This is a common feature of lending in new construction and is usually a condition precedent of obtaining the construction loan. See also *takeout loan.*

take-out loan — the permanent, long-term loan arranged to pay off a short-term construction loan. The availability of take-out financing is often a prerequisite for construction financing. In many cases the same lender provides both loans, albeit at different rates and terms. See also *construction loan, permanent loan,* and *standby loan.*

taking — the involuntary transfer of title to real property by a private owner to a public or governmental entity that is statutorily enabled to exercise powers of *eminent domain* to acquire property for public purposes. See also *before-and-after method, eminent domain, just compensation,* and *partial taking.*

tax — a monetary obligation imposed by a government on its citizens for the purpose of funding the services that the citizens have demanded of their government. A tax may be based on personal or business income and investments, the valuation of real or personal property (*ad valorem tax*), the exchange of goods and services (sales tax), the value of a deceased person's estate (estate tax), and other sources.

tax and lien search — a type of title search undertaken in areas that use the Torrens system to describe and register real property. The search is designed to supplement the property description with a list of liens and taxes owing on the property. See also *Torrens title system.*

tax assessment — (1) same as *assessment;* (2) the dollar amount of tax due on a parcel of real property for the fiscal period as determined by formula or appraisal.

tax assessor — the elected or appointed official at the city or county level who is responsible for determining the amount of tax due on the various types of property taxed at that level of government. The county tax assessor, for example, would determine the tax rate for personal property, business property, and the like. In some states, such as California, the amount of tax on real property may not increase more than a fixed percentage per year. In many others, the property will be reassessed each year, giving rise to the possibility that property taxes can increase or decrease rapidly. The tax assessor may also be the tax collector

in the same jurisdiction. See also *board of equalization*

tax base — in public finance, all of the property, personal and real, that is subject to taxation within the jurisdiction of the taxing authority. It is the rough equivalent to an asset in private financial matters.

tax basis — the "cost" of a depreciable asset for income tax purposes. For example, the tax basis of a principal residence generally would be the initial purchase price of the property plus the cost of any capital improvements, such as room additions, swimming pools, etc. See also *adjusted tax basis.*

tax benefits — generally, deductions from or credits toward one's tax liability resulting from special incentives for owning certain types of property or engaging in certain types of businesses or investments. It is currently possible to take a deduction for income tax purposes for depreciation of certain classifications of real and personal property. This provision allows for a reduction in tax liability for income derived from a commercial property, for example, by virtue of the assumption that the asset gradually decreases in value or utility over time (depreciation) and that such nonmonetary loss may be used to offset certain other income. These types of tax benefits are subject to legislative change and administrative interpretation, and therefore must be carefully analyzed for avail-

241

ability. See also *tax credit.*

tax bracket – in progressive systems of federal and state income taxation, tax bracket is that percentage at which the top full tier of individual or corporate income is taxed. For example, most of John Doe's income is taxed at 15%, but the last $300 is over the maximum amount for the 15% bracket, and is taxed at 28%. John's tax bracket is 15%; his marginal tax bracket is 28%. See also *income taxes* and *marginal tax bracket.*

tax certificate – a document issued to a person (other than the owner) by the tax collector indicating that the bearer has paid delinquent taxes on real property owned by another and is subsequently entitled to a tax deed subject to the delinquent tax payer's statutory right of redemption. See also *tax deed.*

tax clearance – a statement from a taxing authority that there exist no delinquent taxes, that tax returns have been filed for the required periods, and that no liens are filed on a taxpayer by the issuing agency. A tax clearance is very desirable, if not required, upon the sale of a business so that a purchaser is assured that there are no delinquent sales or franchise taxes, employment-related taxes such as withholding or disability fund contributions, property taxes on fixtures or equipment purchased with the business, and the like. It may also be required where the estate of a decedent seeks to transfer property

from the estate. It verifies that there are no outstanding estate tax liens.

tax credit – a dollar-for-dollar offset of the amount of tax due; a tax benefit resulting from a special inducement to participate in a legislatively favored program. Examples would be a tax credit allowed for hiring the unemployed or a person on welfare, or building a plant or store in a specially designated area where the building of such facilities provide construction jobs or long-term employment opportunities. Each dollar spent on the favored activity reduces the actual amount of the tax owed by one dollar.

tax deed – a deed given by the taxing authority to a person who purchases real property in a tax sale. Such a deed will only pass the interest held by the delinquent taxpayer and may be subject to certain rights of redemption depending on the jurisdiction. See also *right of redemption* and *tax sale.*

tax district – the largest area over which a taxing authority has the power to levy and collect taxes. A tax district may consist of more than one assessment district. See also *assessment district* and *property tax.*

tax lien – a lien attached to property, real or personal, to secure delinquent taxes. A lien may be placed on the property on which the tax is due, or in the case of a lien attached by the Internal Revenue Service for delinquent income taxes, it may attach to all other property owned by the taxpayer. See also *lien*.

tax preference – tax-favored items considered in the calculation of the federal alternative minimum tax (AMT). Examples include accelerated depreciation, excess charitable contributions, and tax-exempt interest. See also *alternative minimum tax*.

tax rate – the percentage applied to the assessed value of property to determine the amount of tax. For example, a $100,000 property subject to a 2% tax rate would be taxed $2,000/year. Colloquially, the "rate" is often a blended rate that is comprised of the rates due schools, improvement districts, water and sewer bonds, and other jurisdictions such as the county or regional firefighting authority. See also *property tax*.

tax roll – the public record database or list of all properties, assessments, and owners that comprise the tax base. See also *tax base*.

tax sale – a forced sale of privately owned real property by a government agency to satisfy unpaid property tax liens. See also *right of redemption, sheriff's sale*, and *tax deed*.

tax shelter – the tax benefit derived from investment in certain types of properties or businesses that have the effect of generating tax "losses" that may reduce the tax on income. Ownership of real estate is "sheltered" because of favorable rules re-

garding capital gain on a personal residence, interest and property tax deductions and depreciation, as well as special rollover provisions for investment property. See also *capital gain*.

tax stamps – a point-of-sale taxation on qualified transfers of real property, evidenced by the application of stamps to the recorded deed. Tax stamps constitute an *ad valorem* (based on value) tax. A tax rate is applied to the sale price to compute the amount of the tax. In California, for example, the rate is currently $1.10 per $1,000 of purchase price.

tax-deferred exchange – See *Section 1031 exchange*.

tax-free exchange – See *Section 1031 exchange*.

tear-down –a property whose structure has no functional or economic value and that is bought for the potential development of the underlying land.

teaser rate – low rate of interest offered for a very short time (weeks or months) at the start of a mortgage loan as an inducement to the borrower to accept the loan and to provide a lower mortgage payment for easier borrower qualification. For example, if fixed rate loans are offered at 8%, an adjustable rate mortgage with a teaser rate might be offered at "2.9% for the first 3 months." After the first few months, the rate will adjust dramatically upward. Teaser rates are usually associated with negative amortization. See also *adjustable rate mortgage* and *negative amortization*.

tenancy — the right to occupy and be in possession of real property. Owners hold title in some form of tenancy. Renters occupy property subject to tenancy agreements. See also *joint tenancy, month-to-month tenancy, periodic tenancy, tenancy at sufferance, tenancy at will, tenancy by the entirety*, and *tenancy in common*.

tenancy at sufferance — the possession of premises by a tenant after the expiration or termination of a lease. Such possession is usually without explicit landlord consent, and carries with it no right to possess, only what is sometimes called naked possession. See also *tenancy*. See by contrast *adverse possession* and *squatter*.

tenancy at will — permission to enter on and occupy property for an unfixed period of time. For example, Abel might allow Baker to use Abel's fishing lodge "as long as I don't need it." See also *tenancy*.

tenancy by the entirety — an estate created by the conveyance to a husband and wife with the right of survivorship. Upon the death of either the husband or the wife, the title to the entire property passes to the survivor to the exclusion of the deceased's other heirs. The termination of this estate requires the joint action of both husband and wife. Compare with *joint tenancy*, which may be broken by the conveyance of an interest by either the husband or wife. States usually do not recognize both tenancy by the entirety and joint tenancy. See also *tenancy*.

tenancy for life — See *life estate* and *tenancy*.

tenancy for years — the estate created by a lease or demise which grants possession of real property for a specific, fixed period of time. It need not be a year or a multiple of years. For example, a lease of a vacation home for "the month of September 2001" is a tenancy for years. See also *demise, leasehold estate*, and *tenancy*.

tenancy in common — a form of ownership recognizing concurrent possession of more than one person, with each having an undivided interest in the entire estate. Unlike joint tenancy, tenancy in common may be established by separate instruments. No co-tenant can exclude the other co-tenants from any portion of the property, or partition possession of the property. The shares may be unequal, and the co-tenant may sell or will his or her share without disturbing the co-tenancy relationship. Each co-tenant bears his or her proportional share of maintaining the property and is entitled to a proportional share of the income from the property. See also *community property, joint tenancy*, and *tenancy*.

tenancy in severalty — (also called *sole tenancy*) ownership by one person or entity. The confusing term derives from the notion that the owner's interest is severed from that of other persons. An individual may hold sole title in several forms: as a single (never married) man or woman; as an unmarried (divorced or widowed) man or woman; or as a married man or woman as his or her sole and separate property. See also *joint tenancy, tenancy,* and *tenants in common.*

tenant — (1) in its most general sense, one who holds or occupies real or personal property by any kind of right or title, whether in fee or by lease. See also *fee* and *lease.* (2) more commonly, a renter of real property; the lessee. See also *landlord, lessee,* and *lessor.*

tenant improvement (TI) — construction project or remodeling of leased space to accommodate the specific needs of a lessee. These may include the installation of interior walls, special wiring, flooring, signage, lighting, etc. The cost and responsibility for tenant improvements is usually a matter of rigorous negotiation. In new construction, such as a shopping center, the owner/builder will grant the tenant an allowance (budget) for certain improvements, beyond which costs the tenant may be liable.

tenant mix — in retail environments such as shopping malls, the composition of tenants and the range of goods and services they provide. Typically, the shopping center owner or developer seeks to attract retail tenants representing the optimum of complementary but diverse purveyors of goods and services consistent with the area demographics.

ten-day escrow law — See *Bulk Sales Act*

tender — (1) the unconditional offer of performance on one party's obligations under a bilateral contract. For example, a tender of performance by a buyer of real property might be the act of placing funds equal to the full purchase price plus costs into escrow. A tender is often performed to provide convincing evidence of a contract breach by the other party. For example, if the buyer has placed all necessary funds into escrow, and the seller refuses to deliver a deed, the seller may be in default and subject to suit. See also *bilateral contract* and *breach of contract.* (2) the act of performing a contract obligation or completing the performance of such an obligation.

tenement — (1) all things permanent, whether tangible or intangible, that are part of and pass with the land. Examples include houses, buildings, rights to receive rents, etc. (2) in common parlance, an urban apartment building serving low-income renters.

tentative map — a preliminary

map for a project or subdivision submitted for comment and negotiation with a planning authority. Once the ultimate plan is determined, a final map is submitted, approved and recorded. See also *subdivision map act.*

tenure – the nature or classification of one's possessory rights; an artifact of feudal land law used primarily to distinguish between freehold and leasehold interest.

term – (1) the length of time stated in a contract for the performance of its requirements. Examples include the duration of a lease, the period over which loan payments are due, etc. (2) a provision in a document, especially a contract. The term limits or defines some right of the parties.

terminable interest – property interests or estates that terminate upon the death of the holder, or upon some other event. Life estates, and estates subject to a reversionary or remainder interest are terminable. See also *life estate, remainder,* and *reversion.*

termination of listing – the cancellation of a broker–seller listing agreement. The agreement may be terminated mutually prior to the expiration date. Depending on the language of the listing contract, the seller may be able to cancel the listing prior to the expiration either for cause or upon sufficient notice. Absent such language, the seller may be liable to the listing broker for pay-

ment of the agreed compensation if the property sells during the period of the listing contract. See also *listing.*

termite – a type of wood-destroying insect. Drywood termites live in hives above ground and may swarm periodically. Subterranean termites build underground colonies and travel in tubes constructed of mud above the surface to prey on wood structures. Both types can cause considerable damage to wood structures and are very common in the southwestern United States, although they may be found in every state.

termite clearance – a document prepared by a pest control company indicating that a particular property is free of active infestation by wood-destroying organisms. Termite clearance may be required by a lender prior to the funding of a real estate loan. See also *termite, termite inspection,* and *termite report.*

termite inspection – sometimes also called a pest control inspection. A professional physical investigation of a property by a pest control specialist for the purpose of determining the presence of termites and other wood-damaging organisms, including fungus, wood-boring beetles, carpenter ants, etc. See also *termite clearance* and *termite report.*

termite report – the written findings of a termite inspection. A termite report will generally follow a format adopted by the applicable state pest control board. It will disclose the presence or absence of active infestations of termites and other wood-destroying organisms and identify any wood structurally compromised by such damage. It will offer recommendations, and, usually, an estimate for the work needed to eradicate the organisms and repair any structural damage. Methods of eradicating termites include local chemical treatment, whole-house fumigation, microwaves, heat, and cold. See also *termite, termite clearance,* and *termite inspection.*

termite shield — a metal flashing at the base of a structure to prevent termite infestation at the foundation.

terms — conditions, duties, requirements, and promises contained in an agreement. See also *term.*

terra cotta — "baked earth"; a hard, fired clay material used for tiles and pots for plants.

terrace — (1) a balcony; (2) a flat area adjacent to a building designed for walking, sitting, or relaxing; (3) to cut a series of flat areas into a hillside using bulldozers for the purpose of planting crops or building structures.

terrazzo — flooring made of small pieces of tile, granite, marble, shells, or stone set in cement or grout, sanded flat, and polished to a high sheen.

testament — originally referred to the disposition of personal property.

Now the word "will" covers the disposition of both real and personal property. See also *will.*

testamentary trust — a trust that takes effect upon the death of the testator. See also *living trust* and *testator/testatrix.*

testamonium clause — a clause in a deed or will assuring that the proper parties are signing the instrument.

testate — (1) the condition of having created a valid will; (2) one who dies leaving a valid will

testator/testatrix — (1) a man/woman who makes a will; (2) a man/woman who dies leaving a valid will.

therm — a measure of heat equal to one hundred thousand British thermal units (BTUs). See also *British thermal unit.*

thermal window — a window designed to resist the passage of heat from inside to outside, or vice versa. Many thermal windows have two or more sheets of glass separated by a vacuum or airspace. Some are coated with a material designed to reflect heat.

thermostat — an electronic or electro-mechanical device used to control a heating and air-conditioning system. The thermostat acts as a temperature-sensitive switch, turning on heating or cooling systems at preset intervals or when the temperature reaches an adjustable predetermined level.

thin market — (1) a real estate market in which buying and selling activity is low, making comparable sales data scarce; (2) a real estate market in which few properties are available for sale, causing buyers to make higher offers.

third party — a person or entity not a part of a contract, agreement, or transaction, but who may have rights that are affected thereby. For example, real estate brokers are not typically parties to a real estate purchase contract, but may have the right to be compensated when the transaction is consummated. See also *parties.*

three phase wiring — a system of electrical supply allowing a series of simultaneous heavy uses, most often seen in factories and industrial settings.

threshold — (1) a covering strip attached to the floor in a doorway to conceal the joining of two dissimilar materials, and, in the case of exterior doors, to prevent water intrusion; typically made of wood, metal, stone, or concrete; (2) a breakpoint on which something else depends. In real estate, for example, some lenders require that a certain percentage of the units in a condominium complex be owner-occupied before they will consider lending on a unit in the project. That minimum percentage is a threshold.

tide — the rising and falling levels (occurring twice a day) of large bodies of water such as oceans, seas, and large lakes, due to the unequal gravitational attraction of the sun and moon on different parts of the earth.

tidelands — land that is covered and uncovered by water resulting from the ebb and flow of tidal action. See also *tide.*

tie beam — a timber that attaches to and holds together other structural elements. See also *collar beam.*

tie-in contract — a contract that depends on another contract involving the same or related parties. For example, Abel may agree to sell Baker a farm if Baker sells Abel his lakefront property. Some tie-in contracts or agreements are benign. Others may violate various antitrust laws. For example, a contract to sell a property that required the buyer to sign a commitment to resell the property through the same listing broker might be an illegal tie-in agreement. See also *antitrust laws.*

tile — (1) any small flat material that may be used in conjunction with similar materials to cover a surface. Commonly, tiles are ceramic, stone, clay, cement, or vinyl, but they may be made of virtually any material. (2) the pattern or placement of squares or other compatibly shaped objects to form a surface such as a ceiling, floor, or wall covering.

timber — a large, roughly squared

piece of wood used structurally in a building or other improvement to land, distinguished from lumber by its relative lack of finish surfacing.

time interval maps — maps of different eras used to show the growth or development of an area over a period of years.

time is of the essence — a common phrase in contracts putting signatories on notice that the time limits stated in the contract are critical to the contract and should be strictly adhered to. A failure by one party to perform a contractually required act within the specified time frame may be regarded as a breach by the other party.

time value of money — a financial principle holding that money received sooner in time has greater value than money received later. See also *discounted cash flow* and *interest*.

time-share — a development project in which ownership is in the form of an "interval ownership" estate permitting occupancy for a specific time or times throughout the year. Units are sold in blocks of one week at a time. Each of the many owners holds title to the property as tenants in common under a separate use agreement. Prices may vary depending on the specific time of year purchased. Summer periods are most expensive in temperate areas, whereas winter periods command the highest prices for ski resorts.

Time-share salespersons generally require a real estate license, and their sales practices are often strictly regulated by the states.

title — (1) the right to ownership of land or personal property; (2) the rightful means under which one claims ownership or a possessory interest in land; the union of all elements of ownership; (3) the written evidence of ownership. See also *deed*, *estate*, and *tenancy*.

title defect — a question concerning the validity of title that affects its marketability. See also *cloud on title*, *marketable title*, *title*, and *title insurance*.

title insurance — an insurance or indemnity contract purchased from a title insurance company to guarantee that the policyholder will be protected from loss due to challenges to the title or estate acquired. The title company warrants that any losses caused by defects in title *unknown to the insurer or the parties at the time of the issuance of the policy* will be indemnified In general, title insurance will protect against unknown problems in the past, such as forged deeds, mental incompetence of a person in the chain of title, undisclosed heirs, etc. There are several forms of title insurance. Not all policies protect against all risks. See also *American Land Title Association*.

title insurance company — a company in the business of insuring title to real property. See also *title insurance.*

title order — the formal written request, usually made at the opening of escrow by an escrow officer, that a title company research the title to a parcel of real property for the ultimate purpose of issuing insurance on it. See also *title insurance* and *title search.*

title report — [also called *preliminary title report (prelim.)*] a document produced by a title company (the result of a title search) identifying the current owner of record, the estate under which the title is held, and all encumbrances of record affecting title. It forms the factual basis on which a title insurance company relies when offering title insurance. See also *encumbrance, liens, marketable title, preliminary title report (prelim.), title insurance,* and *title search.*

title search — the process of researching the current state of title to real property. See also *abstract of title* and *preliminary title report (prelim.).*

title theory states — states that have adopted the common law concept that when property is mortgaged, the title is divided between the borrower and lender. The legal title is held by the lender. Equitable title is held by the borrower. The borrower "perfects" its title to full vesting when the mortgage is retired. In a title theory state, the lender may demand immediate possession of the property upon default. In a "lien theory" state, the lender must foreclose on the property to assert its rights. See also *foreclosure, lien,* and *title.*

toenailing — the technique of nailing at an angle to create more friction or gripping action.

toll road — a public or private road on which charges are assessed for each use by a vehicle. Modern toll roads use electronic devices linked to the driver's credit card to assess tolls without requiring the driver to stop at a tollbooth.

ton — (1) a measure of weight equal to 2,000 pounds in the United States; (2) a measure of the cooling capacity of an air conditioner. One ton is equivalent to 12,000 British thermal units (BTUs).

tongue and groove — a method of joining wood by butting pieces of lumber, one having a protruding flange (tongue) to another with a receiving slot (groove).

topographical survey — a map showing the variations in elevation or level of a parcel of land. See also *topography.*

topography — the nature or condition of the surface contour of land.

topsoil — loose surface soil containing a high concentration of organic nutrients on which plants depend.

Torrens' title system — named after

Sir Richard Torrens, a nineteenth-century reformer of Australian land laws. States that have adopted this system of title registration require a property owner to "register" his or her land and apply to a court of competent jurisdiction for a certificate of title. The certificate of title, issued after a search for encumbrances and publicized notice for those who may assert a claim, is intended to provide conclusive assurance as to the validity and nature of the title. This system is used in place of recording and title insurance in "title theory" states.

tort — an act or omission (other than breach of contract) that causes injury or damage to another and for which the judicial remedy of damages is available. A tortious act is not generally subject to criminal prosecution, but rather, is subject to laws of civil litigation. The elements of a tort are the existence of a legal duty from defendant to plaintiff, the breach of that duty, and proximate damages to the plaintiff as a result of the breach. A failure by a real estate broker to inform a buyer of a known defect in a property being purchased might be actionable as a tort.

town — any municipal area smaller than a large city. Like many terms that formerly had specific meanings (village, street, road), the meaning of the term "town" has become more general.

townhouse — an architectural style;

a dwelling characterized by two-story construction with a common wall or walls. The common form of ownership is similar to a condominium project in that the property owner not only owns his or her respective unit, but also an undivided interest in any common area. Townhouse ownership sometimes differs from condominium ownership in that the townhouse owner possesses the physical structure rather than just the airspace between the walls, floor, and ceiling. However, in many areas "townhouse" now refers to the physical style rather than the form of ownership. See also *condominium* and *planned unit development*.

township — the primary unit of measurement in the government rectangular survey method representing a 6-mile-square area that is further subdivided into 36 equal sections each comprising 640 acres. See also *base line, government rectangular survey method, meridian, range lines, section,* and *township lines*.

township lines — the survey lines that border a township on the north and south sides. The east–west boundaries are range lines. See also *range lines* and *township*.

track record — an informal expression meaning the past experience and history of success that a borrower, developer, or other business entity has in a particular area of business.

tract — any parcel of land. Primarily a parcel of land acquired or assembled for subdivision into lots or smaller tracts for development or building of homes or commercial buildings. See also *lot, block, and tract (subdivision)*.

tract home — a home built as one of a series of homes of similar architectural style on adjoining lots within the same area by the same builder. A mass-produced home. See by contrast, *custom home*.

tract map — a map or plat filed with the appropriate agency as a public record. It illustrates the numbered lots, blocks, streets, and other matters of public interest within a planned or existing subdivision. A tract map is often referred to in documents of transfer to identify the subject parcel by lot number, block number, and tract map number. See *lot, block, and tract (subdivision)*.

trade fixtures — personal property consisting of equipment, furniture, and other systems that are specific to a trade or business that have been placed in or on the premises for a specific purpose associated with the use of the property. If placed or installed on leased premises, there is a presumption that such items will be removed by the tenant at the expiration or termination of the lease. See, by contrast, *fixture*.

trade down — to purchase a replacement property lower in value

than the property one has most recently sold. Federal tax law has recently changed and now allows persons of all ages to freely trade primary residences up or down without adverse tax consequences, provided that certain dollar limitations and occupancy criteria are met. See also *capital gain, principal residence*, and *trade-up*.

trade in — the practice of offering real property as partial or full consideration toward the purchase of a replacement. A trade-in program is most commonly found in new home developments where the builder will purchase the current home of the new home buyer and apply the net proceeds as a down payment toward the purchase price of the new home. The property offered for trade-in must have an appraised value within an acceptable range, be in marketable condition, and be located in a market area where the property will be sold relatively quickly. Compare with *exchange* and *tax-deferred exchange* for properties other than a primary residence.

trade up — to purchase a replacement property higher in value than the property one has most recently sold. Federal tax law has recently changed and now allows persons of all ages to freely trade primary residences up *or* down without adverse tax consequences, provided that certain dollar limitations and occupancy criteria are met. See also *capital gain,* *principal residence,* and *trade-down.*

tradesperson, tradesman — a service provider experienced in a craft, such as plumbing or carpentry.

traffic count — the tabulation of vehicles passing a given location or between two points during a specified period. Such information is used to determine the commercial viability of a site, or to analyze an area for improvements for traffic flow, such as street widening, turn lanes, traffic signals, and the like.

trailer — any unpowered wheeled device towed by another vehicle. Mobile homes are sometimes inaccurately referred to as trailers. See also *mobile home.*

trailer park — (1) an area designated for temporary occupancy by persons with vehicles towing trailers; a campground with facilities for trailers; (2) a mobile home park; an area designed to accommodate mobile homes on a permanent basis. See also *mobile home.*

transaction — (1) commonly, a purchase and sale; (2) any contract calling for some type of exchange.

transfer — to convey, sell, or give, as in a transfer of title. See also *convey.*

transfer fee — See *tax stamps.*

trap — the lowest portion of the S-shaped pipe found under plumbing fixtures. Its function is to trap water in the curve of the S, thereby preventing the escape of sewer gases into the structure.

traverse window — a window in which one sash moves past the other sash horizontally.

tread — the flat portion of a stairway on which one walks. See also *riser.*

Treasury bill (T-bill) — an interest-bearing debt instrument sold by the federal government at weekly sales. They bear maturities of up to one year, shorter than those of Treasury bonds. T-bills are purchased at a discount to the full face value. The investor receives the full value when they mature. The difference, or discount, is the interest earned. The average rate on 26-week T-bills is commonly used as an index for certain adjustable rate mortgage loans. See also *adjustable rate mortgage, index,* and *Treasury bonds.*

treasury bonds — long-term obligations of the U.S. Treasury. They carry maturities of from 10 to 30 years. Interest is paid semiannually. As interest rates rise, the value of the existing bonds tends to fall. As rates fall, the values tend to rise. See also *Treasury bills.*

treble damages — a court award of three times the actual damages in a lawsuit. They are required by statute in certain settings, and are intended to serve as a punishment and a deterrent to similar future conduct. Examples include antitrust awards, awards for bad checks, and certain egregious conduct by landlords. See also *damages* and *punitive damages*.

trespass — in real estate, entering on or placing anything on the property of another unlawfully and without the consent of the owner of the property. Trespass, depending on the jurisdiction and the nature of the trespass, may have both criminal and civil implications and remedies. See also *adverse possession* and *nuisance*.

trim — certain decorative or finish materials in or around a building. For example, moldings are considered trim.

triple-A tenant — See *AAA tenant*.

triple net lease — (also called "net-net-net") a commercial lease in which the tenant assumes many of the expenses of ownership—taxes, insurance, and maintenance—in addition to a fixed rent payment. There are many varieties of "modified" triple net leases, ranging from the tax-insurance–maintenance model all the way to leases in which the tenant pays the mortgage, taxes, and insurance, all operating expenses, and a profit override to the owner.

triplex — a three-unit multifamily structure.

truck high — an area of a commercial building or warehouse where the floor is at a level even with the bed of tractor–trailer vehicles to facilitate the loading and unloading of cargo.

truss — a prefabricated structural

component used in roof construction as an alternative to on-site framing. Light framing lumber is combined with engineered metal fasteners to build a lightweight and strong supporting structure for the roof.

trust — an arrangement in which legal title to property is held in the name of one entity or individual for the benefit of another. Legal title is held by the *trustee*, while equitable title, (the right to the benefit of the property) is held by the *beneficiary*. It may be established voluntarily, or by operation of law, as where one person has obtained control of property belonging to another. See also *equitable title*, *legal title*, *trustee*, and *trustor*.

trust account — an method of accounting requiring separate deposit accounts and separate records for monies under the control of a fiduciary for the benefit of another. See also *fiduciary*.

trust beneficiary — the person entitled to enjoy the benefits or income of property held in a trust. See also *beneficiary*, *trust*, and *trustor*.

trust deed — an alternative to a mortgage, a financial instrument used in conjunction with a promissory note to establish the collateral in a loan secured by real property. In contrast to a two-party mortgage agreement, a trust deed requires a three-party agreement involving a trustor (borrower), trustee (neutral functionary), and beneficiary (lender), in which the trustee holds legal title until the promissory note is paid in full (or defaulted). In the case of full performance (i.e,. satisfaction of the promissory note held by the beneficiary), the trustor will demand cancellation of the note by the beneficiary and a deed of reconveyance from the trustee to the trustor. In the case of a serious breach (i.e., non-payment for a specified period), the beneficiary may order the trustee to begin foreclosure proceedings against the trustor as specified in the trust deed. See *beneficiary, mortgage, promissory note, trustee,* and *trustor.*

trust instrument – the formal document that creates a trust and establishes the responsibilities and powers of the trustee, typically a trust deed or a declaration of trust. See also *trust* and *trust deed.*

trustee – (1) one who holds property for another as a fiduciary; a person who has the obligation to protect the subject of the trust for the benefit of the beneficiary. He or she may be named in the trust instrument or may be designated by a judge. (2) a neutral third party, as in the trustee of a trust deed, who holds bare legal title to a property, until such time as the terms of the underlying note secured by the trust deed have either been performed or breached.

trustee's sale – a form of nonjudicial foreclosure, in which the trustee is empowered by the terms of the note to sell the property at public auction in the event of a breach by the borrower. In many states, if the lender elects nonjudicial foreclosure, the recovery is limited to the collateral. The lender may not pursue the borrower for any shortfall. See also *antideficiency laws, foreclosure, judicial foreclosure, nonjudicial foreclosure,* and *nonrecourse loan.*

trustor – the borrower/purchaser of real property who deeds the property being purchased to a trustee as security for a note. See also *beneficiary, trustee,* and *trust deed.*

Truth in Lending Law (Regulation Z) – (also called the "Federal Truth in Lending Act") the Truth in Lending Act (TILA), Title I of the Consumer Credit Protection Act of 1969, implemented by Regulation Z of the Federal Reserve Board, intended to promote the informed use of consumer credit by requiring disclosures about the true costs of the loan.

This regulation applies to most individuals or businesses that offer or extend credit to consumers when the credit is secured by an interest in real property. It also applies to many, but not all, consumer loans secured by personal property. TILA is intended to enable the customer to compare the cost of a cash versus credit transaction and to make sense of the varying costs of credit among different lenders. See also annual percentage rate.

tsunami – Japanese for a very large

ocean wave generated by severe seismic activity.

tuck pointing – the finishing of joints between bricks or masonry by the application of grout or mortar with a trowel.

turnkey – a build-to-suit construction project where the finished product is such that the end user/purchaser need only "turn the key" in the lock to begin functional utilization of the building.

turnover – (1) the rate at which the inventory of a business is sold; (2) the number of times a property is sold or leased in a given time frame.

turnpike – a toll road or freeway characterized by limited access points and high speeds.

two-hour door/wall – a door or wall constructed in such a way as to resist fire for two hours.

U

UBC – See *Uniform Building Code.*

UCC – See *Uniform Commercial Code.*

ULI – See *Urban Land Institute.*

ULSPA – See *Uniform Land Sales Practices Act.*

ultra vires – acts undertaken that are beyond the power of a corporation as defined by law or corporate

charter. See also *corporation.*

unclean hands doctrine – a legal principle which holds that one who has defrauded another in some particular matter cannot obtain equitable relief through judicial action on the matter. See also *laches.*

unconscionability – a legal doctrine applied to the enforcement of contracts. If the contract is so one-sided as to oppress or deny meaningful choice to one party, it is deemed unconscionable, and the court will not enforce it. See also *adhesion contract* and *contract.*

underimprovement – an improvement to real property that does not lead to the highest and best use of the property. An example is the construction of a small two-bedroom house in a neighborhood of larger, more expensive homes. See also *improvement.*

undersigned – the person(s) whose name(s) appear signed at the end of a document.

undertenant – See *subtenant.*

underwrite – the act of assessing financial risks and setting related prices accordingly. See also *underwriter.*

underwriter – (1) in real estate lending, underwriters determine the acceptability of a borrower's loan application and determine the loan amount, rate, and terms for which the applicant qualifies; (2) in insurance, underwriters price insurance policies according to their analysis of the risks involved; (3) in financial securities, underwriters price securities (stocks, bonds, limited partnerships) according to perceived risk and then bring the securities to market.

undisclosed agency — a circumstance in which an agent fails to disclose the existence of an agency agreement to a party in a transaction. Agents may be bound personally to perform on a contract if they fail to properly disclose their role as agent. See also *agency*.

undivided interest — (1) the interest that a co-owner has in a parcel of real property. The interest is a fractional interest in the entire property, not a 100% interest in a portion of the property. (2) the interest that a condominium owner has in the common areas of the condominium project. See also *joint tenancy* and *tenancy in common*.

undue influence — an improper or oppressive constraint or persuasion of another such that the will of the other party is overcome, and he or she is induced to perform or refrain from some act that he or she would not otherwise have done. Misusing a position of confidence, or taking unfair advantage of an infirmity or the desperate circumstance of another may give rise to a finding of undue influence.

unearned income — personal income derived from sources other than the labor of the person. Examples include rents, dividends, and royalties. See also *passive income*.

unearned increment — an increase in the value of real property

due to forces beyond the control of the owner and unrelated to any improvements made by the owner to the property. Examples include a favorable change in zoning or a sudden surge in population.

unencumbered property — (also called "free and clear") real property free of debt, but not necessarily free of liens such as current taxes and utility easements. See also *easement* and *lien*.

unenforceable contract — a contract that may be valid in form but which will not be enforced by a court of law. Examples include certain contracts with minors, oral contracts subject to the statute of frauds, contracts against public policy, and contracts that exceed an applicable statute of limitations. See also *adhesion contract, Statute of Frauds, void,* and *voidable*.

unethical actions — actions in conflict with accepted business or professional standards of conduct. Real estate licensees may be subject to discipline and loss of license for engaging in unethical conduct. See also *agency, Code of Ethics,* and *duties of care*.

unfair and deceptive practices — a term used by the Federal Trade Commission (FTC) to prohibit sales practices that fall short of fraud but which nonetheless offend public policy, or are oppressive, unscrupulous, or unethical. The FTC has broad powers over interstate land sales.

unfinished office space — space in an office building that is without dividing walls, floor coverings, or any other amenities or *tenant improvements*. Commercial leases often provide various allowances for finishing the space to suit the tenant. See also *tenant improvement*.

Uniform and Model Acts — a variety of comprehensive laws that have been adopted or proposed for adoption throughout the nation as controlling state law in a number of areas. The goal is to establish uniformity among states in such areas as commercial law, building codes, land sales, consumer credit, partnership, and landlord/tenant law. These Acts are drafted or reviewed and approved by the National Conference of Commissioners on Uniform State Laws. See also *Uniform Building Code, Uniform Commercial Code, Uniform Land Sales Practices Act, Uniform Partnership Act, Uniform Residential Landlord and Tenant Act, and Uniform Simultaneous Death Act.*

Uniform Building Code (UBC) — a national set of building and construction regulations published by the International Conference of Building Officials. It has been adopted extensively in the western United States and is slowly being adopted or adapted throughout the nation. It has also served as the code of El Salvador and was the basis for the national codes of Japan and Brazil. See also *building codes*.

Uniform Commercial Code (UCC) — a body of law that codifies and governs commercial transactions such as sales of goods, bank deposits and collections, bulk transfers, ware-

house receipts, commercial paper, letters of credit, certain investment securities, and secured transactions. Of primary importance to real estate are the bulk sales rules (Article Six), which cover the sale of the inventory of a business in the course of the sale of that business, and the secured transactions rules (Article Nine) which cover fixtures purchased on credit.

Uniform Land Sales Practices Act (ULSPA) — adopted as federal law in 1968 as the Interstate Land Sales Full Disclosure Act. The Act applies to large subdivisions of unimproved land in which sales are accomplished through the use of mails or other indices of interstate commerce. It provides for registration of the subdivision with the Department of Housing and Urban Development (HUD), certain uniform disclosures and a cooling-off period of seven calendar days for purchasers. There are many exemptions form the registration requirements for smaller subdivisions, subdivisions that are sold primarily to residents of the state in which the lots are located, and bulk sales of lots to a developer.

Uniform Partnership Act (UPA) — a widely adopted model act that establishes the legality of partnerships and provides for partnership ownership of real property.

Uniform Residential Appraisal Report (URAR) — a form on which residential appraisals must be made for HUD, the VA, the FHA, the FHLMC, and FNMA. Because of its wide use by government lenders and guarantors, it enjoys widespread use in the lending community at large. See also *appraisal*.

Uniform Residential Landlord and Tenant Act (URTLA) — a

model act that provides for consistency of interpretation and regulation of residential leases. It has been widely adopted and adapted throughout the United States. The Act covers the obligations of landlords and tenants in detail, and prescribes specific remedies for breaches of those obligations.

Uniform Settlement Statement —

a federal law, 12USC Sec. 2603, Chapter 27 and Real Estate Settlement Procedures, that requires a standard form, commonly called a HUD-1, that discloses costs, fees, and other expenses associated with the purchase and sale of certain residential properties. See *RESPA*.

Uniform Simultaneous Death Act — a model act adopted by most

states to cover the situation in which two or more joint tenants are killed in a common accident or disaster. The Act provides that joint tenants who are deemed to have died simultaneously are treated as tenants in common. The effect of this rule is that the heirs of the decedents will take title to the property. If, however one joint tenant remains, the Act does not apply. See also *joint tenant* and *tenancy in common*.

unilateral contract — (1) a con-

tract in which one party performs or promises to perform some act for another without receiving a recipro-

cal promise from the other party. A court may determine that a reciprocal agreement is implied by law or by the circumstances. For example, a property owner may be ordered to reasonably compensate a volunteer fire department if it has saved his or her property from destruction. (2) a bilateral contract that has been fully performed by one party. For example, if Abel tenders full payment to Baker for his property under a purchase contract that calls for a grant deed to be delivered to Baker, the contract becomes unilateral until Abel actually delivers the grant deed, when it is said to be fully executed. See also *bilateral contract, contract,* and *executory contract*.

unimproved property — (also

called *raw land*) land without human-made structures such as buildings and streets.

unincorporated area — land

within a county, but not within an incorporated city. Public services such as fire, water, and police are often provided by the county.

unincorporated association — an

organization of people who are associated for some charitable, religious, scientific, fraternal, or recreational purpose. These associations may be tax-exempt. Many homeowners' and condominium associations are unincorporated associations. See also *homeowners' association*.

unit — (1) a part of a larger property

that is intended for individual use; (2) within an apartment building or a condominium complex, a room or group of rooms that are designed for individual occupancy. Usually characterized by a private entrance. Title to a condominium is generally described in terms of a particular unit. See also *condominium*.

unit value — a price or value denominated by a unit of measurement, for example, price/square foot, price/acre, etc.

United States Geological Survey (USGS) — an agency within the U.S. Department of the Interior that is charged with the responsibility of mapping, surveying, and conserving lands within U.S. borders.

unities — the legally required characteristics of joint tenancy. In essence, the joint tenants must take title to the property at the same time and by the same instrument. They must have the same title (all joint tenants) and must each enjoy an undivided right of possession and enjoyment. A failure of one or more of these conditions will usually result in the creation of a tenancy in common. See also *joint tenancy*. See for an explanation of the unities: *unity of interest, unity of possession, unity of time*, and *unity of title*.

unit-in-place method — an appraisal method for calculating the replacement cost of a structure. The installed prices of each individual component of the structure are estimated on a per square foot basis, than added together and multiplied by the total square feet of the structure. For example, labor and materials for framing, roof, tile, carpet,

painting, and the like would be estimated, then totaled and multiplied by the total square footage to determine the replacement cost of a house. See also *appraisal*.

unity of interest — a required element of a joint tenancy. Interests in the real property must accrue by the same conveyance. In other words, a joint tenancy cannot be created through a series of conveyances in which individual joint tenants are added. See also *joint tenancy, unity of possession, unity of time*, and *unity of title*.

unity of possession — a required element of a joint tenancy. Each joint tenant must enjoy an undivided right to possess and enjoy the entire property. No tenant can claim a specific part of the property as his or her own to the exclusion of the other joint tenants. See also *joint tenancy, unity of interest, unity of time*, and *unity of title*.

unity of time — a required element of a joint tenancy. All joint tenants must take title at the same time. See also *joint tenancy, unity of interest, unity of possession*, and *unity of title*.

unity of title — a required element of a joint tenancy. All joint tenants must hold the same title. In a tenancy in common, the tenants may have taken possession by several titles. See also *joint tenancy, unity of time, unity of interest*, and *unity of possession*.

unjust enrichment — a legal principle that a person should not be allowed to retain money or benefits which in justice belong to another. It is applied in a variety of circumstances, including in real estate transactions in which one party conveys property rights to another based on a mistake of fact induced by a nondisclosure.

unlawful detainer action – a legal action brought by a property owner to regain possession of a property from one who initially occupied the property lawfully, but who is now in breach of the possession agreement or who has stayed beyond the term of the agreement. See also *ejectment*.

unmarketable title – a state of title to real property that is so fraught with questions as to its validity that a reasonable person acting prudently would not purchase the property. See also *marketable title*, *title*, and *title insurance*.

unrealized gain – appreciation of an asset that has not yet been sold. If Abel purchases an apartment building for $500,000, and five years later the property is worth $700,000, Abel has an unrealized gain of $200,000. When the property is sold, the gain is realized and may or may not be recognized for income tax purposes. See also *gain* and *taxable gain*.

unreasonable – irrational, unwise, arbitrary, or foolish. Contract law generally imposes a standard of reasonableness on the parties concerning areas of conduct that are not specifically defined in the contract. See also *reasonable* and *unreasonably withheld consent*.

unreasonably withheld consent – the capricious or arbitrary refusal by a party to a contract to consent to an assignment of rights to the contract. In contracts such as leases that permit subleases, there may be a contract clause prohibiting the landlord from unreasonably withholding consent to a sublease to a credit-worthy and otherwise appropriate tenant.

unrecorded instrument – a deed or other document affecting real property that has been properly executed but not recorded. It is binding between the maker and others with notice of its existence, but may not be binding on the world at large. See also *bona fide purchaser*, *notice*, and *recording*.

unsecured loan – a loan that is not backed by collateral. Unsecured loans are typically backed only by the good credit of the borrower. See also *collateral*.

unsecured note – a note (the written evidence of a loan) that is not backed by collateral. See also *collateral* and *unsecured loan*.

UPA – See *Uniform Partnership Act*.

upgrades – (1) improvements to a newly built property that are specified by the buyer before the escrow closes. These are items that are not included in the basic purchase price. Examples include more expensive carpet, added space, optional air conditioning, tile or granite countertops in place of Formica™, etc. (2) less commonly, improvements made after closing to a new property by an original owner.

up-leg — See *replacement property*.

upside potential — the expected appreciation over a particular period of time of a parcel of real property.

upzoning — a change in zoning from lower to higher density or from a less intensive to a more intensive use. See also *zoning* and *downzoning*.

URAR — See *Uniform Residential Appraisal Report*.

Urban Land Institute (ULI) — a nonprofit research and educational organization founded in 1936, dedicated to improving the standards for land planning and development. The institute publishes numerous books and articles covering the fields of land use and planning.

urban property — real property located in or close to a city. Urban property is typically characterized by high-density development. See also *rural*.

urban renewal — the process of recovering, restoring, or replacing large numbers of urban structures that have deteriorated or have become obsolete. In a broader sense, urban renewal often includes the social goals of drawing people back to underutilized urban centers and improving the economic lives of those who live there.

urban sprawl — the haphazard growth of a city into surrounding areas.

URTLA — See *Uniform Residential Landlord and Tenant Act*.

usable area — (1) in a single-tenant building or a single-tenant floor in a multistory building, the gross area of the building or floor minus the building lobby and penetrating shafts, such as stairways, elevators, and air ducts; (2) in a multitenant building or floor, the gross area of the building or floor minus the lobby, penetrating shafts, public corridors, rest rooms, janitorial closets, and utility rooms.

use tax — in real estate, a tax imposed on the presumed use by a property owner of a public utility or good. Examples include sewer and street taxes.

use value — the subjective (not market) value that a special-purpose property has for its owner. The concept is applied to properties that serve a particular owner or purpose well, but that may have little or no market value beyond that use. A sports stadium, for example, may have great value to the owner of a football team, yet be essentially valueless to others not in a position to use it.

useful life — (1) the period of time over which an improvement to real property produces net value to its owner; (2) the period of time over which the IRS determines that it is appropriate to depreciate a physical asset such as a building. At the end of that time, the asset may still have economic value but will produce no further tax benefits. See also *capital asset, depreciation,* and *improvement*.

USGS — See *United States Geological Survey*.

usufructuary rights – the right to use enjoy, or profit from the property of another. An easement is an example. See also *dominant tenement, easement,* and *servient tenement.*

usury – the lending of money at rates in excess of those permitted by applicable law.

utilities – public and certain private services to real property. Sewer, water, electricity, gas, telephone, and cable are all utilities. Companies providing these services may be publicly or privately owned, and are generally regulated by the states.

utility – value or usefulness.

utility easement – the right of a utility provider to pass over or use property not owned by them for the purpose of building, maintaining, or providing the utility. The property affected need not benefit from the utility. See also *easement* and *utilities.*

utility room – a room within a building that contains equipment or supplies necessary to maintain the building.

V

VA loan – See *Veterans Administration Loan.*

vacancy – an empty place; often, a property that is available for rent.

vacancy factor – an allowance made in a financial analysis or an

appraisal for the portion of a building or other rental project that is expected to be unrented over a specified period of time. It is expressed as a percentage. For example, if an apartment building with 100 units could be expected, on average over the course of a year, to have 95 units rented, it would have a vacancy factor of 5%.

vacant land – land without buildings but not necessarily without improvements such as sewers or utilities. See also *unimproved property.*

vacate – (1) to leave a premises or move out; (2) to set aside a court judgment or order in favor of a new proceeding..

valid – binding; having the force of law. A valid contract is one that a court will enforce.

valley – (1) that angle in a roof created at the bottom of two downward-sloping sides; (2) the low area formed between two mountains or hills.

valley flashing – the flashing or waterproofing material on the valley of a roof. See *valley roof* and *flashing*

valley rafter – the beam forming the bottom of the valley on a valley roof. See also *valley roof.*

valley roof – a roof or roof section whose edges are higher than its center.

valuable consideration – a legal term meaning a class of consideration (inducement to a contract) that has value sufficient to support terms of the contract. Valuable consideration entitles the promisee to enforce a claim against an unwilling promisor. The consideration need not have actual value to the promisee. It is sufficient that it has perceived value to the promisor. In an attempt to forestall questions concerning the legal validity of consideration, many contracts include a recital that the consideration exchanged is acknowledged by the parties to be valuable. See also *consideration, promisee,* and *promisor.*

valuation – the act of determining the worth of a thing. See also *appraisal.*

value – (1) price or estimated price of an asset; (2) the worth of benefits to be derived from ownership of an asset by an owner or user; (3) abbreviation for "valuable consideration."

vapor barrier – a moisture-resistant material applied to the walls, floors, or roof of a structure for the purpose of preventing water vapor from penetrating. Vapor barriers may consist of paint, plastic sheeting, foil, treated paper, or a combination of these.

vara – (1) unit of length equal to 33 1/3 inches (primarily, Texas); (2) a Spanish and Portuguese word meaning a unit of length ranging from 31 to 34 inches.

variable interest rate (VIR) or **variable mortgage rate (VMR)** – a rate of interest that is subject to change based on an agreed-on formula or index. See also *adjustable rate mortgage, index, margin,* and *variable rate mortgage.*

variable rate mortgage (VRM) – a mortgage in which the interest rate varies according to an agreed-on index (such as the Office of Thrift Supervision's cost-of-funds index (COFI). Same as *adjustable rate mortgage.* See also *cap, index, margin,* and *payment cap.*

variance – municipally determined individual exception or change to a portion of a zoning requirement, such as permission to build an otherwise nonconforming apartment building in a commercial zone. A variance may be granted after an application and hearing. It is designed to add flexibility to a general scheme of zoning. See also *nonconforming use* and *zoning.*

vendee – (1) a purchaser of personal, or more commonly, real property; (2) a purchaser under a land contract. See also *land contract.*

vendee's lien – an unusual form of lien placed on a property by a buyer under a contract of sale prior to the close of escrow. It is intended to secure a buyer's deposit by placing other potential purchasers on notice that the property is subject to an agreement to sell.

vendor – (1) a seller or personal or real property; (2) a seller under a land contract. See also *land contract* and *vendee.*

vendor's lien – a equitable legal concept rather than an actual recordable lien. It arises when a seller of real estate has conveyed possession to a buyer with no security other than the buyer's promise to pay. The vendor's lien secures any remaining payment due from the buyer.

veneer – a thin layer of material applied over another substance, to give the appearance that the area is composed entirely of the uppermost material. Examples include wood veneers, and brick facings applied to a concrete surface.

vent – an opening, such as that made by a pipe or a duct that allows passage of air (or other gas or fumes or smoke, etc.), through or out of a building. See also *duct, vent pipe,* and *vent stack.*

vent pipe – a pipe attached to the trap in a plumbing fixture, designed to release sewer gases to a rooftop vent stack. See also *trap* and *vent stack.*

vent stack – the portion of a vent pipe that projects through a roof. See also *vent pipe.*

ventilation – a system of providing fresh or conditioned air to the interior of a structure. See also *heating system.*

venture capital – money provided by a third party for the start-up costs of a new business. Because these funds are considered to be at high risk, they typically command high rates of return. Often, these funds are advanced in exchange for a significant equity stake in the new business instead of a stated rate of return.

venue – the court having appropriate legal jurisdiction over a claim or action.

veranda – long covered open porch running along the side of a structure. See also *patio* and *porch.*

verbal – pertaining to words, either written or oral. In recent years it has come to have the same meaning as "oral," referring to spoken words. Verbal contracts for the sale of real property may not be enforceable. See also *Statute of Frauds, oral,* and *oral contract.*

verbal contract – See *oral contract.*

verdict – the formal finding or decision made by a jury.

verification – sworn statement as to the truth, accuracy, or authenticity of an instrument's contents. Verifications may be made by oath, affidavit, or deposition.

vested – fixed, settled; not contingent. See also *vested interest.*

vested interest – present right or title to something, which allows the holder to sell or give away the right or title, even if the right or title may not be enjoyed until a future date. For example, if Abel has a reversionary interest in a home that he has deeded to Baker as a life estate, Abel's interest is a vested interest. Abel may sell or otherwise alienate his reversionary interest in the property, even though he will not be able to possess the property until Baker dies. See, by contrast, *contingent interest.* See also *alienation, life estate,* and *reversion.*

vestibule – small room or entrance hall leading to a larger space. See also *lobby.*

Veterans Administration (VA) loan

– (also called "GI loan" or "VA loan") a loan partially guaranteed by the Veterans Administration under the Servicemen's Readjustment Act of 1944 and later, made to an eligible veteran or to an unremarried widow or widower of an eligible veteran for the purchase of real property. The purpose of the loan guarantee program is to encourage private lenders to make low-down-payment or no-down-payment loans to eligible veterans by guaranteeing a portion of the loan. Eligibility is determined by the veteran's length of active service, but generally varies between six months and two years. See also *certificate of eligibility.*

via – Latin for "road" or "way."

viable – feasible; workable.

vicarious liability – the legal responsibility of one person for the acts of another because of a presumed relationship of control between the persons. For example, real estate brokers may be vicariously liable for the tortious acts of their agents. See also *liability* and *tort.*

village – small assembly of houses and other structures. In some jurisdictions a village is a technical term meaning a municipal corporation smaller than a town.

violation – an act or a condition not in accordance with the law or private rules (such as CC&Rs) relating to permissible uses of real property. Examples include allowing trash to accumulate on a property, or in the case of a homeowners' association with CC&Rs, painting the exterior of a condominium a color not permitted by the association.

VIR – See *variable interest rate.*

visual rights – (1) right to a scenic view, free from obstruction created by erection of a structure.; (2) right to deny permission for erection of a structure that would block visibility at a traffic intersection.

void – invalid; not enforceable; having no binding effect or legal force. Contracts for an illegal purpose are void. See, by contrast, *voidable.* See also *unenforceable contract.*

void *ab initio* – Latin term for a contract that is void from the moment of its creation because it is illegal or counter to public policy. See also *void* and *voidable.*

voidable – contract that may be valid, but that is capable of being voided (disaffirmed) if certain circumstances, actions, or conditions should occur. A contract in which fraud has occurred may be voidable by the defrauded party. A contract by a minor for an item not deemed a necessity (such as food or shelter) may be voidable by the minor or a guardian.

volt – measure of electricity. One volt is the force necessary to cause 1 ampere of current to flow through a wire with a resistance of 1 ohm. Most household current in the United States is 110 to 120 volts, with 220-volt circuits sometimes provided for heaters, clothes dryers, and stoves. See also *watt.*

voluntary deed — See *deed in lieu of foreclosure.*

voluntary lien — lien placed on property with consent of or at the request of the property's owner, or as a result of a voluntary act by the owner. Mortgages and trust deeds are examples of voluntary liens. See also *lien.*

VRM — See *variable rate mortgage.*

W

wainscoting — the covering of a lower portion (usually, one-third to one-half) of interior walls with a wood or tile surface. The upper portion of the wall may be painted, wallpapered, or covered with some other material different from the material below.

waive — to relinquish a right or claim voluntarily. See also *waiver.*

waiver — (1) the relinquishment of a right or claim; (2) the written evidence of a relinquishment of a right or claim. For example, a buyer may sign a waiver document relinquishing his or her right under a contract to inspect a property.

walk-through — the final physical inspection of a property prior to closing escrow by a buyer, or to taking possession by a tenant. The purpose of the walk-through is often limited to determining that the property is in the same condition as that contemplated in the contract, that nothing material has been removed, and that any agreed-upon repairs have been made. See also *inspection.*

wall — a flat vertical structure that divides or encloses an area. Walls may be interior, exterior, or both. They may also be load-bearing, meaning that the wall serves as a support for the structure, or non-load-bearing, meaning that the wall serves as a partition or a decoration, without a structural function.

wall heater — a small electric, gas, or fueled device installed between the studs of a wall and designed to heat the immediate area only.

wall plates — the top and bottom horizontal wood members of a wall, to which the vertical studs are attached. The bottom member is often called a sole plate and the top member is the top plate.

wall tile — tile that is designed to be placed on the surface of a wall. Tiles that are designed for this purpose may not be suitable as floor or countertop tiles. The surface may be too delicate to wear well or too slick to walk on.

wallboard — See *drywall.*

wall-to-wall carpeting — carpet that covers the entire floor area of a room.

ward — a person, especially a child or one judged mentally incompetent, placed in the lawful care of a guardian. See also *guardian* and *incompetent.*

warehouse — a structure used for storage of materials, equipment, merchandise, etc.

warehousing loans — the depositing of loans by a lender or other financial institution into a bank to serve as collateral for a loan or to be held for later sale. See also *seasoned loan* and *secondary mortgage market*.

warrant — (1) to assure that title to a particular parcel of real property is good and that the buyer's possession will remain undisturbed; (2) to represent in a contract that certain facts are as they are represented to be; (3) an order by which a drawer authorizes one person to pay a particular sum of money to another.

warranty — a binding promise by a seller to a buyer as to the condition of a property. Real estate contracts often contain certain basic warranties to be made by the seller. See also *as-is* and *implied warranty of habitability*.

warranty deed — a deed used in some states for the purpose of conveying fee title. The seller makes certain "warranties" concerning the condition of title in the granting instrument. The increasingly widespread use of title insurance has made warranty deeds less common in recent years. See also *deed, grant deed* and *title insurance*.

waste — destruction of property by a tenant, mortgagor, or other person who is rightfully in possession of the property but is either not the owner or who holds less than fee ownership. Waste generally lessens the value of the property and may occur through a number of means, including material alterations in the property, failure to pay required property taxes or insurance, and fire. See, by contrast, *ameliorating waste*.

waste line — a pipe that carries wastewater from any kitchen, bath fixture, or other water-using fixture, such as a clothes washer, except a toilet. Toilets are connected to separate sewer lines. See also *sanitary sewer*.

wasting assets — (1) any asset that tends to deteriorate and diminish in value over time. Most improvements to land are wasting assets, because they will not last forever. The land itself is deemed to have a potentially unlimited life. (2) assets such as oil, lumber, minerals, etc. that are diminishing or being depleted. Includes the diminishing of patent rights and fixed-term franchises.

water mains — large pipes carrying fresh water to a structure.

water mark — (1) the mark on a shore that shows the highest and lowest normal levels of the water; (2) faint mark on paper used to identify an original document, a source of a document, or a brand of paper.

water power — the power created by the movement or fall of water, to which a riparian owner has rights. See also *riparian rights*.

water rights — rights to use and/or control water. See also *riparian rights*.

water table — the level below the natural grade of land at which water can be found in a particular location. If the natural water table is too high, construction may be difficult or expensive.

watercourse – a natural or artificial open channel through which water flows. A river is a watercourse, as is a concrete flood control channel.

waterfront property – land or improved property that borders a body of water.

water-holding capacity – the capacity of a given amount of soil for absorbing and holding water, expressed as a percentage of the soil's dry weight.

waterproof – a characteristic of a material that will not be damaged by exposure to water or moisture. See also *water-resistant*.

waterproofing – the act of applying a material or materials to a portion of a structure with the goal of preventing water completely from migrating from one side of the barrier to the other. Waterproofing is commonly applied in basements and other below-grade areas.

water-resistant – a characteristic of a material designed to repel water. It is not necessarily waterproof. See also *waterproof*.

waterscape – (1) a water or sea view; (2) an aqueduct.

watershed – (1) a drainage area of a river or stream; (2) a natural barrier separating two river systems.

watt – a unit of electrical power; the equivalent of the flow of one ampere created by 1 volt of pressure. See also *volt*.

way – a street, alley, path, or easement that carries pedestrian or motor traffic. Like many other words defining what had formerly been distinct types of streets or roads (boulevard, avenue), it may now be used to designate virtually any type of street, road, or other thoroughfare.

wear and tear – gradual deterioration of the improvements to real property resulting from use over time. Normal or ordinary wear and tear results from a reasonable use of the property. Most commercial and residential leases contain a clause anticipating that the tenant will cause only normal wear and tear, which is chargeable to the landlord. Excessive wear and tear is generally the responsibility of the tenant under terms of the lease.

weathering – the deterioration of the exterior of a house or other building or structure caused by exposure to rain, wind, and sun.

weatherstrip – a strip of felt, plastic, metal, or other material applied to air gaps, such as those between doors and door jambs or windows and frames, to prevent air from passing in or out. The purpose is to make a structure more airtight, so that heating and cooling systems will operate efficiently. See also *insulation*.

weephole – a small hole left or drilled in a wall, usually a retaining wall, to allow drainage and avoid or decrease pressure from the weight of water buildup.

weir – a dam that diverts water to a mill, pond, etc.

weir box – a box containing a measuring device, often placed in an irrigation ditch to measure water flow. See also *weir*.

well – a pit or hole dug or drilled into the ground, usually to reach and extract water, gas, or oil. An artesian well is a well in which water flows up under pressure, as in a fountain. Access by well to a sufficient supply of fresh water can be a significant determinant of value for rural land. Many states include clauses in real estate purchase contracts that allow the buyer to test the production and capacity of a well before committing to purchase a property.

wetlands – a type of environment in which the land consists of wet, soggy soil, such as in swamps, bogs, and marshes. Wetlands may contain environmentally sensitive plants and animals and are often subject to development restrictions.

wic – a place on a seashore or on the bank of a river.

widow – a woman whose husband has died and who has not remarried.

widower – a man whose wife has died and who has not remarried.

widow's election – in some states, the principle that a widow may choose to take her share of property under a husband's will, or the share that would come to her by state statute, whichever she deems best. See also *community property* and *widow*.

widow's quarantine – from old English law. The period after a husband's death, usually 40 days, during which a widow could stay in the husband's house free of rent. See also *widow*.

widow's walk – a platform or deck on or around the roof of a Cape Cod-style home, having a view of the sea, so called because it offered a vantage point to wives of sailors from which they could watch for their husbands to return from a voyage.

wild deed – a deed in the chain of title in which the grantor does not have a prior recorded interest. This sometimes happens when a party's name changes after acquiring a property, as in the case of women who take the husband's surname on marriage, or when the legal description of a property is incorrect.

wild interest – interest in a property that is not fully traceable in the chain of title. See also *wild deed*.

wild land – land not being used for a specific purpose such as cultivation or construction; land in its natural state.

will – a written expression of a testator's wishes with regard to disposition of his or her property, possessions, and rights after his or her death. It must meet certain criteria, which vary by jurisdiction, to be considered valid. See also *beneficiary*, *codicil*, *probate*, *testator/testatrix*, and *witness*.

windbreak – a structure (e.g., a wall) or natural barrier (e.g., line of trees or hill) that protects an area from the force of winds.

window – an opening in an exterior

wall of a structure made for the purpose of allowing light and/or air to pass into the structure.

window covering – any of a variety of materials (wood shutters, cloth drapes, metal blinds, etc.) applied to or attached to or around the inside of a window for decorative or light control purposes. In many states, attached window coverings are treated as real estate and are conveyed with the property. See also *window*.

window jamb – a structural frame designed to receive a window. See also *window*.

window pane – the glass element of a window. See also *window*.

window sash – a movable frame containing the glass of an opening window. See also *window*.

windowsill – the bottom horizontal structural element of a window. See also *window*.

window trim – thin decorative elements applied to cover the joints between a window jamb and the interior or exterior wall surface. See also *window*.

without recourse – (1) in lending, a loan in which the security is limited to the collateral. If the borrower defaults, the lender may obtain the return of the collateral, but may not proceed further against the borrower. See also *nonrecourse loan*. (2) in a negotiable instrument, a qualified endorsement relieving the endorser of personal liability. For example, in the case of a third party check, an endorsement including the phrase

"without recourse" is intended to prevent liability on the part of the endorser in the event that the check is dishonored.

witness – (1) to sign one's name to a document such as a deed or a will for the purpose of attesting to the authenticity of a document or to the authenticity of the signature of other persons. See also *attest*. (2) the person providing such testament; (3) a person whose declaration under oath is received as testimony in an official proceeding, such as a trial or a hearing.

Women's Council of Realtors® – a professional organization within the National Association of Realtors®.

wood – the hard fibrous substance that makes up the bulk of the branches and trunks of trees. See also *board*.

wood frame construction – a type of construction using wood lumber for the structural members of walls, roofs, and upper floors. Other materials, such as stucco, wood, or brick, often cover the framing.

wood products – any of a variety of materials consisting in whole or in part of materials derived from trees. Examples include paper, cardboard, plywood, cellulose insulation, and fiberboard. Modern wood products include such items as decking made from sawdust and recycled plastic.

wood-destroying insect – an insect that eats or bores into wood, weakening it. Termites and wood-boring beetles are common examples. Many states now require an inspection by a licensed pest control company of wood frame residential properties when they are sold. See also *termite*.

work letter – an addendum to a commercial lease that defines the improvements to be made at the landlord's expense and the work to be done at the tenant's expense.

working capital – assets (usually money) available to a business on short notice for the purpose of conducting daily business activities..

workinghouse – a structure that houses the machine that operates a grain elevator, usually situated on the top of the elevator.

workout plan – a plan developed to help avoid foreclosure. A workout plan may include such strategies as an extension of a loan term or a reduction in the interest rate.

worthier title – a **common**-law doctrine, pertaining in cases where a person would inherit exactly the same interest in a given property *either* by right of descent in the absence of a will or by devise (i.e., through a will). Acquisition of the title by descent is considered to prevail, or to be the "worthier" title.

wraparound mortgage – (also called a "wrap") a junior mortgage having a face value of the amount it secures plus the balance due on the first mortgage. The mortgagee collects payments based on the face value of the wrap-around mortgage, makes the payment due on the first mortgage, and keeps the difference. The "wrap" often carries a rate of interest higher than that of the underlying first mortgage, thereby profiting the holder of the wrap. Wraparound mortgages are generally used in an environment in which interest rates have risen rapidly, making it attractive to leave an older low-interest mortgage in place when the property is sold. The seller is typically, but not always, the maker of the wrap. Note that a due-on-sale clause in the underlying first mortgage may affect this strategy. See also *due-on-sale clause* and *mortgage*.

writ – a type of written order by a court.

writ of attachment – See *attachment*.

writ of certiorari – See *certiorari*.

writ of ejectment – a writ prepared in an action to recover real property, usually from a tenant. See also *eviction*.

writ of execution – a writ ordering an officer of the court to carry out a decree or judgment, often to levy and sell a defendant's property.

write off – (also called "charge off") to remove an asset from a financial account, as in instances of a debt that is not collectible.

write-off – a tax deduction representing a real or legislatively determined financial loss that is recognized by federal or state income tax law. Real estate offers many tax-favored options, such as the ability to depreciate investment property. See also *depreciation.*

wrought iron – a form of decorative iron, forged, bent or hammered into shape, then welded into gates, fences, and the like.

wye ("Y") – the merging of two railroad tracks that meet at an angle into one; more recently, the merging of two highways or freeways that meet at an angle into one.

X

X – (1) a mark used as substitute for a signature in certain instances. A person who cannot sign his or her full name on a document may mark an "X" on the signature line; a notary or witness must then attest to the identity of the signatory; (2) a mark on a map made to indicate a location of significance.

X-bracing – cross bracing within a wall.

xeriscape – (1) a dry or arid landscape; (2) a human-made landscape designed, using native plants, to require a minimum of water. An increasingly popular alternative to traditional landscape design in arid areas of the southwestern United States.

xylophagous – feeding on or in wood or wood products. Termites and carpenter ants are xylophagous.

Y

yard – (1) a unit of distance, the equivalent of 3 feet; (2) an open area between a property line and a wall of a house or other building. The three types of yard are front, side, and back.

year-to-year tenancy – a form of periodic tenancy in which the term runs one full year or a multiple of years. See also *periodic tenancy* and *tenancy.*

yield – (1) the rate of return on an investment, expressed as a percentage of the original investment; (2) for an income property, the ratio of a property's annual net income to its cost. For example, an apartment building with a price of $1,000,000 and a net annual income of $90,000 would have an annual yield of 9%.

yield to maturity – the internal rate of return (IRR) of an investment, considering the cost, all cash flows, and the selling price. See also *internal rate of return.*

yuppie – a slang term meaning "young urban professional," intended to describe a largely single, upwardly mobile demographic with significant disposable income.

Z

zero lot line — the placement of an exterior wall of a building on the lot line. Zero lot lines are generally used by developers to allow residential properties to have one large side yard, rather than two smaller yards. The result is often increased density. See also *zero side yard*.

zero side yard — a type of subdivision in which the houses are built with zero lot lines, sometimes used to provide more usable yard area (on one side) for homes built on narrow lots. See also *zero lot line*.

z-lot — a lot that is not set perpendicular to the street it faces, but rather is set at an angle. It is generally flanked by similarly configured lots. They tend to result from a decision by a builder that the angled look of the lots from the street will give a greater feeling of space between houses.

zone — area whose land use is restricted or defined by zoning ordinance. Types of zones include residential, high-density residential, commercial, agricultural, and industrial. See also *zoning*.

zone theory — an area of nuisance and trespass law dealing with aircraft overflights of real property.

zoning — the division of a city or county into areas of different permissible land uses. Some of the many types of zoning theories and practices include:

aesthetic zoning – designed to preserve the appearance or character of an area.

cluster zoning – allows intensive land use in exchange for the dedication of public parks, open space, or other public needs.

conditional zoning – a type of cluster zoning in which the total open space for an area is determined legislatively. The details of individual land use decisions within the parameters of the plan are left to a planning commission.

spot zoning – fine tuning of a zoning area through individual land use decisions which are inconsistent with the zone generally. Spot zoning may also be the result of strong political pressures.

bulk zoning - an attempt to control density through the use of setbacks, building envelopes, and a required percentage of open space.

zoning estoppel — rule that prevents the government from carrying out a downzoning ordinance because of substantial expenses incurred by a landowner in reliance on a previous zoning designation. See also *downzoning* and *upzoning*.

zoning map — a map showing current zones as set by zoning ordi-

274

nances. See also *zone* and *zoning ordinance*.

zoning ordinance – local law that determines land use and construction in a particular area (zone), usually set by a city or county. See also *zoning*.

zoning variance – land use exception made by a local government agency for a particular property within a zone. An example would be a reduction in the minimum setback requirement for a proposed construction project where the small size of the lot makes the official setback impracticable. See also *setback* and *variance*.

zygocephalum – a crude measure of land comparable to the area that a yoke of oxen could plow in a day.

Appendices

Keystrokes for the Real Estate Master IIx®

Keystrokes for the TI-BA Real Estate™

Keystrokes for the HP10B®

Keystrokes for the HP12c®

Mortgage Payment Table

Cost per $1,000 Borrowed

Selected Real Estate Related Web Sites

Real Estate Master IIx® and Qualifier Plus IIx®
Calculated Industries, Inc

Finding a monthly loan payment for a $100,000 loan at 8.25% amortized over 30 years

Steps	Keystrokes	Display
Clear the registers	[On/C] [On/C]	0.00
Enter the loan amount	100,000 [L/A]	100,000
Enter the term in years	30 [Term]	30
Enter the Interest rate	8.25 [Int]	8.25
Compute monthly payment	[Pmt]	751.27

Texas Instruments BA Real Estate™
Finding a monthly loan payment for a $100,000 loan at 8.25% amortized over 30 years

Steps	Keystrokes	Display
Clear TVM*	[2nd] [CLR TVM]	0.00
Set payments/year*	[2nd] [P/Y] 12 [=]	P/Y=12.00 switching to C/Y=12.00
Finish setting payments*	[=]	12.00
Set payment to end of period*	2nd [BGN/END] once or twice	BGN will disappear
Enter the term in years	30 [TERM]	TRM=30.00
Enter the interest rate	8.25 [I%]	I%=8.25
Enter the loan amount	100000 [LOAN]	LN=100,000.00
Compute monthly payment	[CPT] [PMT]	-751.27**

* These steps only need to be performed once to set the defaults for a typical mortgage loan. After they have been entered, they will remain in memory until the user changes them. Subsequent calculations may be performed using just the last four steps of the above example.

** This calculator represents payments as a negative number.

Hewlett Packard 10B®

Finding a monthly loan payment for a $100,000 loan at 8.25% amortized over 30 years

Steps	Keystrokes	Display
Clear TVM	[Gold] [CLEAR ALL]]	0.00
Set Monthly Payment	12 [Gold] [P/YR]	12.00
Enter the loan amount	100000 [PV]	100,000.00
Enter the term in months	360 [N]	360.00
Enter the interest rate	8.25 [I/YR]	8.25
Compute monthly payment	[PMT]	-751.27*

*This calculator represents payments as a negative number.

HEWLETT-PACKARD 12C®

Finding a monthly loan payment for a $100,000 loan at 8.25% amortized over 30 years

Steps	Keystrokes	Display
Clear display, stacks and registers	[Gold f]+[CLEAR CLX]	0.00
Enter the loan amount*	100000 [CHS] [PV]	-100,000.00
Enter the number of years	[Blue g] [n (blue 12x)] 30	360
Enter the rate of interest	[Blue g] [i (blue 12÷)] 8.25	0.69
Press Payment key	[PMT]	751.27

Changing the sign, pressing the CHS key, of the loan amount will result in the payment amount being shown in the display as a positive number.

MONTHLY PAYMENT MATRIX FOR A 30-YEAR AMORTIZING LOAN

ANNUAL INTEREST RATE

PRINCIPAL	5.00%	5.50%	6.00%	6.50%	7.00%	7.50%	8.00%	8.50%	9.00%	9.50%
$100,000	$537	$568	$600	$632	$665	$699	$734	$769	$805	$841
$105,000	$564	$596	$630	$664	$699	$734	$770	$807	$845	$883
$110,000	$591	$625	$660	$695	$732	$769	$807	$846	$885	$925
$115,000	$617	$653	$689	$727	$765	$804	$844	$884	$925	$967
$120,000	$644	$681	$719	$758	$798	$839	$881	$923	$966	$1,009
$125,000	$671	$710	$749	$790	$832	$874	$917	$961	$1,006	$1,051
$130,000	$698	$738	$779	$822	$865	$909	$954	$1,000	$1,046	$1,093
$135,000	$725	$767	$809	$853	$898	$944	$991	$1,038	$1,086	$1,135
$140,000	$752	$795	$839	$885	$931	$979	$1,027	$1,076	$1,126	$1,177
$145,000	$778	$823	$869	$916	$965	$1,014	$1,064	$1,115	$1,167	$1,219
$150,000	$805	$852	$899	$948	$998	$1,049	$1,101	$1,153	$1,207	$1,261
$155,000	$832	$880	$929	$980	$1,031	$1,084	$1,137	$1,192	$1,247	$1,303
$160,000	$859	$908	$959	$1,011	$1,064	$1,119	$1,174	$1,230	$1,287	$1,345
$165,000	$886	$937	$989	$1,043	$1,098	$1,154	$1,211	$1,269	$1,328	$1,387
$170,000	$913	$965	$1,019	$1,075	$1,131	$1,189	$1,247	$1,307	$1,368	$1,429
$175,000	$939	$994	$1,049	$1,106	$1,164	$1,224	$1,284	$1,346	$1,408	$1,471
$180,000	$966	$1,022	$1,079	$1,138	$1,198	$1,259	$1,321	$1,384	$1,448	$1,514
$185,000	$993	$1,050	$1,109	$1,169	$1,231	$1,294	$1,357	$1,422	$1,489	$1,556
$190,000	$1,020	$1,079	$1,139	$1,201	$1,264	$1,329	$1,394	$1,461	$1,529	$1,598
$195,000	$1,047	$1,107	$1,169	$1,233	$1,297	$1,363	$1,431	$1,499	$1,569	$1,640
$200,000	$1,074	$1,136	$1,199	$1,264	$1,331	$1,398	$1,468	$1,538	$1,609	$1,682

PRINCIPAL	10.00%	10.50%	11.00%	11.50%	12.00%	12.50%	13.00%	13.50%
$100,000	$878	$915	$952	$990	$1,029	$1,067	$1,106	$1,145
$105,000	$921	$960	$1,000	$1,040	$1,080	$1,121	$1,162	$1,203
$110,000	$965	$1,006	$1,048	$1,089	$1,131	$1,174	$1,217	$1,260
$115,000	$1,009	$1,052	$1,095	$1,139	$1,183	$1,227	$1,272	$1,317
$120,000	$1,053	$1,098	$1,143	$1,188	$1,234	$1,281	$1,327	$1,374
$125,000	$1,097	$1,143	$1,190	$1,238	$1,286	$1,334	$1,383	$1,432
$130,000	$1,141	$1,189	$1,238	$1,287	$1,337	$1,387	$1,438	$1,489
$135,000	$1,185	$1,235	$1,286	$1,337	$1,389	$1,441	$1,493	$1,546
$140,000	$1,229	$1,281	$1,333	$1,386	$1,440	$1,494	$1,549	$1,604
$145,000	$1,272	$1,326	$1,381	$1,436	$1,491	$1,548	$1,604	$1,661
$150,000	$1,316	$1,372	$1,428	$1,485	$1,543	$1,601	$1,659	$1,718
$155,000	$1,360	$1,418	$1,476	$1,535	$1,594	$1,654	$1,715	$1,775
$160,000	$1,404	$1,464	$1,524	$1,584	$1,646	$1,708	$1,770	$1,833
$165,000	$1,448	$1,509	$1,571	$1,634	$1,697	$1,761	$1,825	$1,890
$170,000	$1,492	$1,555	$1,619	$1,683	$1,749	$1,814	$1,881	$1,947
$175,000	$1,536	$1,601	$1,667	$1,733	$1,800	$1,868	$1,936	$2,004
$180,000	$1,580	$1,647	$1,714	$1,783	$1,852	$1,921	$1,991	$2,062
$185,000	$1,624	$1,692	$1,762	$1,832	$1,903	$1,974	$2,046	$2,119
$190,000	$1,667	$1,738	$1,809	$1,882	$1,954	$2,028	$2,102	$2,176
$195,000	$1,711	$1,784	$1,857	$1,931	$2,006	$2,081	$2,157	$2,234
$200,000	$1,755	$1,829	$1,905	$1,981	$2,057	$2,135	$2,212	$2,291

Cost per $1,000 borrowed on a fully amortized 30 year loan with equal monthly payments

2.50%	2.75%	3.00%	3.25%	3.50%	3.75%	4.00%	4.25%	4.50%	4.75%	5.00%
$3.95	$4.08	$4.22	$4.35	$4.49	$4.63	$4.77	$4.92	$5.07	$5.22	$5.37
5.25%	5.50%	5.75%	6.00%	6.25%	6.50%	6.75%	7.00%	7.25%	7.50%	7.75%
$5.52	$5.68	$5.84	$6.00	$6.16	$6.32	$6.49	$6.65	$6.82	$6.99	$7.16
8.00%	8.25%	8.50%	8.75%	9.00%	9.25%	9.50%	9.75%	10.00%	10.25%	10.50%
$7.34	$7.51	$7.69	$7.87	$8.05	$8.23	$8.41	$8.59	$8.78	$8.96	$9.15
10.75%	11.00%	11.25%	11.50%	11.75%	12.00%	12.25%	12.50%	12.75%	13.00%	13.25%
$9.33	$9.52	$9.71	$9.90	$10.09	$10.29	$10.48	$10.67	$10.87	$11.06	$11.26
13.50%	13.75%	14.00%	14.25%	14.50%	14.75%	15.00%	15.25%	15.50%	15.75%	16.00%
$11.45	$11.65	$11.85	$12.05	$12.25	$12.44	$12.64	$12.84	$13.05	$13.25	$13.45
16.25%	16.50%	16.75%	17.00%	17.25%	17.50%	17.75%	18.00%			
$13.65	$13.85	$14.05	$14.26	$14.46	$14.66	$14.87	$15.07			

Selected Real Estate Related Web Sites

Real Estate News
Real Estate ABC.com : Award-winning information site. Includes extensive information of consumer interest, including real estate finance.
http://www.realestateabc.com

Inman News: Well known real estate news site. Includes content with residential, commercial, and consumer interest.
http://www.inman.com

International Real Estate Directory (I.R.E.D.): Extensive information of national and international interest.
http://www.ired.com

RealtyTimes: Timely articles of interest to agents and consumers.
http://www.realtytimes.com

Selected Associations
American Homeowners Association: Information and services for homeowners. Partners with mortgage, utility, publishing, real estate, and consumer financial services industries.
http://www.ahahome.com

National Association of REALTORS®: Resource center for consumers and real estate professionals
http://www.onerealtorplace.com .

Illinois Association of REALTORS®: Example of state association site. State legal, professional development, economic, and legislative updates. IAR Magazine on-line. Member profiles and industry links.
http://www.iar.org

Real Estate Finance
Ginnie Mae (GNMA; Government National Mortgage Association): GNMA helps provide affordable homeownership opportunities for all Americans; facilitates secondary market activities for federally insured or guaranteed mortgages.
http://www.ginniemae.gov

Fannie Mae (Federal National Mortgage Association; FNMA): FNMA is a large diversified financial company and the nation's largest source of home mortgage funds. Fannie Mae does not lend money directly to home buyers; but rather makes sure that mortgage lenders have money to lend to home buyers. Site includes financial and home-buying information.
http://www.fanniemae.com

Freddie Mac (Federal Home Loan Mortgage Corporation; FHLMC): FHLMC is a shareholder-owned corporation which works to provide homeowners and renters with lower housing costs and better access to home financing. Site includes financial and home-buying information.
http://www.freddiemac.com

Bankrate.com: Bankrate.com provides current market rates and analysis.
http://www.bankrate.com

Real Estate Education

Appraisal Institute: Residential and commercial appraisal education, research, publishing, and professional designation programs.
http://www.appraisalinstitute.org

Urban Land Institute (ULI): The Urban Land Institute is a nonprofit education and research institute that is supported and directed by its members. Its mission is to provide responsible leadership in the use of land in order to enhance the total environment.
http://www.uli.org

Institute for Business and Professional Ethics (IBPE), DePaul University: Programs and resources to explore and further ethical practices in business.
http://www.depaul.edu/ethics

The Real Estate Research Institute (RERI): Part of the Indiana University Center for Real Estate Studies, the RERI conducts and/or supports research on real estate investment performance and market fundamentals to improve the quality of real estate decision making.
http://www.reri.org

HUD and Other Real Estate Related Government Sites

Department of Housing and Urban Development (HUD): HUD is the Federal agency responsible for national policy and programs that address America's housing needs, improve and develop the nation's communities, and enforce fair housing laws. HUD's business is helping create a decent home and suitable living environment for all Americans, and it has given America's cities a strong national voice at the Cabinet level.
http://www.hud.gov
See especially http://www.hud.gov/hudprog.html

Department of Veterans Affairs: The Veterans Affairs site provides information on benefits and services, including home loan guaranty services.
http://www.va.gov/
See also General Services Administration (GSA)
http://www.gsa.gov
Especially http://www.gsa.gov/staff/pa/cic/housing.htm

The National Council on Disability (NCD): NCD, an independent federal agency, makes recommendations to the President and Congress on issues affecting Americans with disabilities. NCD's overall purpose is to promote policies, programs, practices, and procedures that guarantee equal opportunity for those with disabilities, regardless of the nature or severity of the disability; and to empower them to achieve economic self-sufficiency, independent living, and inclusion and integration into all aspects of society. http://www.ncd.gov

States have sites specific to their departments of real estate. For example: State of California Department of Real Estate http://www.dre.ca.gov

Corporate Real Estate Sites

Examples of large corporate real estate sites:

RE/MAX
    http://www.remax.com

Century 21
    http://www.century21.com

Prudential
    http://www.prudential.com/realestate/

Home Search Sites

Realtor.com
    http://www.realtor.com

Home Advisor (Microsoft)
    http://homeadvisor.msn.com

HomeSeekers.com
    http://www.homeseekers.com

Commercial Real Estate

Commercial Source
    http://www.commercialsource.com

CCIM
    http://www.ccim.com

Loopnet
    http://www.loopnet.com

About the Authors

The authors bring to this work a unique set of experiences, styles, and perspectives—academic, practical, pedagogical, conceptual, linguistic. Barbara Cox worked in language research, communications education, and real estate instruction. Jerry Cox brings a strong commercial and institutional real estate background with tremendous experience in contracts and development. And David Silver-Westrick adds strengths of legal training and years of exceptional success in residential real estate. Here's more ...

BARBARA COX earned a doctorate in education and psychology from Stanford University. Her professional life includes work as educator and researcher at college/university level, corporate trainer, and textbook author. She has conducted extensive research on language acquisition and development, and is author of *Vocabulary Basics* (Prentice Hall, Second Edition, 2002).

As Director of Technology for the Orange County Association of Realtors® in California for 3 years, Dr. Cox established and directed the Technology Education Center. Among the 22 real estate technology courses she developed were DRE-approved Internet Marketing and E-Mail How-To, Real Estate (Agent) Finance, Contact Management, and basic computing. Her real estate titles include *Learning the Language of Real Estate* and, with Wm. Koelzer, *Internet Marketing in Real Estate*. She currently teaches Real Estate Principles, Real Estate Practice, and Real Estate Finance at Saddleback College in Mission Viejo, CA.

JERRY COX is a principal of Cox Realty Advisors, a consulting firm in asset management, entitlement, and development feasibility. With over 28 years' experience in the real estate profession, primarily in institutional environments, Jerry's emphasis has been creating, managing and disposing of property portfolios. More recently he has added residential brokerage to his activities with a national brokerage firm in San Clemente, CA.

As a former Director and past-president of Mary Erickson Community Housing, a nonprofit corporation established for the assurance of affordable rental housing for very low income residents of southern Orange County, Jerry continues his work in the acquisition, management and development of multi-family projects.

Jerry holds a bachelor degree from the University of California at Riverside (UCR) and completed post-graduate programs in real estate at the Universities of California, Los Angeles (UCLA) and Berkeley (UCB) as well as The Wharton School of the University of Pennsylvania. Through the National Association of Realtors® Jerry earned the GRI designation as a Graduate of the Realtor® Institute.

DAVID SILVER-WESTRICK has been a practicing Realtor for 15 years, and was named *2002 Realtor of the Year* by the Orange County Association of Realtors (OCAR). In 2002, David was president of the Southern California Multiple Listing Service Corporation, one of the largest MLS providers in the U.S., serving over 23,000 subscribers in Los Angeles, Orange and Riverside counties. In 2001, David was president of the 6,800-member Orange County Association of Realtors. David is a Director of the 100,000-member California Association of Realtors and of the million-member National Association of Realtors. He is advisor to Saddleback College's real estate program, and he has taught OCAR's new agent orientation program. David is also a contributing editor for the Realtor News, an OCAR publication.

Prior to joining Century 21 OMA, he was associated with Tarbell Realtors for 7 years and was their top high-end agent. David is consistently honored for the outstanding service that he provides to his clients. For the past 5 years, he has earned Century 21's most prestigious award for sales production—*The Centurion*.

David attended UCSD and the Law School at USC.